Woman
Changing
Woman

Woman Changing Woman

*Feminine Psychology Re-Conceived
Through Myth and Experience*

V I R G I N I A

B E A N E

R U T T E R

HarperSanFrancisco
A Division of
HarperCollins
Publishers

Except for the friends and family who have given permission to appear in this book, the names and identifying characteristics of the women whose stories are told have been changed in the interest of patient confidentiality.

Photo credits appear on page ix.
Acknowledgment is gratefully made to Princeton University Press for permission to use quotations from C. G. Jung's *The Archetypes and the Collective Unconscious,* Collected Works, vol. 9, part 1, copyright © 1969 and from *Psychology and Alchemy,* Collected Works, vol. 12, copyright © 1968; to Charles Boer for permission to quote from his translation of the "Hymn to Demeter" in Homeric Hymns, rev. 2nd ed., Spring Publications, Dallas, copyright © 1980; to the University of Arizona Press for use of songs from Leland C. Wyman's *Blessingway,* copyright © 1970; to Wesleyan University Press by permission of University Press of New England for use of songs from Charlotte Johnson Frisbie's *Kinaaldá,* copyright © 1967; to Knopf, a division of Random House, Inc., for quotations from Thomas Mann, *The Black Swan,* University of California Press, copyright © 1990; to June Rachuy Brindel for use of quotations from *Ariadne,* St. Martin's Press, copyright © 1980; and to Professor Bruce Lincoln of the University of Minnesota for use of his work on women's puberty rituals from *Emerging from the Chrysalis,* Harvard University Press, copyright © 1981.

FIRST EDITION

Library of Congress Cataloging-in-Publication Data
Rutter, Virginia Beane.
    Woman changing woman : feminine psychology re-conceived through myth and experience / Virginia Beane Rutter. — 1st ed.
        p. cm.
Includes bibliographic references.
ISBN 0–06–250748–6 (alk. paper)
    1. Women—Psychology.   2. Women—Religious life.
3. Feminist psychology.   4. Feminist therapy.   5. Women—mythology.   6. Initiation rites.   I. Title.
HQ1206.R85 1993   92–56422
305.42—dc20   CIP

    93 94 95 96 97 ❖ RRD(H) 10 9 8 7 6 5 4 3 2 1

This edition is printed on acid-free paper that meets the American National Standards Institute Z39.48 Standard.

for my mother,
Justine Centomain Beane
and my father,
Lt. Col. James Bishop Beane II

Contents

List of Illustrations, *ix*
Acknowledgments, *xi*
Prologue, *xiii*

P A R T I

Containment

1 Creating the Feminine Container, *3*

2 Adorning a Woman, *31*

3 Molding a Woman, *57*

P A R T II

Transformation

4 Knowing the Power of the Womb, *89*

5 Encountering the Goddess of Death, *111*

6 Divining the Dark, *129*

P A R T III

Emergence

7 Healing With Compassion, *153*

8 Celebrating the Mother-Daughter Mystery, *171*

9 Emerging Through Ritual Separation, *197*

Notes, *229*
Bibliography, *239*

List of Illustrations

Cover illustration. *The Altar,* by Lynn Taber-Borcherdt, Tucson, Arizona.

Figure 1. *Conversation.* Detail of a marble votive relief, dedicated by Xenocrateia, fifth century B.C. Athens, National Archaeological Museum. No. 2756. Courtesy of Athens Archaeological Museum.

Figure 2. *Twin Goddesses.* Painted terra-cotta statuette from Corinth, late seventh century B.C. Courtesy of British Museum, London.

Figure 3. *The Ideal Woman Washing the Initiate's Hair in the Navajo Girl's Puberty Ceremony.* For figures 3–6: Photographs taken during a Navajo Kinaaldá Ceremony, 1986. Permission and photos by Kenji Kawano. P.O. Box 1922, Window Rock, Arizona 86515.

Figure 4. *The Ideal Woman Combing the Initiate's Hair in the Navajo Girl's Puberty Ceremony.*

Figure 5. *The Ideal Woman Washing the Initiate's Jewelry in the Navajo Girl's Puberty Ceremony.*

Figure 6. *The Ideal Woman Molding/Massaging the Initiate in the Navajo Girl's Puberty Ceremony.*

Figure 7. *Maiden/Mother* goddess figure. White marble statue from Çatal Hüyük, shrine VI.A.10, seventh century B.C. Archaeological Museum, Ankara, Turkey. Photo by Mrs. M. A. Mellaart. Courtesy of Professor James Mellaart.

Figure 8. *Childbirth.* Terra-cotta figurine from Cyprus, sixth century B.C. Courtesy of the director of the Department of Antiquities, Cyprus Archaeological Museum, Nicosia.

Figure 9. *Hecate: Triple Moon Goddess* (The Hecaterion of Marienbad). Frontispiece drawing, M. Esther Harding's *Woman's Mysteries: Ancient and Modern.* Photo by Peter B. George, San Francisco. Courtesy of the C. G. Jung Foundation, New York.

Figure 10. *Kuan Yin.* White porcelain statue, author's collection. Photo by Peter B. George, San Francisco.

Figure 11. *Demeter and Persephone at Eleusis* (Exaltation of the Flower). Marble votive relief, fifth century B.C. from Eleusis, Greece. Louvre Museum, Paris. Photo by Alinari. Courtesy of Art Resource, New York.

Figure 12. *Persephone Rising from the Ground* (Head of Demeter). Terra-cotta relief, Greek Hellenistic period. Museo Nazionale delle Terme, Rome. Photo by Alinari. Courtesy of Art Resource, New York.

Acknowledgments

I would like to sing the praises of all who helped bring this book into being. Within the Jungian community, my appreciation extends to the Scholarship Committee of the C. G. Jung Institute of San Francisco, chaired by Tom Singer, whose awards from the Van Loben Sels Fund helped to support the early stages of research; to Harry Prochaska, Michael Flanigan, and Ann Paras of ARAS (Archive for Research in Archetypal Symbolism) at the C. G. Jung Institute of San Francisco, who gave invaluable assistance with the visual images; to Anmari Romberg of the C. G. Jung Institute in New York for setting me on the permission-seeking path for use of the works of art; and to Florence Grossenbacher, Elizabeth Osterman, Mary Jo Spencer, and Jane Hollister Wheelwright, honored mentors. Thanks also to Jean V. Naggar, my literary agent.

My gratitude goes to Mark Bahti, Meinrad Craighead, Sue Nathanson Elkind, Peter B. George, Joseph Henderson, Barbara Moulton, Marion Russell, Donald Sandner, and Lynn Taber-Borcherdt, whose work and presences are part of the fabric of this book. They are all acknowledged for their specific contributions either in the prologue or in other places in the text. In addition, I am obliged to the following people who sustained me while I was writing: Jan Berry-Kadrie, Barbara Custer, JoAnne Dellaverson, Jyoti Elias, Ernest Pierucci, Blanca Rivera, and Frances Tobriner. My women's ritual group deserves special tribute for their creation of a beautiful Summer Solstice ceremony, celebrating the first draft of the manuscript, that renewed my strength for the next stage of work.

Just as I completed the final manuscript, my aunt and namesake, Theresa Virginia Centomain Pierucci, my mother's sister, died peacefully at the age of eighty. While growing up, I spent many hours in Aunt Theresa's kitchen listening to stories of her Italian-American girlhood. In true oral tradition, she handed down to me our Italian feminine heritage. I can only hope that my writing has been graced by her spirit of honesty.

My husband, Peter, above all, deserves thanks. He encouraged me to take on this project and generously gave of his time when asked to edit at critical stages in its development. I could not have brought this book to fruition without his and our wonderful children's love nurturing me all the way along.

Figure 1.
Conversation.

Prologue

*T*he core of the psychotherapeutic relationship between two women is a feminine mystery. The mystery lies at the heart of the
mother-daughter relationship; its positive essence is based on an
intimacy whose depth transcends time. *Woman Changing Woman* evolved
out of this mystery during my experience of being pregnant while practicing psychotherapy and out of my deep involvement with the unique psychological terrain of women therapists working with women patients. I use
the term *patient*, rather than *client*, because the Latin root of *patient* means
"to suffer or endure" and "to be under someone's care," while the word
client has a commercial connotation in our society. As a Jungian analyst I
feel suffering and caring are fundamental aspects of therapeutic work.

My observations in clinical practice led to my researching anthropological studies on women's rituals. In these studies I found collective celebra-
tions of the positive mother-daughter relationship that I had experienced
with my own mother. I was raised in the heart of an Italian Catholic maternal tradition; a statue of the Virgin Mary was ever present in our home.
Even my Scots father, an avowed agnostic, tacitly honored Her presence.
Perhaps he sensed that my mother's loving strength derived in some way
from her spiritual affiliation with the archetypal energy of the Madonna.
My relationship to my mother included much physical affection as well as
quiet devotion to the Virgin Mary. My mother connected me, both bodily
and spiritually, to my prehistoric roots in the Great Mother.

During my research I discovered Changing Woman, the chief deity of the Navajo people, the daughter of First Man and First Woman. She is "the woman who is transformed time and again,"[1] growing old and becoming young again with the change of the seasons. Changing Woman created corn and gave the Navajo instructions for its cultivation.[2] And she gave them the *Kinaaldá,* the puberty ritual for every girl in the tribe to enact when she comes of age. The myth says, "After that, time passed on merely by changing her. Changes would occur with her in four-day periods."[3] As a feminine archetype[4] of transformation and fertility, both physiological and spiritual, Changing Woman's energy permeates the work of psychotherapy between two women.

In February of 1990 three events coincided that led to my writing this book. The first was the death of my first therapist, Magda Proskauer, at the age of seventy-nine. Magda, a German Jewish refugee, was a wisewoman whom I had first met twenty years earlier when she was teaching a breath and movement group. She initiated me into Jungian psychology and into the relationship between psyche and body, mediated by breath. She died of lung cancer, ironically, still asserting an indomitable will.

I was privileged to participate in the last few weeks of her life and honored in accompanying her to the threshold of death. At her memorial service, I described my last visit with her:

> I came to visit Magda early on Friday morning. She was sitting
> up in bed, her breath labored; she had refused oxygen the night before.
> She smiled radiantly when I walked in. Her voice was almost gone,
> and in its absence I found myself reaching out to touch her, the only
> communication possible. I massaged her shoulders and neck, then held
> her hands. She gripped my hands tightly with her own and caressed
> the design on my bracelet, over and over. Just before leaving, I anointed
> her dear face with oil; she closed her eyes, leaned back, and received
> my blessing. And I received the gift of her acceptance. She died that
> afternoon, undaunted.

The second event that led to the creation of this book was guiding my six-year-old daughter through the ordeal of minor surgery. Preparing her, psychologically and emotionally, for the operation involved many small rituals, such as taking her to meet and question the doctor who would be doing her surgery and showing her the hospital where it would take place. Seeing my daughter through a trauma that entailed general anesthesia and its concomitant threat of death moved me again to an appreciation for the gift of life.

The third event was meeting Marion Russell, then commissioning editor at Mandala Books, an imprint of Unwin Hyman, in London. I had accompanied my husband on a week's book tour to England that she had arranged and found, unexpectedly, a colleague and friend in Marion. She and I had an instantaneous mutual attraction and intellectual rapport. Out of our discussions about our feminine/feminist concerns, the possibility of a book emerged.

These three events each involved an intense dyadic[5] relationship between two women: between a mentor/wisewoman and myself, between my daughter and myself, and between a soul sister and myself. The first relationship was fraught with the power of the archetype of death for a woman who had fully lived; the second, with the fear of death for a beloved child; and the third, with the conception of an idea, a child of the mind, a spiritual entity. Each event involved ritual elements—some more elaborate and conscious than others.

Once conceived, this book was blessed with life. When Marion left the publishing world to train as a psychotherapist, the proposal for *Woman Changing Woman* fell into the capable hands of Barbara Moulton, editor of feminine spirituality books at Harper San Francisco. Barbara and I also met in a powerful way around this material. Her keen mind and discerning editing have kept me focused on the book's essence. With her exquisite sensibility to feminism and feminine spirituality, she has provided an invaluable bridge between my inner creative life and the outer world. We incarnated this book together.

One-to-one relationships between women call up uterine existence—deep, intense, primordial feelings—"the knowledge flowing between two alike bodies, one of which has spent nine months inside the other," as the poet Adrienne Rich says.[6] Mother-daughter, sister-sister, granddaughter-grandmother constellations reach backward and forward in an unbroken line of generational connectedness. Scientists have discovered a component of mitochondrial DNA that has been passed down unchanged from mother to daughter since the beginning of human existence.[7] Thus it is present in all women. This essential psychobiological relationship between mother and daughter, daughter and mother is the unconscious ground of feminine psychology and of a modern woman's life. These depths of feminine psyche stir between any two women who are working together in the intimate container[8] of psychotherapy.

The interaction between woman therapist and woman patient involves an intrinsic quality of shared nature, of basking in the feminine bath together, of merging and separating, and of subtle change occurring in each of them during the process. In depth psychotherapy there is an unconscious mutuality of exchange, whether or not this mutuality is consciously acknowledged. Although my role as the guardian of the work is mandated and necessary, I am influenced: my psyche is acted upon by the psyches of my patients. On a conscious level, I also learn from my patients—about myself, about life, about culture.

Depth-oriented psychotherapy is an experience of initiation—a rite of passage from one stage of consciousness to another. In my work I have seen that psychological initiation for a woman is intrinsically interwoven with the physical initiatory experiences originating in her own body: menstruation, defloration, fertility, conception, childbirth, nursing, and menopause. These fundamental real-life events also appear as body-embedded images in women's dreams and unconscious material laden with both literal and symbolic meaning. Her body and psyche reflect her blood mysteries. Such images represent threshold experiences that demand the sacrifice of a woman's previous *physiological* state of being and a concomitant sacrifice of her *psychological* identity at the previous stage. Each transition in a woman's life is a dramatic event arising from a bodily source and simultaneously affecting her mind and her soul. Therefore, each process of feminine development or change inherently calls for a ritual response that acknowledges its meaning.

Ritual is also inherent in psychotherapy. Even if no one names it as such, each analytic hour and the extended process of analysis constitute a healing ritual in which the unconscious, the source, is being honored. In April 1989 I was fortunate to participate in a conference at the C. G. Jung Institute of San Francisco with two of my mentors in Jungian psychology who have written about initiation and ritual. Dr. Joseph Henderson's book *Thresholds of Initiation* is a classic study of the archetype of initiation as it appears in analytical work. Although much of his material amplifies male psychology, he also includes the psychological work of several women. Dr. Donald Sandner apprenticed himself to a Navajo medicine man and has studied and participated in extant healing ceremonies in many parts of the world. His book *Navajo Symbols of Healing* delineates the Navajo system of chant healing and draws parallels to Western psychotherapy. At the conference, I presented material illustrating the Navajo girl's puberty ritual, the Kinaaldá. While preparing for this program, I was encouraged by reading Bani Shorter's book *An Image Darkly Forming* and Sylvia Brinton Perera's paper "Ceremonies of the Emerging Ego in Psychotherapy." I learned that both of these Jungian analysts were also seeing the spontaneous development of ritual in their work with women patients.

Subsequently, I discovered Bruce Lincoln's superb anthropological study of women's puberty rituals *Emerging from the Chrysalis: Studies in Rituals of Women's Initiations*. For many years I had been studying and working with two of the five ceremonies he discusses in his book, the Kinaaldá and the Eleusinian mysteries. In the other three rites, I was delighted to find descriptions of additional ritual elements that paralleled women's psychological processes I had observed in my clinical hours. I also found that many of the psychological initiatory experiences of women in psychotherapy were similar to Lincoln's interpretation of the meaning of puberty rituals for girls and their cultures. Lincoln defined a threefold pattern of enclosure, metamorphosis or magnification, and emergence for women's initiations in contrast to male initiation patterns, which follow a process of separation, liminality (transition), and reincorporation.[9] The threefold patterns for both female and male initiations parallel the alchemical process examined in detail by Jung as the essence of all analytic work.[10] The structure of this book—containment, transformation, and emergence—is the pattern of change I have seen in women's development in my analytic practice. My work with men forms a different alchemy. Within this initiatory pattern, a multitude of individual rituals take place.

In psychotherapeutic work a woman is contained or enclosed in a healing process of ritual relationship—honoring body, ego, and self—that effects a psychological transformation. The psychological unfolding may involve physical, emotional, or spiritual transformation. The therapeutic enclosure is therefore naturally suited to feminine development and provides the ritual container for development that our culture generally lacks.

Some feminist schools of thought reject the spirit inherent in women's biological gift of life on the grounds that such valuing reinforces the patriarchal wish to keep women at home to bear children and adapt to the role of the "good mother." I believe it is a great loss to deny the essence of woman's nature—her relation to her body and its wisdom—because from that wisdom she brings forth her own power and creativity in every realm of life. All puberty rituals recognize that a woman's fertility, whether it is expressed physically or spiritually, symbolizes life for the family, the community, and the cosmos.

I will focus on two of women's physical initiatory experiences in this book—menstruation and birth—in order to elaborate the interrelationship among body, soul, and mind in the ritual of psychotherapy. I will discuss, as the archetypal ground for these initiations, the Kinaaldá, the Navajo girl's puberty ritual, which is still being practiced today; the Neolithic birth-giving Goddess culture of Çatal Hüyük; and the myth of Demeter and Persephone in ancient Greece as it was enacted in the Eleusinian mysteries. The myths and rites from these cultures illuminate the meaning of modern women's dreams and emotional experiences.

Modern women lack a rich tradition of story telling in which to place their own experience. Television soap operas and romance novels are superficial and wholly inadequate substitutes. Significant feminine rituals are also missing. Even their remnants, such as baby showers and intimate lunches or teas, are often denigrated and dismissed as trivial by both men and women. Women need to find their own voices and tell their own stories.[11] Woman-to-woman psychotherapy is a place for a woman to find her own voice, to uncover and make conscious the motivating stories and myths in her individual psyche. In the collaborative work of psychotherapy, the woman and her therapist together remake the original family and cultural myths into a new story, creating, as Jung said, "healing fiction."[12] Through fantasy, dreams, tears, and ritual experience, a woman in psychotherapy articulates life as story—integrating ordinary and traumatic events into meaningful experience.

I always feel grateful to each individual who bares her soul and shares her inner life with me. After I have listened to a woman's story, I feel responsible for the sacred knowledge she has disclosed; shared knowledge over time weaves the bond between us. In this spirit I offer immeasurable thanks to the three women who have agreed to share their labors with those who read this book. Their psyches, as well as mine, illumine these pages. Each woman gave wholehearted permission for the use of her material. Entering the process of presenting her personal psychological work to the world, each chose her own new name. By taking a name especially for this book, Beatrice, Carmina, and Sarah enacted a ritual of renaming that occurs in many initiatory ceremonies at the age of puberty. In the Catholic church a girl selects a name when she is confirmed at the age of twelve, a name intended to reflect her conscious dedication to the spirit. In the myth of Demeter and Persephone, Kore is renamed Persephone after her sojourn in the underworld. When she was abducted from the Elysian fields, she was a girl, a maiden; after her return she is a woman, a queen. Changing Woman could change her name as she wished by changing her dress from white shell to turquoise, to abalone, to jet.[13] Her two most important names are Turquoise Woman and White Shell Woman. Each of the women whose tales I tell renamed herself according to her own particular psychological intention. BEATRICE, CARMINA, and SARAH join with me in offering our stories for others to glean something for themselves.

PART I

Containment

Figure 2.
Twin Goddesses.

1

Creating the Feminine Container

$\mathcal{A}$ woman invokes the feminine mystery at the heart of the mother-daughter relationship when she chooses a woman therapist. She seeks a feminine other, a mother, a sister, a grandmother, a lover. Her conscious reasons for entering therapy involve both suffering and a sense of imbalance beyond her immediate understanding. She feels isolated, out of control, afraid, as if she is falling apart. She is conflict-ridden about her love relationship to a man or a woman. She hates her job. She is overwhelmed by a pregnancy, or by caring for young children or negotiating with teenage children. Or she feels the loss of older children leaving home, the death of a parent or friend.

The external stresses mirror a change pushing up from within; it is time to move from one place to another. An initiatory threshold has been reached, or life has been dammed up at an old stage. A new developmental task requires attention to inner reality. Only when that task is being performed will the relationship between inner and outer reality come back into balance. From a Jungian perspective, the Self[1] is striving to be realized. At such a time, much like the prepuberty stage of adolescence when longings press for realization from within, a woman seeks the enclosure or container of the therapeutic relationship in which to experience her transformation. If she forms a relationship with a female other she will be able to affirm her deepest nature in an initiatory process that belongs to the modern world but holds the power of ancient rites.

A woman brings her personal, cultural, family, and religious experiences to the psychotherapeutic encounter. The feelings associated with her upbringing are constellated immediately in the new situation in which she finds herself. This is a container unlike any she has previously encountered—a quiet, closed sacred space with the attention of a single woman focused completely on her. It is a place of self-attunement; it can be a place of self-realization. In the quiet of that enclosure, the woman has the opportunity to listen to her own voice at last.

The therapeutic space between two women partakes of ancient Greek dream incubation, in which a woman (or man) sought healing from the divine physician Asklepios. A patient went to the god's temple at Epidaurus, where under the guidance of the *therapeutae*, priests or priestesses, she carried out a prescribed ritual. She first purified herself in the holy fountain or spring, then went to sleep in the underground labyrinth of the temple, where she awaited a healing dream. In her dream Asklepios appeared, in serpent or dog form, touched the affected part of her body, and then vanished. When she awoke, she was healed. The serpent, who wreathes Asklepios's staff, has keen sight and rejuvenates itself by shedding its skin, which symbolizes "becoming free of illness." [2] From prehistoric times the snake was associated with the Great Goddess as a symbol of the renewal of life.

Eye diseases were frequently reported cured at Epidaurus.[3] To heal the eyes is to restore or change vision; the result is a new way of seeing the world. A woman comes to psychotherapy seeking a new perspective on her life. She encloses herself in a relationship with another woman and turns her attention inward; she closes her eyes in order to see that which she has not seen before. In her dreams she receives visions that alter her perception of herself and others. Her vision changes through brooding on her dreams and her life.

My goal as a therapist is to help a woman become herself by honoring and holding what arises from within her. Devoid of personal investment in the course of her development or outer life, I am set apart from other female figures she has known. Yet as a feminine dyad, we partake of the essential mother-daughter bond as it has existed for centuries. Prehistoric cultures, as well as extant matrilineal cultures, show a female way of being, but modern women's psyches show the use of these ancient sources in the service of developing a new way for the future that includes both the fact of our own patriarchal domination for thousands of years and a desire for a new relationship to men and maleness. One could say that our whole culture is in an initiatory process. We are going through a metamorphosis in many different arenas—psychological, political, and social—as many women and men press toward a different way of life.

My identity as a woman is the center of my identity as an analyst. I bring to the therapeutic relationship my own personal and cultural experiences and values as well as the skills I have acquired through my training. Years of personal analysis and analytic training have led to my own initiations, but in order for my work with people to be genuine and alive, it is imperative that I engage with the other, the patient. For the process to truly matter in both an objective and a subjective way, the relationship between us must be authentic. Both therapist and patient must be deeply affected by the work if it is to have value.[4] Sometimes it is important to share my personal history, experiences, or feelings with a patient. But what is more important is that I share my being; otherwise the process remains sterile. Women embody their psyche, soul, and spirit in a different way from men. The woman patient and I create a unique dyadic relationship, a ritual dyad, that parallels the relationships in her external life but forms the container for the process of initiation and development that she is seeking.

This initiatory process takes many forms. Sometimes a woman requires simply the "container" of therapy and a supportive, objective feminine presence to facilitate change; she need only see her situation differently from how she has been taught in her family or cultural milieu in order to remove the internal obstacles hindering her life flow and development. Other women are called to therapeutic work by traumatic childhood experiences or by an inner compulsion to individuate, that is, to become fully themselves. Such women embark on a long, deep journey toward a total reordering of the personality.

Emergence from the journey does not come about simply with the cessation of troubling symptoms such as anxiety or depression but takes a different form. Where previously the woman had been suffering a kind of death in life, in deep psychotherapy she consciously comes to terms with the source of her suffering. She actively undergoes a dark descent that involves confronting the elements of the collective unconscious and its archetypal contents. Her conscious taking up of her own fate, of loss of soul, of her own personal unconscious energy and its psychic meaning, holds the promise of psychological rebirth. She actively encounters the spirits of the collective unconscious as life-giving or life-destroying. When these deep contents of the psyche are stirred, all known beacons disappear, and she and I struggle together to find signs of the new path her Self is unfolding.

From time to time during our work, miraculously, a third entity beyond the two women in the room is activated: the entity of a powerful feminine being. This figure may take the form of Changing Woman, the Great Mother, Kuan Yin, Demeter/Persephone, Hecate, Psyche, or any other mythic heroine, goddess, or divinity. Sometimes the third in our trinity appears as a real woman: a favorite aunt, grandmother, or teacher who emanated a quality of the divine herself. Although the figure belongs to the patient and arises from her unconscious through the work of the analysis, she also comes to stand behind the therapist in both a supportive and a compensatory way. This entity or goddess-power in the therapy may remain unconscious for many years, yet she becomes the motivating archetype in the process of the work. The therapist may develop a relationship to this figure and find a corresponding energy activated in herself that meets or meshes with the archetype constellated in the other woman.

In the course of long-term therapy, many motivating archetypal figures manifest in dreams and other psychic material, and they can be amplified with mythological and ritual material from other cultures. As two women working together, we acknowledge these presences consciously and attempt to understand how these entities in the patient's psyche are functioning in either a creative or a destructive way.

The grandmother-mother-daughter relationship at the heart of the feminine archetype is addressed by Carl Jung in the concept of the "Kore":

> Demeter and Kore, mother and daughter, extend feminine consciousness both upwards and downwards. They add an "older and younger, stronger and weaker" dimension to it and widen out the narrowly limited conscious mind bound in space and time, giving it intimations of a greater and more comprehensive personality which has a share in the eternal course of things.... The psyche pre-existent to consciousness (for example, in the child) participates in the maternal psyche on the one hand, while on the other it reaches across to the daughter psyche. We could therefore say that every mother contains her daughter in herself and every daughter her mother, and that every woman extends backwards into her mother and forwards into her daughter. This participation and intermingling give rise to that peculiar uncertainty as regards *time:* a woman lives earlier as a mother, later as a daughter. The conscious experience of these ties produces the feeling that her life is spread out over generations—the first step towards the immediate experience and conviction of being outside time, which brings with it a feeling of *immortality*. The individual's life is elevated into a type, indeed it becomes the archetype of woman's fate in general. This leads to a restoration or *apocatastasis* of the lives of her ancestors, who now, through the bridge of the momentary individual, pass down into the generations of the future.[5]

This matrilineal sense of time and flow of life is reflected in the threefold aspect of the Kore: maiden, mother, and crone. The process in woman-to-woman psychotherapy awakens the inherent trifold structure of a woman's psyche and reconnects her to her own generational feminine history. In the intimate analytic relationship, maiden, mother, and grandmother energies flow back and forth between the two women. As we reweave our heritage of lost feminine wisdom in the context of an initiatory ritual, a new consciousness is born, a new vision is created. Both restoration and creativity play a part in the modern feminine identity that eventually emerges.

In my lineage of analytic training, Barbara Hannah was the grandmother, the wisewoman elder who inducted me into the mysteries of Jungian psychology. Miss Hannah had worked with Carl Jung for thirty years before his death in 1961. When I went to Zurich to enter analysis with her and study at the C. G. Jung Institute, I was thirty years old, and she was eighty. Several weeks before I had my first meeting with her, I had this dream:

> Magda, my first therapist, has arranged for me to meet Barbara Hannah. I am sitting between the two of them at a table where a meal is being served. Miss Hannah says, "The thing that interests me is your name, Beane. It's so unusual." And I say, "Yes, I always disliked it as a child, but I can't imagine giving it up now." Miss Hannah responds, "I can't understand why women change their names at all." I want to go on and tell her about the Scottish origin of my name, but I feel inhibited, that I would be taking advantage of her by not waiting for our official analytic hour.
>
> The next thing I know, Magda, Miss Hannah, and I are riding in a car. Miss Hannah is driving toward "home" on a narrow road through the woods, through incredible lightning and thunder, going very fast. It is *very* dangerous. Suddenly we are at the edge of the road, and a great bolt of lightning flashes. We see a huge precipice below. Miss Hannah's screaming face is outlined, but she doesn't or can't swerve away from the edge. I am desperately clutching at both of them as they fall into the abyss, while trying to save myself at the same time. Then I find myself standing at the edge of the precipice with a letter to Miss Hannah not yet mailed, trying to figure out how they have both managed to tumble into it . . . Terrified, I awake in shock.

Although I did not understand what this dream foreshadowed at the time, it proved to be my introduction to the emotional reality of the unconscious as it was lived in analysis in Zurich. My initial encounter with Miss Hannah triggered a storm of feeling and turmoil along with resistance to being led into that storm. The whirlwind continued in the second dream I had of her a few weeks later:

> Somehow, somewhere, I am enduring an incredible assault. Every time I stand up, wind and water deluge me and knock me over. In the background I know Miss Hannah is responsible for this. When I finally arrive at Miss Hannah's house, I tell Dr. von Franz, who opens the door, "I had a dream in which Miss Hannah was teaching me the power of the unconscious." Dr. von Franz just nods, as if to say she understands.

Storms, lightning, and thunder herald change. In the Navajo Blessingway myth, dark clouds gathered for four days preceding Changing Woman's birth on a mountaintop.[6] Changing Woman's power appeared here at the beginning of my initiation into my profession, my soul, my Self. Studying and undergoing analysis in Zurich for a year and a half was a complete immersion in my inner life. Magda, my psychological mother, was responsible for my going to Zurich to study Jungian psychology at the source. Barbara Hannah, daughter of an English vicar, had been an artist living in Paris until she read an article written by Jung in 1927. In the article, "Woman in Europe," Jung addressed the psychological emancipation of modern women.[7] Jung's ideas had such a profound impact on Miss Hannah that a year later, at the age of thirty-nine, she decided to go to Zurich and find him. Subsequently, she devoted herself to Jungian analytical psychology and became an analyst.

In the dream, my relationship with Miss Hannah is immediately established on the basis of my maiden name, an abbreviation of a Scotch clan name. Miss Hannah also had Scottish ancestors. Our relationship was maiden to crone. Her headlong plunge from the precipice, taking Magda with her, represented her willingness to engage in my descent whether my ego accepted it or not. I still want to save myself; the process once she and I meet goes forward with frightening rapidity, which proved to be true. Looking back on this dream, I see another meaning in the vision of Magda and Miss Hannah being lost to me. They have both died in the last ten years, and I am left to carry on the work of re-visioning feminine psychology.

There was no holding myself aloof after I had this dream, which I told Miss Hannah in our first hour. Once the container of our relationship was established, the descent began, and there was little discrimination between the archetypal world and the everyday world in which I was living. In the intensity and isolation of immersion in a different culture, the archetypal world was activated in every moment. Relating to an analyst who was born in the previous century provided depth and a sense of history to my therapeutic understanding; Barbara Hannah became my psychological grandmother.

Coming from a background of art history, I found my understanding of the interpenetration of myth or archetype and daily life had been illuminated by ancient art. In Greek painting and sculpture, the iconography of the sacred and the mundane merge, infringe on, and embellish each other. Women in scenes on friezes or vases can be legendary or mythical, professionals or family women. Psychologically, the archetypes of the collective unconscious infuse personal life with power—positive or negative. They are a source for an individual to draw on. The interpenetration of personal and archetypal realities is a guiding motif of analytic work.

For a woman, psychotherapy with a woman provides a place for the primordial relationship of mother, daughter, and grandmother to be renewed.

The mutuality and mirroring that occur in a pure feminine container hold the possibility for an honoring and validating of woman's irrational as well as rational forces, both physical and spiritual. An emphasis on insight alone alienates women already denied their place in patriarchal culture, because the model of insight therapy is based on neutrality, distancing, isolationism, and self at the expense of others. By contrast, the "self-in-relation" model for therapy developed by the women psychologists and psychiatrists at the Stone Center at Wellesley College in Massachusetts stresses mutual empathy and empowerment in therapeutic relationship. Their model challenges the inherent male bias in previous psychotherapeutic systems, where women's femininity has been pathologized. Jean Baker Miller points out women's strengths to tolerate feelings of vulnerability, to nurture the development of others, to be cooperative, and to continue to be creative in emotional relatedness even in a patriarchal system where they are continually treated in a subordinate and degrading way.[8]

For women, change often involves not only a corrective emotional experience in therapy but a reeducation in specifically feminine values and a repudiation of patriarchal ones, which have usurped the relationship of women to their own natural cycles. A feeling of connectedness to her own intrinsic value supports and furthers a woman's developmental journey. When the personal mother-daughter-grandmother relationship has failed to embody that value, a woman may find ancient sources to revitalize her femininity in ways that support her modern womanhood.

The earliest artistic representation of the mother-daughter pair is depicted on frescoes excavated at Çatal Hüyük in ancient Anatolia (now Turkey) dating from the seventh millennium B.C. The Goddess of regeneration—a birth-giving figure with arms and legs upraised—is the central image represented at this Neolithic site, where religion was a part of people's daily lives.[9] She is often doubled—that is, two identical figures are shown side by side, one smaller without breasts, one larger with breasts. The double aspect is thought to refer both to the mother-daughter pair and to the Goddess in her dual aspect of maiden and mother.[10] One marble statue dating from 2200 B.C. shows the mother-daughter pair fused at the bottom with two heads, two sets of breasts but only two arms between them (figure 7). I take these images of the fusion of mother and daughter at Çatal Hüyük to mean that, as a given and necessary component of the culture, mother and daughter were interrelated in an immediate, helpful, and productive way from birth until death. The third aspect of the Great Goddess, the receiver of the dead, is represented by the symbol of a vulture at Çatal Hüyük.[11]

I have observed, in rural areas of Greece and in El Salvador, a matrifocal pattern in family life similar to what probably existed in prehistoric communities, where mother and daughter functioned as a unit. Initially, the little daughter is an adjunct to the mother in the home, helping with food preparation and housework and caring for younger siblings. In prehistoric times a daughter must have rarely left her mother's side. Today, in Greece and El Salvador, in addition to learning domestic work, she may attend school and prepare herself for a wider horizon. If, when the daughter reaches maturity, she leaves home to work or to attend college in a city, she still remains intimately connected to her mother. She sends support to her aging parents, returns home to help them, or takes her children to their home to be cared for. After marriage, the grandmother may move to the city to care for the children while her daughter works. Grandmothers are highly respected in these cultures. In this way the daughter remains psychologically within the mother.

This arrangement works beautifully in rural cultures that function in an interdependent and largely unconscious way. Fundamental to such cultures is the potential for the natural loving relationship between mother and daughter to express itself throughout life in mutually supportive ways. Each is able to see the life force of the feminine mirrored, expressed, and magnified in the other.

Artists tend to objectify archetypal and spiritual forces in the form of divinities. At Çatal Hüyük the divine feminine is everywhere visible in symbolic form. In modern Greece the divine feminine is expressed in ancient sculpture and paintings as well as in ritual devotion to the Virgin Mary. In El Salvador the Virgin Mary is the central figure in religious life. The art of the people in El Salvador also reflects an honoring of women's work in spiritual form. When I was in San Salvador recently, I found crosses painted with a central figure of a dancing woman, arms outstretched, with small vignettes of women's daily life filling the rest of the space. The overall effect of this brightly colored work is one of related, joyful, abundant life. The cross has become a symbol of cooperation and fertility instead of isolation and suffering.

With increased consciousness, however, the problem for modern women has become very different. Archetypal feminine images have almost completely vanished from our culture. With the exception of some museum art, some works by modern women artists, and shrines to the Virgin Mary in Roman Catholic churches, women have had no spiritual or archetypal framework in which to feel contained. Many Catholic women find no inspiration in an insipid, idealized Madonna, devoid of earthy female energy, sexuality, and life.

The eradication of the feminine from spiritual life has led to the patriarchal devaluation of the traditional female roles of childbearing and housekeeping and the trivialization of women's relationships with one another. The place of women in the world of work is still limited by discrimination, and our society does not support women's double role as homemaker and career woman. Equality of roles in the home between husband and wife has yet to be realized. Women in our culture are born into an unequal society and are raised to suffer patiently their second-class status.

A woman seeking psychotherapy today usually feels denied her wholeness by both society and family, whether her mother gave herself to child-rearing, had a career, or did both. Internally a modern woman still bears the weight of centuries of degradation. The patriarchal attitude of woman as inferior is so deeply ingrained in our psyches that it has become a repressive force of archetypal proportion.

The marble statue at Çatal Hüyük (figure 7) with only one pair of hands, therefore, is no longer simply a positive image of the archetypal wholeness of the mother-daughter pair. Instead, it psychologically represents a symbiotic mother-daughter relationship in which the power to act, to do, to effect, is lost. Where the feminine is repressed and the female denied her fullness, such deformation, fusion, and lack of ability is inevitable. The image comes to represent the two halves of one woman, one of which can only be expressed at the expense of the other. The mother voice in a woman tells her to accept the conventional values and standards that keep her subservient to men *for her own good;* the daughter voice tells her to fight for the authenticity and power that is her feminine right. Whether a woman chooses to fulfill herself as a single woman, as a woman in relation to another woman, as a wife, as a mother, and/or as a career woman, the internal division will make itself felt in both inner and outer life. It may be expressed externally in a single woman's inability to balance her relationship to a lover with her all-consuming job demands, or in her inability to form satisfying love relationships or to find meaningful work in the world, or in her frustration at trying to meet the overwhelming demands of both her children and her profession. Struggling with patriarchy within and without, women find themselves divided and bound in many ways.

Internally, the single pair of hands in the Çatal Hüyük double image manifests in a woman's negative mother complex, in which the daughter's feeling of being incomplete is projected outward into negative mother feelings. The daughter is caught in identifying with her mother in negative ways. She feels trapped by her mother and longs to separate; she wants to develop herself, but she remains dependent. Where the mother has devalued the feminine in herself, she cannot bequeath the secure femininity that her daughter needs or provide a role model for her in the world. In her search for herself, the daughter clings to her mother, who, she feels sure, has her missing feminine essence. In some cases, the mother, in her emptiness, also turns toward the daughter to fulfill herself. In others, the mother distances herself or actively rejects her daughter. They become locked in a love-hate relationship. Sometimes the death of the parent is the only release from this negative bond. The dependency between them reflects a failed search for the wholeness they each wish to find. In a culture that valued the feminine, they would naturally be finding it in each other. But, tragically, this feminine wholeness is nearly invisible in our society.

Woman-to-woman psychotherapy offers hope for the restoration of this wholeness. After some years of work, a woman is sometimes able to reconnect with her mother or her daughter on new emotional ground. On a personal level, such a reunion brings about a precious healing of the mother-daughter relationship for each of them. On a collective level, the new consciousness between mother and daughter restores and renews a link in our generational feminine heritage.

The shift from unconscious matriarchal fusion of mother and daughter to more differentiation and consciousness between mother and daughter begins to be represented in early Greek art. Instead of the fusion seen in the Çatal Hüyük statue, the mother-daughter pair is rendered side by side as nearly identical (figure 2). Toward the fifth century B.C., the archetypal deities of Demeter and Persephone become a mother with nursing baby at her breast. A statue of Demeter nursing Persephone is still found in Enna, Sicily, serving as Virgin and Child in a local church.[12] In the friezes depicting Demeter and Persephone at Eleusis of the early fifth century B.C. (figure 11), mother and daughter face each other in direct communion, instead of staring out at the viewer side by side, each unconscious of the other.

The myth of Demeter and the abduction of her daughter, Kore/Persephone, is articulated in the Homeric "Hymn to Demeter" in the seventh century B.C. This story is the archetype of the mother-daughter relationship in Western culture. The following is my paraphrase of the poem, using much of Homer's language as it appears in the translation by Charles Boer.

> The myth begins with Kore playing with her friends in a meadow, gathering flowers. In the distance is her mother, Demeter. Kore spies a fragrant flower, the narcissus, which Earth caused to grow at her father Zeus' request to entice the girl for Hades. As Kore reaches out her hands to take the lovely blossom, the earth opens, and out leaps Hades, lord of the underworld. He seizes her and bears her away in his golden chariot, weeping and wailing.
>
> As Demeter hears her daughter's cries, "a sharp pain seizes her heart," and she speeds like a wild bird over land and sea, searching for her child. No one wants to tell her the truth. For nine days, she wanders over the earth with flaming torches in her hands, fasting, her hair untied. "Not once did she taste of ambrosia or the sweet draught of nectar,

for she was grieving, nor did she once plunge her body in bath." Hecate, goddess of the crossroads, tells Demeter that she heard Kore's cries but did not see who carried her off. Together they go to the Sun, who tells them that Zeus gave Kore to his brother Hades.

Demeter continues to mourn and travels to Eleusis, where she lives for a time, acting as nursemaid to the baby Achilles. There she unexpectedly finds some relief in laughter at Baubo's bawdy clowning. Demeter then asks to have a temple and altar built in her honor.

As long as Kore is lost, Demeter causes the earth to be barren. When it becomes apparent to Zeus that the human race will perish and the gods be denied their honor should Demeter not be appeased, Zeus is forced to send Hermes to the underworld to bring Kore back. Hades allows her to go but not without affirming himself as a worthy husband and her as Persephone, queen of the underworld. (Up to this point in the myth, she is called Kore, the generic word for "girl" in Greek.) Hades "secretly slipped her a sweet pomegranate seed to eat" so that she would have to return to him. Hermes takes her back to her mother, who is waiting in her temple at Eleusis.

Demeter leaps up, and Persephone runs to meet her mother. Demeter asks to hear the whole story of the abduction and explains to Persephone that if she has partaken of any food in the underworld, she will have to go back and dwell with the shades a third part of the year and live only two parts of the year with her mother and the other gods. "Whenever the earth blossoms with all kinds of fragrant spring flowers, you will come back up again from the mist darkness, to the great astonishment of gods and mortal men."

"They spent the whole of that day, with hearts united, and they warmed each other's hearts with many gestures of affection, and her heart stopped grieving. They gave and received joy from each other." Hecate joins the mother and daughter in their reunion, and from that day on attends Persephone. The ecstatic Demeter makes the ground fertile again and bestows two gifts on the Greek people, the gift of grain, or corn,[13] and the gift of the Mysteries.[14]

Woman-to-woman therapy enacts this matriarchal mystery: the "heuresis" or "finding again" of the daughter by the mother, of Kore by Demeter, the reunion of mother and daughter. As Erich Neumann said, "Psychologically, this finding again signifies the annulment of the male rape and incursion so that the nuclear situation of the matriarchal group, the primordial relation of daughter to mother . . . is renewed and secured in the mystery."[15]

The myth can be read on many levels and still eludes conclusive interpretation. The archetypal level is represented in the unfailing bond between mother and daughter, a bond of unbroken continuity from the beginning of time. The female therapist and patient in psychotherapeutic process enact a psychological mother-daughter reunion in the interest of healing. At the same time, each carries her own psychic mother and daughter within her. This creates a pure and powerful feminine container for the analysis.

The myth of Demeter and Persephone probably originally represented the cycle of an agricultural society with its seasonal changes of growth, Demeter as "Grain Mother,"[16] and her daughter the young fruit of the earth. Later Demeter became more the actual corn and Persephone the life force in the seed that appeared and disappeared into the ground. The mother gradually embodied the earth, physicality, and the daughter the underworld, spirituality.[17] When Persephone's fate is accomplished and she has to spend a third of the year with her husband as queen of his ghostly domain, Hecate, who heard her cries, becomes her constant companion. Hecate provides the third, the moon aspect. Demeter, Persephone, and Hecate form a trinity of feminine earth, underworld, and sky. They also represent the three phases of the moon: new moon, full moon, and waning moon; maiden, mother, and crone. Hecate herself is threefold (figure 9), but for the Greeks, as the dark aspect, she embodied the *power* of the moon.[18]

Gradually the myth took on new dimensions with the establishment of male domination in Athens. It gave voice to women's predicament in classical Greece, at the height of male supremacy, when a girl was separated from her mother and married off as soon as possible after her menarche. This patriarchal practice was enforced even though it was known that the younger the woman, the greater the risk of childbirth. Women who died in childbirth were considered to be heroes like men who died in battle.[19]

This legacy of male domination and female victimization extends into the present and is rigidly resistant to change. Psychotherapy for women today often involves a radical reeducation to the feminine, away from the patriarchal values with which all women have been raised. Because in our culture many women have not had the prepubescent closeness with their mothers that Greek women apparently had, the task in analysis becomes the heuresis, or finding again, of the lost feminine both personally and culturally. This cultural liberation takes place for each woman in the context of psychological development that is driven by a necessity erupting from within. The influence of each woman's development extends outward in ever-widening circles to affect both the other women and the men in her life. Through her own willingness to endure the descent, she becomes a true cultural heroine instead of a sacrifice to the patriarchal system.

Woman-to-woman therapy is the ritual container for the lost feminine in our culture. Her lost femininity must be restored to a woman before she can relate in her fullness to a man again or take up a meaningful place in the world. Two women in psychotherapy share an ongoing personal, cultural, and archetypal experience that includes their mothers as well as themselves. This configuration produces an unusual state of empathy that has the potential to become a ritual experience of the matriarchal mystery.

The reunion of Demeter and Persephone brought two gifts to the Greeks. Demeter first gave them the Eleusinian mysteries as initiation rites into the life of the spirit. Her second gift was the gift of grain, or agriculture. As a consequence of the reunion, the Greek people were enriched both materially and spiritually. Psychologically, the reunion of mother and daughter enriches a modern woman's psyche and her environment.

Woman-to-woman therapy can accomplish an "annulment of male rape and incursion" and restore mother-daughter unity in the mystery. The purpose of this restoration is not to recapture a golden matriarchal age but to renew a woman for her contemporary life. Revitalizing her femininity helps her find a new order of relationship with men and with her own inner maleness. This new relationship is a task that reaches far into the future and will take concerted effort from both women and men. All of us are affected by the patriarchal imbalance in our society. One image that recurs in modern women's dreams is that of giving birth to a baby boy; I believe this is a manifestation of the cultural unconscious [20] in women attempting to give birth to a new way of being in relation to men and maleness.

In the Homeric "Hymn to Demeter," there is no description of the relationship between Hades and Persephone. But I see Hades as more than a force disruptive to the idyllic mother-daughter relationship. With respect to female-male relationship, Hades, a powerful male deity, slips Persephone the pomegranate seed, a fertilizing seed. Kore becomes queen and is *named* after her sojourn in the underworld, which suggests, respectively, maturation and individuality. Their marriage was considered the prototypical marriage, with its guarantee of reproduction. Perhaps the divine marriage of Hades and Persephone was an archetypal intimation of the modern task men and women have inherited of transcending patriarchal roles and finding a new union. Such a union has yet to be realized, has yet to come to light. As an inner symbol the seed is the fertilization of feminine creativity by masculine spirit. Jung called this masculine element the *logos spermatikos,* the fertilizing word.[21] This insemination can happen within a woman as well as in her dialogue with a man. Masculine and feminine each need the other, symbolically, for completion, for fertility. This is true for all men and women, regardless of sexual preference.

From my observation of women's dreams and fantasies, the abduction motif is very powerful for women. The attraction of being carried off, away from the group, on an unknown adventure appeals to the feminine psyche.[22] It seems to be a call to individuation. Psychologically, it is "otherness" that draws a woman. Sometimes the "other" takes the form of a man or a woman; sexuality always promises something beyond the moment. At other times it may take the form of a creative project, a trip, or a compelling cause. But the inner or outer irresistible "other" involves an element of possession, passion, or force. The fascination with the unknown "other" compels a woman to take up her own fate, willing or unwilling, of becoming an individual, of completing or developing herself.[23] Hades is the "other," the unknown opposite in this myth. In the Sumerian myth of Inanna, the descent to the underworld, the call to individuation, is effected by Inanna's dark sister, Ereshkigal.[24] As modern women realize themselves and as both women and men change, new archetypes of feminine development and of the union between masculine and feminine are being created in the unconscious.

The story of Demeter and Persephone has continued to serve as a mythic enactment of patriarchal repression. Culturally, the myth reflects the problem of a woman's natural inclination to influence and affect the world she is born into, only to find herself forced into submission to the dominant male power structure. Personally, it can be seen to reflect the problematic relationship between a woman's sexuality that draws her to a man and her revulsion for that man who will, under the patriarchy, dominate her. After puberty, as she becomes capable of integrated sexuality, it is natural for a girl to be drawn away from the mother, drawn to a man or to a woman lover. If a woman is a lesbian, the mother-daughter problem will still exhibit the effects of patriarchal forces. Sexual development and its subsequent pull toward a relationship outside the family is a normal stage of feminine maturation, a development that brings her closer to her mother in status, a sexually mature woman herself. There is no psychological reason that it should sever a daughter's relationship to her mother.

Seen from this perspective, the second half of the story, the reunion of mother and daughter that produces the fruitful gifts and simultaneously allows her to spend part of her time in the underworld with her husband, to assume her place as queen, has yet to happen culturally for us. We have yet to reach a balance of power between masculine and feminine. And women are only gradually finding themselves in internal reunion with the mother through their own self-nurturing. But the power of the myth, embedded as it is in genetic mother-daughter relationship, has kept and continues to keep the hope alive for women. Psychologically, the first step for our cultural development lies in the reunion of the mother-daughter pair within each individual woman.

Demeter's mourning and her search lie at the center of the therapeutic process between women, as does Persephone's innocence, incomprehension, fear, trauma, and eventual reconciliation. On a developmental level, Kore's abduction and descent can be seen as unconsciously partially by choice, motivated by her own awakening sexuality and desire to mature. It mirrors her initiation through defloration, her second blood mystery. When a girl's hymen is broken, she bleeds; this is significant for her and for the man who has shed her blood. She is forever changed physically and psychologically. Part of that change is accepting separation (not severance) from her mother, becoming queen in her own right. A later, Orphic version, of the myth shows Persephone, secreted in a house by Demeter, weaving a scarf for her mother.[25] Three goddesses, Aphrodite, Athena, and Artemis, come to tempt her out to the meadow where the abduction will take place. Away from the protective circle of her mother's love, her potential will be fulfilled. She will meet her fate. A separation from childhood innocence, a confrontation with the unknown, and a coming to terms with what she has lost and what she has gained through her experience are part of each woman's journey of initiation. As part of her maturation Kore realizes a third dimension of her femininity, the power of the dark moon goddess, Hecate.

Demeter's initiation is in the search and eventual reconciliation with her daughter. Viewed externally, the myth presents the mother-daughter pair as blissfully merged, then as separated and different from each other. Initially they are desperate about being separated, but eventually both come to terms with their individual identities. Viewed internally, the myth can be seen as the separation of a woman from herself, her lost femininity, her lost other, and the necessity for renewal in that reunion.

Usually, by the time a woman enters therapy, the original state of harmony between mother and daughter is already profoundly disturbed, so that both loss of feminine self and a skewed or traumatic experience in relation to the patriarchy feel to her as if destined from birth.

As a result of the cultural bias in favor of men, not only does a woman live in fear of external male violence, criticism, and rejection, but male "forces" reign in her psyche. Often in therapy, what has to be carefully monitored and worked through is the patriarchal complex that is operating within the patient. Whether dealing with male power and glory or male destructiveness, the woman, the feminine, is always on the defensive. Sometimes it takes many years to extricate a woman from the internal oppression of this collective male domination so that she can find her own inner ground. The task is all the more difficult because simultaneously, for her well-being, she has to negotiate relationships with men in her life as well as with inner male figures.

When male forces reign in a woman's psyche, her dreams are preoccupied with male figures who are either threatening, violent, and annoying or powerful, charismatic, and helpful. Rape, assault, burglary, machines, and nuclear war are prevalent themes. Or she may have dreams of heroic, seductive, and powerful men who appear to save the woman in distress. The woman and other female figures appear briefly and tangentially. They are powerless, subdued, in awe, or at best, on the defensive in relation to the male figures. The woman is either terrified of, dependent on, or identified with the internal and external men in her life. This complete preoccupation with maleness is more pronounced in women who have experienced male violence toward the feminine as children, either physical or emotional, in conjunction with mothers who were identified with the masculine or unable to embody the feminine themselves. But all women in our culture have to struggle with this patriarchal complex by virtue of the history we share. Psychologically, the inner profile of even culturally advantaged women often reveals a state of dependence upon the male constructs to which they and their mothers and grandmothers have been bound for centuries. In the most extreme cases, there is no substance to the feminine, no solid female core, no fleshy sexual being, no viable female ego evident in a woman's dreams and inner life. She is a shadow of herself, a brittle persona, cowering and terrified. Male power threatens, intrudes, dismembers, dominates. Hecate's dark power, then, is needed to midwife the birth of a stronger feminine self.

Gradually, the negotiations with male dream figures, as well as external men in a woman's life, first effect a transformation in a woman's ego functioning. She becomes less fearful and more productive, and her relationships improve. Working with this cultural complex consists of undoing or unlearning the patriarchal construct of our society. It is not always an initial or discrete stage in the therapeutic process; sometimes it goes on simultaneously or alternately with the evolution or strengthening of a deeper feminine identification. For some women, it is the singular focus of the initial stage of therapy. But this is only one aspect to the beginning of the profound change that is possible if the initiation into being a woman-identified woman is carried through.

Whereas male presences may make themselves felt in dreams, complexes, and outer relationships in the container of woman-to-woman therapy, such male forces remain peripheral to the two feminine beings face-to-face with body and soul completely present. The therapy becomes a feminine *temenos*,[26] or sacred space. No intrusions penetrate that place. A woman begins to shift her focus to herself, toward her own female center, a movement toward liberating her instinct, passion, and mind. In this way she fills out, enlarges, magnifies, and seeks new ground on which to stand. She is supported in her changing by another woman who already stands on the ground she needs to find.

The mutuality of two women alone creates an environment similar to the ritual spaces throughout history into which only women were allowed, for example, the Jewish *mikveh,* the purification bath for women after menstruation, or the temples of the moon goddess in ancient Greece, where priestesses tended the altar and grounds. In our contemporary world, even the atmosphere in a women's locker room in a gymnasium reflects the subtle altering of feeling that occurs in a context that is exclusively female.

Although envy and competition between women are stereotypical in our society, woman-to-woman therapy confronts those stereotypes as psychic energy realigns itself as cooperation and appreciation between women. When the focus is on the capacity of women to empower one another, envy and competition diminish. The divisive energy of male domination that pits women against one another falls away.

Beyond the societal issues, however, becoming a woman-identified woman is the deeper quest. Within a feminine container, a woman has the possibility of entering an initiation that affirms her deepest nature, including body, psyche, and soul. And sometimes her journey may lead on to a spiritual quest.

One of the richest female initiation ceremonies is the Kinaaldá, performed by the Navajo. Changing Woman is the Navajo tribe's primary deity. She is "the woman who is transformed time and again"[27] growing old and becoming young again with the change of the seasons. As the myth says, "Whatever is on the earth's surface and the means of making life possible have all been given into her charge."[28] According to the Navajo story, Changing Woman, who is also called White Shell Woman and Turquoise Woman, established the Kinaaldá, her menstruation ceremony, as a model for all. Following menarche, each girl is ritually made over according to Changing Woman's model before she takes her place as a woman in the community. In preparation for the ceremony, the initiate must choose an Ideal Woman, or sponsor, a woman she admires, to accompany her through the initiation (figure 3). The initiate's mother is also intimately involved with the ceremony.[29] The relationship between initiate and sponsor is a compelling model for the therapeutic relationship between two women.

The double aspect of the feminine is presented in Neolithic Çatal Hüyük as two undifferentiated halves. The Eleusinian mysteries present the mother-daughter pair as both together or merged and separate or different. The Kinaaldá presents a conscious and differentiated choice of sponsor who tends the girl through the initiatory process. This exogamous[30] choice acknowledges the initiation as a spiritual event as well as an honoring of the girl's physical fertility. All these dyadic forces are operating in woman-to-woman psychotherapy. In the context of a meaningful relationship to a woman analyst, a woman finds a container in which she can unite body, soul, and self-image.

The *temenos* of psychotherapy includes both the physical surrounding of the office space and the unique nature of the relationship between the two women. The space remains constant, as does a temple, synagogue, or church. The relationship with each woman differs according to the conscious and unconscious interaction between our psyches. In my own analytic office, the atmosphere is influenced by a painting that shimmers with desert tones of purple, mauve, sand, and metallic copper and gold. It hangs on the wall behind my chair facing the woman opposite me. Four by five feet, it consists of thirty-six individual squares that illustrate the Greek myth of Eros and Psyche interpreted by Erich Neumann as the psychic development of the feminine.[31] This myth became important to the artist at a time in her life when the creative muse had abandoned her. This painting emerged after a long period of studying the tale in its many versions.[32]

Though there are many myths women identify with in their psychological processes, this painting is witness day in and day out to the psychotherapeutic work that goes on in my office. Working in the presence of this painting has affected me and the women who sit opposite it in mysterious ways. Its powerful imagery evokes responses and mirrors feelings that arise from the unconscious depths of women changing.

In the tale of Eros and Psyche, Psyche's initiation begins when, goaded by her sisters who say her bridegroom, Eros, is a hideous serpent, she lights a lamp in order to see him. Previously, he has hidden his identity from her. By electing to *know* him for what he is—man, beast, or god—pregnant Psyche embarks on a path to consciousness and suffers the immediate loss of both her own comfort and security and her husband's love.[33] Beginning psychotherapy brings light to what previously has been experienced in the dark. Taking the first step is anxiety-provoking for some women, frightening for others. The physical container is unfamiliar; I am a stranger, and the relationship between us has yet to develop.

When CARMINA was beginning therapy at the age of nineteen, she defined her ambivalence this way: "I'm afraid to look into the mirror that you are to me. The therapy relationship is a relief but scary. I'm afraid of the dependency because it might be taken away from me." Carmina was pursuing a bachelor's degree in fine arts when I met her. Her initial dream after seven months in therapy reflected a deep fear and distrust of our relationship.

> You and I are standing facing each other. I know it's me. It feels like me. You have both hands on my back. You turn into someone else, someone who is ugly.

For Carmina, the dream was both erotic and terrifying. She said, "I am afraid of being rejected by you, afraid of damaging this situation, because I value being here. I have vicious, destructive self-hatred. I have a problem drawing the line with women. Sometimes I get obsessed about how ugly I am. Sexually I am attracted to men, but I fear men. With women I get security, communication, closeness, then sex as an extension of those feelings." Carmina feared her father, a research scientist, who, in his cerebral orientation, had failed to appreciate her budding femininity. When she was two years old, a brother was born with muscular dystrophy, a degenerative genetic disease. All her mother's energy had gone toward the newborn, and Carmina had felt abandoned. When Carmina entered therapy, she and her mother were more friends than mother and daughter. But there was an unconscious fusion between them that caused problems. Carmina's first deep love experience had been with a girl a few years older than herself when she was thirteen. She had had subsequent sexual relationships with both girls and boys. It was her difficulties with her self-image and with intimacy that led her to seek therapy.

In her dream, at the beginning of what was to be a ten-year psychotherapeutic relationship, the emotional container is highly charged. We are standing close enough to touch. I am holding her; she is attracted but frightened of her power to turn me/her into something ugly or bad. The shadow side of mother-daughter closeness is evident here: what hurts one hurts the other; boundaries are blurred; what is experienced as wonderful merging transforms into ugliness and hatred. The roles can be reversed at any time. Carmina could not trust our relationship at this point, and in the past she had experienced the power of her own self-destructive complex to alter her self/body image. When she was in the grip of that complex, her perception of her own beauty was so distorted that no actual or symbolic mirror could restore her to herself. I felt steadfast in the face of her fears because from the beginning I felt a strong unconscious connection with this woman, twelve years younger than I was. The message of the dream to me was that initially I had to hold everything for her—her dreams, her fears, her hatred, and her love—until her own individual path emerged.

Six years later, the container was dramatically changed. Although Carmina still worried about the boundaries between us, feared the process of psychotherapy, and struggled with trusting me, the years of psychotherapeutic work had produced a ritual response in the unconscious. The following dream revealed the change in the nature of the work.

> I'm at your house. I'm there for a session in your office. You propose to hypnotize me. I think, "Oh, nothing will happen, it won't work." But something does happen. I realize I am hypnotized and feel suffocated, like I'm succumbing. It is happening to me; I have no control over it. I fall asleep in an intense way. I know I will remember nothing from the experience.

I wake up, and I'm aware of the clock changing, the hands moving with no relevance to real time. While I've been asleep, you've been off busy in your house. I feel like an intruder, uncomfortable. I get my things to leave. But suddenly your children come in, both blonde. I'm looking for signs of you in them; the eyes are yours. I know that one of the boys is bad; the younger one is five, the older, eight. I start playing with them, reading them a story, hanging out with them. We make toast. You keep working, cleaning house. It gets later and later, closer to dinnertime. You're glad I'm amusing the children. It gives you some time.

Suddenly I panic and realize it's time for your husband to come home. I rush out. The house is high on a hill, which is jagged and rocky. Halfway down I find myself among pavilions in a lush garden. I pass your husband sitting on a bench under the arbor near the gate, engrossed in something. I start running. I'm crying. There is broken glass and garbage everywhere. Things have degenerated. On my way up it was well-kept; now it's neglected.

At the bottom of the hill there is an inlet or bay. I go into the water and do a cleansing ritual that you had told me about. I throw off my clothes and wash and wash. I'm still angry with you about the house scene, upset and hurt. You're in the water swimming. We both see what is happening as positive. I run along the sand, and there you are with a pregnant woman. You are explaining the cleansing ritual to her. It's another Carmina, another me. I'm jealous of her. She's so connected to you; I want that. A wave comes swirling over me, feeling like hypnosis, but not safe. I keep waiting for pain or death, but it doesn't come. I'm just inside the wave.

Carmina was unconsciously exploring the nature of the container between us. Boundary and control issues were primary for her. In the dream she has come to my home, crossed a boundary, to see me. With that boundary crossed, she feels forced/seduced into a process over which she has no control. A passive victim of hypnosis in the dream, she fears loss of consciousness in our work. That she falls asleep and remembers nothing means that the therapeutic work was lost. Instead she ends up babysitting my children, a role with which she had been comfortable in relation to other women whom she admired. Falling into that role would have been the end of her analytic work. Carmina had never felt that she could have both herself and a relationship to another person. As long as she resisted active participation in her own process she was psychologically at risk for repeating the dependent relationships she had had in the past with other women. When she flees my home in the dream, she sees the shadow of what her unconscious had lured her into—the garbage. Fear of maleness in the form of my husband forces her into the deeper female experience. She finds a bay in which to perform a purification ritual that she says she learned from me. At this point she lets go of the old pattern of her being either babysitter or lover to her Ideal Woman. Although still fleeing the man, she goes toward *herself* in the woman-to-woman therapeutic container.

The shift in the dream from my home and imaginary family, where Carmina feels passively hypnotized, to nature, where she chooses to perform a cleansing rite, was critical to the deepening of her therapeutic work. The ocean bay is the collective unconscious, the source of all life, which she and I had to both know and share for her work to be viable. In the Eleusinian mystery rite, purification was one of the preparations for the ceremony. On the specified day a great cry went up in Athens where all the participants were gathered: "Initiates into the sea!" Each initiate went down into the sea to bathe herself, carrying her offering of a sow. After bathing herself and her pig, she went on to the temple to make her sacrifice to Demeter.[34]

In the dream Carmina reunites with me at the sea and meets her female double. This shadow[35] figure, who appeared again and again in Carmina's work, often carried the positive, more developed qualities of her psyche. At this stage of therapy, the missing aspect of herself was less susceptible to being projected onto the other woman. Here the double was the one pregnant with new life, the one in right relationship to me. This boded well for the progress of the therapy. It resonated to the separate mother-daughter images at Çatal Hüyük and in ancient Greece. Carmina and her twin were separate but also alike; one was pregnant, one not. Doubling in the unconscious refers to an entity being on the verge of consciousness. A doubled image intensifies the power of a single image. In the atemporal world of ritual, the motivating force of Carmina's work could express itself as rebirth, the powerful reunion of her disparate parts. In the temporal world of personal relationship, she could only reenact the old patterns that had kept her from finding her womanhood.

The reference in the dream to the clock not marking real time refers to the timelessness in ritual experience. Carmina's changing dictated time passing. Carmina said about this dream, "I'm dependent on your compassion. You are so important to me. Analysis is *my* work, but I don't want to feel that involved with you or it. I feel the conflict between the mundane world and symbolic reality. I'm afraid I'll consume you or you'll consume me. In every relationship either I'm absorbed or I absorb." In addition to the two worlds of personal and symbolic significance, the dream's image of lush pavilions represented a third, or middle, level. This magical site was to become Carmina's unique place of being, appearing often in her dreams and fantasies, bringing with it a sense of calm, beauty, and order. But here it is only hurriedly glimpsed. There is still much tension between the different levels and a sense of desperation about her plunge into the sea. But the plunge does bear fruit in the form of her pregnant double who appears with the promise of new life.

A month later new life transformed the container of our work together, as revealed in the following dream. Carmina described it as "an enormous dream, the most amazing one I've ever had, an emotional, physical dream":

> I am in your office. There are some things in it from my house. It is a shared place, steeped in colors I associate with you. I go into a deep hypnotic state voluntarily. I find an internal landscape. You have your arms around me. You are beside me and behind me creating a sleep container. You are not asleep. You are conscious, protecting my condition. I have a completely safe feeling that happens in my heart. I could not draw the feeling. I know there is a confrontation I have to make with IT. I let myself go and do it. I experience agony, a searing pain in the center of my body. I'm breathing into the pain, as in shiatsu. You press my chest, release a point, the heart pain point, and I breathe through it. Then we move physically into a pattern: we are both curved, both lying down; I am looking down into your face. We make a container together.
>
> Then I am still on the ground. You are standing up. I grab at your feet and ankles. I feel I have to be near you. There is something about "Do I have to go? Or not?" Then, "No I don't." At the end a woman materializes wearing a medallion necklace. There is a message from her.

Carmina described how the low, square, mahogany table that is present in our dream space had been her grandmother's and was a cherished possession. Some of her urns and baskets have also joined my objects in the enclosure of my office. The dream was a picture of the therapeutic interaction between us during this period. Carmina had now submitted herself to her initiation. She had put herself in my hands, in my trust, for an initiatory purpose. The dream showed us working through her painful material with her full participation. Unlike the initial dream, where I was the active one reaching out to her, she the passive/receptive one, or the second dream, where I still had the power over her process by hypnotizing her, here we were equally forming the "pattern" of the process. Our two female bodies made a "container" together.

At the end of the dream, Carmina's fear of rejection and need to stay in union with me arises. I break the merger first. But she is told she does not have to go. And a new woman appears in the office wearing a medallion and bearing a message. Although we did not know who this woman was or would be, she foreshadowed the larger motivating force behind the work, the figure on whom Carmina was intrinsically dependent, an archetypal vision of the feminine Self. She can be seen as an aspect of Changing Woman, whose jeweled dresses are intrinsic to her identity.[36] Her appearance was a corollary to the intimate work we two women had been doing. It was Carmina's dawning relationship to this entity over the next four years of our work that would allow her to separate from me, terminate her therapy, and move into life on her own authority.

The woman who chose the name SARAH was at a different stage of life and in different circumstances when she entered therapy. Thirty years old, married, doing a fellowship in endocrinology, she sought therapy because she was distressed about an ongoing power struggle with her husband. A dream early in our work revealed her fear of the path she had chosen:

> I have been set a task that I can't do.

Sarah said that the dream discouraged her, because "I had done good work that day, and I was really flying high." Sarah's ego development was strong. She was the second child and eldest daughter in a Catholic family of five siblings. Her fifteen-months-older brother had been quiet and shy. Bright, charming, and extroverted, Sarah had received much time and attention from her parents. She had helped parent her three younger siblings, two boys and a girl, and identified with her successful father and his patriarchal perspective. Her sister, the youngest in the family, had identified with her mother. As a result, Sarah had accomplished her academic and professional goals and felt competent in the world. The dream's statement that she had been set an insurmountable task revealed how difficult it would be for her to change in her eleven years of psychotherapy.

Six months after this dream, her archetypal guide, the unknown "other" who set the task in the earlier dream, emerged in the therapeutic container between us:

> There is a king and a queen, but the king doesn't have much of a role. The queen, who is very beautiful, has asked me to come to her idealized kingdom, a kind of planned community, to do some endocrinological research. I am living in the community and am nervous about starting work. The queen asks me to come to her castle home. The garden paths are paved with rock. I speak with her in a chamber. We go to a religious service together, perhaps a mass. She has two children and wants to introduce them. Her daughter, the princess, kisses my ring, which features a beautiful pearl. I feel confused about why. What does it mean? The predominant feeling is one of specialness.

Sarah associated the queen with me: "She looked like you; she had red, auburn-colored hair, and the daughter had even redder hair. I feel I have a Jezebel shadow. Although I've always been invested in being my father's good girl, I've been secretly interested in Mary Magdalene, the sinner. I fear masculine judgment when I act out of feminine feeling. I always have to rationalize my feeling. I long for female receptivity."

The psychotherapeutic relationship had taken precedence in the psyche. In the dream, the masculine force is weak, in the background. Those feminine characteristics that had been relegated to the shadow in Sarah—sexuality, beauty, and female authority—are embodied in the queen who summoned her for this work. Mary Magdalene is the instinctual shadow of the spiritual Virgin Mary. The two are part of the Triple Goddess in the form of the Three Maries who watched the crucifixion of Christ.[37] The third is Saint Mary of Egypt, or Mary Gypsy, whose skin was black and who was renowned as a prostitute.[38] The queen in the dream also has a daughter who honors the human Sarah with a gesture of devotion, kissing her ring. The ring symbolizes relationship and suggested that Sarah's relationship with her own archetypal Queen guide as well as with me was already established, even though she herself was unaware of the meaning of the act. The dream introduced the queen as a Self figure and the daughter as a symbol of Sarah's undeveloped feminine shadow and assured Sarah's ego that she was worthy of tribute. Here were the archetypal mother-daughter as Queen and Princess, the doubling and the tripling of the feminine in generational form. The forces of change, of woman changing woman, were activated.

Fifteen months into our work together, we were deeply engaged in therapy. The dream showed us speaking in the Queen's chamber, a symbol for the therapeutic container. We attend a mass, suggesting that our work would necessarily involve a spiritual dimension. We had both been brought up in the Catholic church; the transformation symbolism of the Mass is a potent surviving mystery in Western religion.[39] Wine and bread are transformed during the ceremony into the body and blood of Christ. Sarah's pearl ring in the dream alludes to "the pearl . . . the jewel . . . the treasure hard to attain at the bottom of the water."[40] The search for the treasure was a central task of alchemy, the transformation of base metals into gold. The dream held the archetypal keys to the initiation process that Sarah was embarked on and manifested our connection in the unconscious.

Nearly a year later Sarah dreamed about our container again:

> You and I have been having sessions in a room in a cloister. You
> have changed the day for one session. As we walk together to the
> room, I see a series of altars in recessed chapels along the corridor.
> Nuns are carrying sacred vessels. It is quiet and solemn. We walk into
> the room. People are gathered around the piano, and you ask about
> them. It is a brothers and sisters choir that practices at this time every
> week. You suggest I join the choir. I say, "No, I'm tone deaf." We leave
> to find a room for our session.

The cloister, with its function of housing the sisters, their lives, and their rituals, in Sarah's childhood was an appropriate image of our therapeutic container. Sarah said, "We go deeper and deeper into the unconscious with the ritual of analysis." But there is an intrusion here. The week before Sarah had told me a dream in which she was imprisoned in a classroom of her Catholic grammar school. In the dream she tricks the nuns into coming into the room and smashes two of them in the face as she escapes. She said, "I think of the nuns with reverence. I wanted to be a nun. They were my teachers, my leaders. I idealized them. My goody-goody image was modeled on them." She had smashed her idols in this earlier dream.

Now Sarah and I are meeting in the cloister, and I am imposing something on her that does not suit her nature. She stands up to me and says, "I am tone deaf." I accept this, and we go on to find our individual container again. It made sense that she feared another set of rules being forced on her in the therapeutic context, with its powerful archetypal undercurrents that she had previously only experienced in the context of institutionalized religion. Once a nun had been her role model, and now I was. Her choice of me was exogamous, outside the family, school, and Catholic system. I embodied a sensual femininity in contrast to the nun's pious ascetic femininity. Initially, I carried that earthy feminine shadow for her. I appeared in several early dreams as the redhead, her Mary Magdalene shadow, as the "other woman" in relation to her husband. She needed me in that symbolic mediating role with him. The imagery also suggested that she was unaccustomed to relating directly to a woman without the presence of a man.

After seven years of work, our relationship combined elements of both the archetypal Queen and the woman "sponsoring" her initiation into womanhood:

> I am out in front of my house. You come by in a car and stop. You have come to tell me about a different approach or perspective on what I am doing. It is very helpful. Your hair is redder, longer, more flowing, your skin whiter. Your car is big, stretched out. Everything is exaggerated. You come like a consultant, I'm surprised you're there. We talk out in front for a while. Then I invite you in.

At this time Sarah was turning her attention to her inner world during our sessions, instead of focusing on the external events in her life. In reality, I had gone to Sarah's home for a session that month because she was ill. The dream confirmed that my visit made a strong impression on Sarah's unconscious. She confessed that she had felt more vulnerable after the visit, because it forced her to accept the reality of her illness. Usually, she ignored her body and its needs. The exaggerated imagery in the dream suggested that a new intensity had entered our relationship. This proved to be true in subsequent years as she struggled to allow her female body its self-expression.

Thirty-two-year-old BEATRICE entered therapy with me during a dreadful crisis with a man from whom she had separated. Only once during her five years of psychotherapeutic work did she have a dream that addressed the container of our relationship. The dream occurred about one year after she began therapy, the night before her wedding, when her stepmother called from England and verbally abused her for being pregnant, unwed, and marrying a "horror," her fantasy of Beatrice's fiance. Beatrice was completely distraught. In our session she told me, "That night I dreamt about you—you were a calming mother figure soothing my nerves." Beatrice had been raised in one room in Shanghai by her Chinese mother and maternal grandmother; she had never met her Russian father. At the age of seven she was thrust into an unknown world, handed over to a strange man, and never saw her mother or grandmother again. Between the ages of seven and thirty-two she was alone in the world, at the mercy of whatever man or institution would have her. Her experiences were cruel and traumatic. When she entered therapy with me, she found again her lost mother. In the beginning I often felt as if I were speaking to a seven-year-old girl, as if she had managed to preserve who she had been at the time of separation beneath an external shell of impassivity.

Like Psyche in the myth, each woman, Beatrice, Sarah, and Carmina, embarked on an initiatory journey sparked by an inner impulse toward consciousness and suffered the loss of the secure identity she had previously known. Submitting to a ritual of dream incubation, each sought healing of old wounds and a new vision of herself. All three became engaged in intense, deep therapeutic relationships, with me serving as Ideal Woman/ sponsor, midwife, or priestess. In the context of our unique dyadic container, each woman was pulled into the mystery of the mother-daughter relationship and found at least one inner archetypal guide or Self-figure who guided her initiation into womanhood. My role was to act as a mediator, to stand in for her own inner Self-figure, to help her access this figure directly, and ultimately, help her separate from me. As we worked together, Changing Woman danced in and out of each woman's transformative journey.

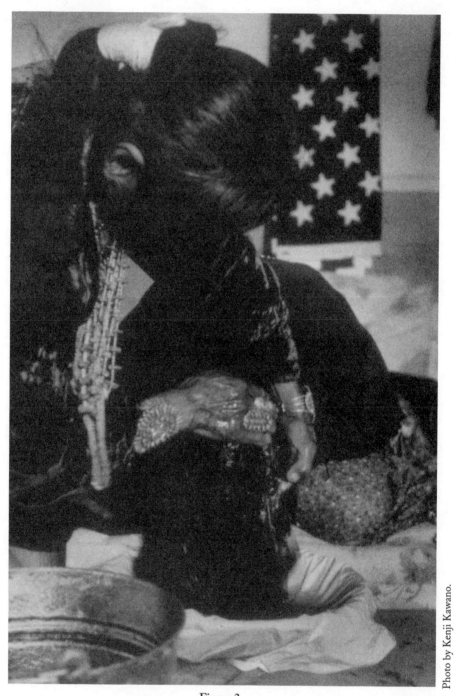

Figure 3.
The Ideal Woman Washing the Initiate's Hair in the
Navajo Girl's Puberty Ceremony.

2

Adorning a Woman

*I*n the collaborative work of deep analysis, a woman and her analyst return to the archetype of initiation inherent in the mother-daughter relationship that each of them experiences in her own body. A woman's first transformation is embodied in menarche, which initiates her pattern of monthly cycles. "In the course of one complete cycle which strangely corresponds to the moon's revolution," as Esther Harding wrote, "the woman's energy waxes, shines full and wanes again. These energy changes affect her, not only in her physical and sexual life but in her psychic life as well. Life in her ebbs and flows, so that she is dependent on her inner rhythm."[1]

In the course of woman-to-woman therapy, a woman's dreams, fantasies, and thoughts and feelings return to her adolescent years. Embarrassment, excitement, awakening, awkwardness intermingle in this transitional period. Images of her first best friend, a favorite teacher, a boyfriend, a change in her hairstyle, or a new piece of clothing that marked the shift from girl to adolescent float in and out of the conscious work in the present. This return to a time of life when great internal physical and emotional changes took place furthers the woman's progress toward psychological initiation.

The conditions surrounding menarche influence all of a girl's subsequent life, creating a pattern of complex psychological attitudes that mark her subsequent initiatory experiences: defloration, pregnancy, childbirth, nursing, and menopause. This pattern also influences and marks her psychological initiation. A woman in psychotherapy has often been subjected to familial reactions of avoidance, shame, and disgust toward her menarche and menstruation. Moreover, a modern woman lacks a rich cultural tradition of story telling in which to place her own experience of sacred blood. In the course of her life, she may struggle with premenstrual distress, menstrual pain, guilt about abortion, sorrow about infertility, anxiety about a distressing pregnancy or a traumatic birth, or inexplicable feelings of loss over the decision not to bear children. Hence her relationship to her menstrual cycles and therefore to her natural rhythmic self is typically disturbed. Parental denigration reinforces the denigration of the feminine in a patriarchal system. Fear of and ignorance about sexuality, pregnancy, and responsibility have become part of a woman's psyche in the wake of such devaluation.

In the midst of her struggle, a woman has found no wisdom in conventional family, community, or religious teaching to guide her. So she has come to therapy with feelings that her body is insignificant, alien, or at war with her spirit. Such alienation from her own ever-changing nature and its intrinsic relation to moon cycles requires a healing that consists of a deep realignment to a basic female spiritual principle.

Women speak of not remembering menarche, this landmark event in their lives, of mothers being secretive about their young daughters' first blood, of fathers being embarrassed and turning away, not wanting to know. At best a girl was able to share the change in her being with peers, joining the ranks of those who had already "started." What possibilities could there be for the development of the mature woman out of such barren ground? If this first phase of a woman's physiological and mysteriological development is thus devalued, what hope is there for the mature woman, for the sexual woman, for the mother, for the woman of age?

When I was a girl, approaching menarche, I was filled with secret anticipation. My budding breasts were a source of shy satisfaction and pride. My mother's blood was familiar to me from the monthly ritual appearance of Kotex in the bathroom. As early as I can remember, I was at times present when she changed the red-stained pad for a pure white one. I was thirteen years old when my first blood appeared. I was away from home, on a bus, on a field trip. But I returned to my mother's loving, caring, competent welcome and her valuing of this first initiatory experience for me. She conveyed the feeling that this was a feminine mystery. I do not remember whether or not she told my father. What I do remember is the profound sense of closeness to my mother those early periods brought me. While my blood flowed I felt inexplicably, irrationally pure, completely contained in my mother's realm. What my mother remembers is both her own sense of loss of her "little girl" and simultaneously her awe and relief that I embraced this transformation so smoothly. She felt my calm as a polar opposite to her own fearful experience of menarche. The fifth child of ten born to Italian immigrant parents, she had faced this important moment of her life with ignorance. But her instinct had led her to the right, natural induction with her eldest daughter. For me, that time was informed with grace.

I was fortunate to have little cramping with my periods so was free to enjoy my primary sense of connection to mother love in them. Innocent and cocooned in relation to her, I was less conscious of the sexuality implicit in this initiation. That was to come later and along with it the internal division that comes with the encounter with "the other." In these feelings of identification with the female realm, I was unconsciously identifying with generations of Italian Catholic women devoted to the Virgin Mary in whom the primordial archetype of the Great Mother still lives.

My feelings of purity during menstruation also echoed an ancient rite of purification. The womb sheds its lining each month: in some cultures this cleansing is celebrated collectively by sweats or in huts of seclusion where women practice purifying rituals. Women who live together menstruate together; they unconsciously synchronize with each other and the moon. A woman often turns inward during her period. During that time "she belongs to herself alone, she is 'one-in-herself.'"[2]

In my first therapeutic relationship with Magda Proskauer I learned to appreciate the ritual of my cycle in a psychological way. Magda taught me that the pull toward the inner world, the withdrawal from the outer world, was a force to be respected in itself. She talked about resting, withdrawing, honoring the incubatory state of menstruating. The result of such attention would be cumulative, she said, in that succeeding periods would be less fatiguing, less stressful, more fruitful and psychically creative. When I worked with Barbara Hannah in Zurich, she told me of her experience in South Africa as a young menstruating woman, where the native taboo on menstrual blood dictated ritual burial of the stained cloths instead of washing them for reuse. Such bits of women's wisdom are important pieces of our genealogical story telling. My feminine identity has been enhanced by such gems of knowledge.

Since that early therapeutic work I have learned that even if I cannot indulge in a retreat from the world during menstruation, I can still change my focus, let my attention move inward for the necessary time. And I have learned to value the chaotic, dark processes that often erupt during that phase of the moon. Whether the eruption produces images that are divine or demonic, I know the feelings will resolve with the end of the flow. And I am always richer for the insights that these images bring.

My own positive experience of menarche left me with a sense of trust and optimism about change that influenced both my physiological and my psychological development. When I felt ready for them, I found sexuality, pregnancy, childbirth, and nursing to be natural and joyful events. The difficulties inherent within these dramatic changes were challenges that I could meet confidently. Psychologically, I was able to embrace psychotherapy, then analysis, while intuitively knowing it portended drastic change, and to see the process through even when it entailed tremendous suffering and pain.

Carmina, Sarah, and Beatrice experienced menarche in different ways. All of them felt alienated from their bodies in some way as adult women. CARMINA related to me the story of the extraordinary events leading to her first bleeding in Barcelona, Spain.

> When I was twelve years old, I was traveling with my family in Spain. I didn't want breasts or femininity. There had been no allusions to menarche in my family. We were looking at all this bloody art in museums and churches—martyrdoms and crucifixions. One day I got my period. That night in my hotel room, I was looking at the stars through a glass cupola and I suddenly disappeared, dissolved into the starry space above me. I realized that religion was all a big lie, that I was going to die. It felt like cosmic death. I went screaming into my parents' bedroom.

Carmina had been raised in the Episcopal church and had just been confirmed before this trip. But when her period came in Barcelona, it was a profound experience; the reality of her own corporeal feminine mystery supplanted that of the church. She was glad to now be like everyone else in her group who had begun menstruating, but she became afraid of men, because she felt she didn't know the rules of relationship with them and was afraid of "being damaged." In her early years of menstruating, she said, "I lived in virginal fantasy, regenerating myths, bemused." Carmina's sense of feminine self-containment was amplified in her erotic relationship with another girl at the age of thirteen. She retained her sense of belonging to herself by shutting men out.

For Carmina, the onset of menarche and the loss of her spiritual belief system happened simultaneously. She opted for her own physical experience as truth. In subsequent years Carmina's body consciousness and her spiritual awareness were always inextricably intertwined. She could never ignore her body or her soul. Her body sense and sexuality always pulled up her deepest psychological suffering and its transcendent meaning.

Carmina's relationship to her body was complicated by her attitude toward her younger brother, who was affected with muscular dystrophy. Not only had the baby, born when Carmina was two years old, absorbed all her mother's attention and time, but Carmina had grown up helping to care for her handicapped sibling. She suffered from an identification with his disabled body. A third child was born when Carmina was four, a bright, healthy boy. Her father's positive attention shifted completely toward him, away from Carmina. At the time we started our work, Carmina wanted in her heart to be an artist but feared familial disapproval if she pursued her art seriously because in her father's scientific eyes, art was perceived as a frivolous pursuit. Over the period of ten years we worked together, she followed a serpentine inner path to fulfilling her vocation and resolving the conflict around her sexuality.

Unlike Carmina's vivid memory of her first blood, SARAH's memory of her menarche in the context of her Catholic school girlhood was vague. She remembered her mother leaving pamphlets about menstruation on her bed and seeing a movie at school about girls' bodies changing. More immediately she remembered anticipating menarche because her best friend, who was physically more developed, had already started her period. "I wanted to have it so I could be like her. But I was tall and skinny with no breasts yet. Once I borrowed a padded bra from my mother's drawer just to feel better about lagging behind."

When Sarah did have her first period, there was no sense of joy or special acknowledgment from her family, just the needed trip to the store with her mother to buy a belt and pads. Like Carmina, she was glad to join her friends in menstruating, but the lack of importance attached to it had other consequences later in her life. Sarah had been raised to respond to external demands, to be responsible and to achieve. She had been a good student, teacher's pet, a leader in class activities, and a star athlete. In all these areas, she outdistanced her less-assertive brother, fifteen months older, and became her father's favorite child. As an adult she still identified with being her father's "good girl."

The dark shadow of this self-image came up at the beginning of therapy. As an adolescent girl she had had a secret sexual relationship with her older brother. It had consisted of exploratory play at night while she pretended to be asleep in her bed. Sarah felt guilty about it because she had avoided taking responsibility for the encounters. She had stopped the interaction one night when she pretended to wake up and told him to get out of her room. She felt she had "put all the guilt on him." Sarah felt the responsibility keenly because of her competitiveness with him—always outdoing him in order to please their father. Now at the age of thirty, she was concerned that some of the same power struggles were going on between herself and her husband.

Sarah had a strong and consistent tendency to repress her body needs and signals, overriding them for the sake of external demands. Her body often revolted against her refusal to listen to her inner feelings. She recalled her shame at her first wedding at the age of twenty, in which she unexpectedly began bleeding during the ceremony. She had known the marriage was wrong for her, but once it was planned she could not bring herself to spoil the plan or admit she was wrong. Now she saw the blood staining her dress as confirmation of her unacknowledged feelings. "I was going against myself." The marriage lasted only a year. At the wedding her body had dramatized her folly.

Some years later, in her mid-twenties, her body asserted itself in a different and more sustained form after she had been pushing herself beyond her limits in a fund-raising job for a large charitable organization. Working extended hours, eating and sleeping very little, she was riding on the excitement of being needed in such an important capacity. After eighteen months of this work, she began experiencing weakness, intestinal pain, and abdominal distress. She was diagnosed with Crohn's disease and was forced to stay home for two years in order to convalesce. For Sarah, the task of her analytic work over a period of eleven years involved withdrawing energy from the father-world of achievement in order to access her inner feminine core and listen to her body and her feelings.

BEATRICE's experience of menarche was traumatic. She spoke of having awakened in a sea of blood at boarding school in London, thinking she was dying. Afterward she was plagued with terrible cramps, vomiting, and fainting during her irregular menstruations. At the age of seven, Beatrice's biological mother had put her on a boat in Hong Kong bound for England in the care of a male acquaintance. She was told she was being sent to a paternal uncle and that her mother would join her later. Seven months later, the uncle died of cancer. Attempts were made to trace her mother, but she had disappeared. Beatrice never heard from her again. She was made a ward of the court and was sent to an orphanage at the age of eight. "Then I stopped talking for several months, until I finally had to start asking for food and drink; hunger loosened my tongue." She began her first formal education at the orphanage.

Subsequently, she was sent from the orphanage to many homes for trial stays. When she was eleven, the widowed judge who had presided over her wardship adopted her. He was ostensibly kind, but he remarried after a few months, and his wife, now Beatrice's stepmother, was subject to fits of rage. Beatrice endured both physical and psychological cruelty. Her adoptive father sent her to boarding school to remove her from the abuse. Neither her biological mother nor her stepmother had informed Beatrice about the natural development of her own body. The fear with which she met her menarche correlated with her traumatic experiences of the loss of a maternal guide in her life. In her isolation, she did not have even the comfort of a peer group.

When Beatrice was seventeen, she was seduced by a sixty-year-old journalist and moved with him to Thailand. They went on trips to Vietnam, where he reported on the war. Beatrice became addicted to heroin and twice almost died of overdoses. On their last trip into the jungle near the Cambodian border, her lover was badly wounded, and three other members of their party were killed. One man, an American, survived and went for help. Her lover, realizing he was fatally wounded, persuaded Beatrice to put the gun in his mouth and kill him. When the American returned, she was taken to Saigon, arrested, interrogated, and released.

Beatrice was returned to her adoptive parents in England. Her stepfather discovered her drug addiction and had her committed to a mental hospital. She was locked up for a week in a padded cell until she was "cured." Some months later, at the age of twenty, Beatrice married an American man who was visiting relatives in London and returned to San Francisco with him. She said the marriage was an "arrangement," not a love affair. During the ten years they were married, she learned computer programming and supported them both for most of that time. Her adoptive father died suddenly of a heart attack; the relationship with her husband deteriorated, and prior to their divorce, she made a suicide attempt by overdosing on sleeping pills. After that she withdrew to a small apartment, speaking to no one and often going without eating. Gradually, she resumed a facade of normalcy, got another job in a software company, and began dating again. She sought therapy because she was disturbed about the way in which she had always submitted to men in her life. For Beatrice, psychotherapy was a refuge, a haven, a beginning of hope and possibility that there could be healing for the deep wounds she had suffered in her life.

Each of these women entered an initiatory process in the ritual of psychotherapy that included a realignment to a basic feminine principle: embodied spirit. In order to accomplish this realignment, the therapy had to touch deep levels of the psyche where women are connected to other women, from mother to daughter throughout history. The archetypal image is at one end of the spectrum in the collective unconscious—living psychic images that we all share by virtue of shared history. At the other end of the spectrum is instinct, felt and enacted by the body.[3] Through a woman's biological periodicity and life-giving potential, she embodies a bridge between archetype and instinct.

Puberty rituals are one kind of drama in which the fusion of archetype and instinct has been expressed. In women's initiation rites, ceremony is crucial for bestowing social and religious maturity in addition to physiological maturity. Basic elements from such ceremonies appeared in the experience, dreams, and conscious imagery of Carmina, Beatrice, and Sarah that held the healing potential for the psychotherapy.

The Navajo Kinaaldá dramatizes several fundamental feminine clusters of meaning that emerge as patterns in the course of women's therapies in relation to a woman therapist. The Navajo girl views her first blood as a joyous event in the context of the mythological life of her people. From the time she is born, the Navajo girl hears stories about the creator of her people, Changing Woman. Through the power of story in song, the girl slowly learns her female part, her relatedness to this complex female deity. Changing Woman's mother and father are Mother Earth and Father Sky. Mother Earth contains sacred plants, especially corn, in her body. Father Sky is filled with sun, moon, and stars. Their daughter is taken to the home of First Man and First Woman and raised by them.[4] Changing Woman's other names are Turquoise Woman and White Shell Woman. Turquoise Woman is associated with earth; White Shell Woman, with water.

The Navajo girl learns that the song ceremonial complex Blessingway tells the story of how Changing Woman was born, how she matured, became pregnant, and gave birth to twin boys. Blessingway is used in rites to protect and ensure long life and happiness. It includes blessings for a new home, for childbirth, for puberty, and for marriage.[5] The adventures of Changing Woman's sons, the twins, are told in Enemyway, the other major song ceremonial, which is used in rituals for the control of evil, like war, possession, and illness.[6]

From the age of four a Navajo girl helps her mother with the daily household chores: building a fire, cooking, weaving, and raising lambs.[7] The girl is told the story of Changing Woman's menarche, when the first Kinaaldá was held for her, with all the deities in attendance, at Emergence Rim—the center of the earth and also its vagina, from which the Holy People first issued forth. The girl is told that Changing Woman established her Kinaaldá as the model for all girls to follow, telling the first Navajo,

> After this, the girls born to you will have periods at certain times when they become women. When the time comes, you must set a day and must fix the girl up to be Kinaaldá. You must have these songs sung and do whatever else needs to be done at that time. After this period a girl is a woman and will start having children.[8]

The Navajo girl hears these stories, hears these songs, and attends initiation ceremonies for sisters, cousins, and friends as she feels herself ripen toward maturity. When she sees her first blood, she rejoices and knows that it is cause for general rejoicing, because it indicates that she is ready to bring forth new life. She knows also that for her people her reproductive power depends on more than her physiological maturity. Like her grandmother and mother before her, she "must also be ritually transformed, made over, before she takes her place as a woman."[9]

As Kinaaldá, the girl will *become* Changing Woman, responsible for both the vegetative cycle of seed, plant, food, and seed, and the human cycle of life, growth, death, and rebirth. The fertility of the Kinaaldá girl, of her people, and of the crops, especially corn, depends on her accomplishment of the ceremony.

The purpose of Blessingway holy songs is to restore all that is "good, harmonious, orderly, happy and beautiful"[10] to the girl and the participants in the ceremony. The Navajo word *hozho* includes these concepts as part of a positive or ideal environment.[11] During the Kinaaldá, negative thoughts, words, or actions are prohibited. The girl is said to be "Walking into Beauty/*Hozho*"[12] throughout the ritual, which lasts four nights and five days.

Plans for the ceremony are made when the girl informs her grandmother or another trusted older woman in her family clan that her first bleeding has begun. The ritual takes place the following summer. By that time, the initiate has already been menstruating for some months. The initiate chooses an Ideal Woman to sponsor her ritual transformation, and a medicine man is engaged for the sing.

Most of the ceremony takes place within the initiate's family hogan. A blanket is hung in the doorway of the hogan to notify the Holy People—Talking God, Sun, and Changing Woman—that a Beautyway ceremony is in progress inside; thus the enclosure or container is created. The hogan songs dedicate the hogan to its ritual purpose and make it holy.[13]

> *he neye nana*
> Here at this house, it is a sacred place,
> Here at this house, it is a sacred place,
> > *holaghei.*

The house under the east is a sacred place,
Now the home of Talking God is a sacred place,
The house made of dawn is a sacred place,
The house made of white corn is a sacred place,
The house made of all kinds of soft fabrics is a sacred place,
The house made of gathered rain waters is a sacred place,
The house made of corn pollen is a sacred place,
Now it is the house of long life and everlasting beauty;
> it is a sacred place.
Here at this house, it is a sacred place,
Here at this house, it is a sacred place,
> it is said.[14]

The girl chooses her sponsor, or Ideal Woman, whose qualifications must fit those originally possessed by First Woman. These attributes include being a skillful rug weaver, a good cook, and a mother. Strength and beauty are also important.[15] The sponsor grooms, dresses, and adorns the initiate throughout the ceremony. Bodily adornment is central to the girl's transformation. The girl is adorned to emulate Changing Woman: loose hair, ceremonial sash, white shell and turquoise jewelry. As she is gradually enriched by her sponsor with these symbolic pieces of clothing and jewelry, she becomes a woman through identifying with the Goddess. The songs chanted for her and the myths repeated in her presence accomplish her initiation in the course of the ceremony.[16]

As part of re-creating the initiate in Changing Woman's image, the Ideal Woman washes the girl's hair with yucca root shampoo and brushes it with ceremonial grass (figures 3 and 4). It is combed to hang down her back and held by a buckskin thong. Then her sponsor washes the girl's turquoise and white shell jewelry (figure 5). After the preliminary purifications, the Ideal Woman ritually dresses the initiate.[17] The dressing is accomplished by songs like the one that follows, in which the initiate is identified as the child of Changing Woman.

> Now the child of Changing Woman,
>> now she has dressed her up,
> In the center of the Turquoise house,
>> now she has dressed her up,
> On the even turquoise floor covering,
>> now she has dressed her up,
> On the smooth floor covering of jewels,
>> now she has dressed her up,
> Turquoise Girl, now she has dressed her up,
> Her turquoise shoes, now she has dressed her up,
> Her turquoise clothes, now she has dressed her up,
> Now a perfect turquoise having been placed on her forehead,
>> now she has dressed her up
> Her turquoise head plume, now she has dressed her up,
> Now at its tip there are small blue female birds,
>> truly beautiful;
>> it is shining at its tip,
>> now she has dressed her up,
> They call as they are playing; their voices are beautiful,
>> now she has dressed her up.
> She is decorated with jewels, now she has dressed her up,
> She is decorated with soft fabrics, now she has dressed her up.
>
> Behind her, it is blessed; now she has dressed her up,
> Before her it is blessed; now she has dressed her up,
> Now the girl of long life and everlasting beauty,
>> now she has dressed her up.

Photo by Kenji Kawano.

Figure 4.
The Ideal Woman Combing the Initiate's Hair in the
Navajo Girl's Puberty Ceremony.

Now she has dressed up her child,
Now she has dressed up her child, it is said.[18]

As Turquoise Girl, the initiate is being remade in Changing Woman's image; Turquoise Woman is a jewel aspect of Changing Woman.[19] The hair-washing and hair-combing rituals in the Kinaaldá reflect the universal valuing of women's hair as a symbol of feminine power. The ritual attention to hair is also a reflection of the intimacy between mother and daughter in such grooming. By the time she is five years old, a Navajo girl has learned to comb and tie her mother's hair into a traditional knot.[20]

Sylvia Brinton Perera describes a hair-combing ritual with one of her patients, which began when the woman brought her a comb as a gift. The woman's painful childhood memories of her mother pulling, scratching, and hurting her head when combing her hair were assuaged through Perera's combing her hair ritually several times. Perera also discusses how the enactment brought up both positive and negative mother-daughter feelings for both therapist and patient. Working through these feelings became a deeply healing experience for the woman.[21]

CARMINA's dreams about her hair as she developed in the course of her analysis reflected a struggle to find her own self-image separate from her mother's view of her. Seven years into our work she had the following dreams:

> I'm an in-between age person, trying to grow up but also aware of stunted qualities. I'm washing my hair, and I realize it has grown. It has grown very fast, and I let it down to my knees. My mother is either skeptical or she does not like it.

> I am at a beach lying in the sun, sensually aware and sensitive. I have a little snake, a gift from my mother. I'm apprehensive; it won't behave. I try to put it in the water, but it won't go. There is a flame nearby. I'm afraid it's going to get burned. My mother is behind me. She takes my hair and pulls it up. She says, "You've got to get your hair cut," and I say, "Why!" I'm very upset, as always when she said that or wanted to change my image.

In these dreams the implication is that long hair is "too much," too powerful, attracts too much attention. It doesn't fit in a society that says a woman must curb her femininity, edit herself, fit a smaller pattern. The dreams revealed both the cultural complex around women's identity as well as Carmina's own mother's influence. The snake is an allusion to the archetypal mystery between mother and daughter elucidated in the Eleusinian mysteries. While the mother-daughter conflict at the cultural and personal level manifested in a tug of war about how Carmina should wear her hair, the uncontrollable sacred snake insisted on making itself known. It was this level of the unconscious that Carmina would have to engage with in order to find her way to the self-image she was asserting in the dreams. Medusa's snaky hair threatened patriarchal power in the ancient Greek pantheon. The snake suggested the healing motive of the incubation ritual of psychotherapy. Carmina saw her mother as being uncomfortable with her daughter's female power, especially as it had radiated in seven years of therapy.

The Kinaaldá girl is provided with the appropriate hairstyle to express her movement from girl to woman in the image of her people's deity, Changing Woman. Carmina had to find her own way, her individuality, her style, by retrieving aspects of the lost feminine from her own unconscious. In the process of this retrieval, she, like many other women, would have to deal with a particular aspect of the shadow: Carmina projected the desirable feminine characteristics into other women. When she saw in other women qualities that she wanted to express, she felt left out, insecure, robbed of her feminine heritage. Her dreams revealed a shadow figure who was beautiful and did everything right, while she felt unattractive, awkward, and ignorant in relationships, especially with men.

A year after the long-hair dreams, Carmina raged in therapy, feeling angry and distressed that whatever she wanted she could not have, that therapy was making her worse instead of better. She dreamed:

I am following a blonde woman with beautiful hair. Her hair is up in a tortoiseshell comb. I'm like a slug behind her, doing everything wrong.

Although Carmina experienced this dream in a negative way because she was consciously suffering, the dream presented a positive shadow figure in the unconscious. Carmina is dark; the shadow here is light. The shadow is usually thought of as containing negative qualities, but in Carmina's case, all the positive attributes belonged to the "other woman," a living entity in Carmina's psyche that she eventually would be able to recognize as her own. This is critical in therapy, where the idealized "other woman" is also often projected into the woman therapist. She saw me as embodying what

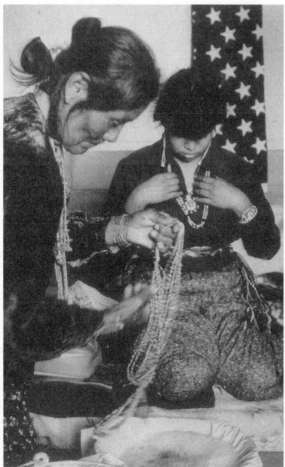

Photo by Kenji Kawano.

Figure 5.
The Ideal Woman Washing the Initiate's Jewelry in the
Navajo Girl's Puberty Ceremony.

she wanted to become. Though this is sometimes a necessary part of analysis, in order to take back that projection, Carmina had to realize the blonde/light/positive in herself. The blonde's tortoiseshell comb alluded to White Shell Woman, the third aspect of Changing Woman, who, in one variation of the myth, is the creator of shells.[22]

In the most extreme form of the "other woman" shadow in women, a woman becomes preoccupied with the fantasy of the other woman or women in her husband or lover's life. The typical focus in a triangle situation is on the jealousy the mate feels, but often it is neither possessiveness nor love for her partner that motivates her jealousy. Rather, it is her fascination and envy of the "other woman" for those feminine qualities that she wishes to realize in herself.

The adorning of her body with clothes and jewelry also figures dramatically in a woman's therapeutic process, especially in her relationship to her mother. When a woman is experiencing a psychological metamorphosis in therapy, the shift in body/ego/self image demands a new physical expression. She finds herself wanting to change her style of dress or being fascinated by a numinous piece of jewelry in a store window.

Six months after her blonde shadow appeared, Carmina returned to therapy after a hiatus, because she had the following dream:

> I come into a courtyard and find Juliet's balcony in Verona. It's cool and wet. I see a doorway and look up. You are standing in the doorway, and I realize it is your house. You have a ten- or eleven-year-old girl with you, your daughter. I think, "I know she doesn't have a daughter." I feel a series of very powerful emotions, pain, envy, wanting to be close to you. I feel lonely, shut out, not there. I'm wearing a long refugee-like dress, menstruating copiously. I turn and start to walk away. A man comes up, following me, and talks to me. I realize he's your husband. I am freaked out. I don't want to know him or to talk to a man. I say, "Look, I'm a dyke, leave me alone."

Carmina said that she woke feeling acceptance, a giving up. "My period started, and I needed to talk to you." The dream spoke to the necessity for her to reenter the symbolic relationship, the ritual enclosure, that held the healing mother-daughter potential. Her body, her blood, was bringing her back to the container in spite of her resistance. The daughter in the dream is herself at an earlier age, premenarche, an age that Carmina had to regain internally in the course of her psychological initiation. Lyn Mikel Brown and Carol Gilligan have defined this age as that at which the girl child is still in touch with her own power and initiative before the societal pressures to conform to a limited view of womanhood have begun to be felt in their extreme.[23]

The resistance to my husband in the dream spoke both to Carmina's desire for the container to be uncontaminated by masculine intrusion and to her ambivalence about the lesbian lifestyle she had become committed to at this time. During these years Carmina had abandoned her artistic vocation. After graduating with a bachelor's degree in fine arts, she continued her schooling and earned a master's degree in business administration. Qualified and competent, she worked in a bank in a high-level administrative capacity. She stopped therapy again during this period when it seemed that her current love affair and her job were both going well.

Almost two years later, she returned to psychotherapy after a disastrous relationship with a woman. In the intervening time she had realized that she wanted a relationship with a man that would lead to marriage and children. She had also realized that she painfully missed her art. At this point in her life and therapy, Carmina dropped into the depths of analysis. She was now twenty-five years old and had lived out what had been necessary in reaction to her family system. She had returned to face the hardest work, her deepest fears: her fear of her own power and creativity and her fear of men. In the face of those fears, the unconscious took up her initiation into womanhood through the symbolism of clothes and jewelry.

Four months after her return to therapy, she had the following dream:

> I'm in a waiting room wearing an old raincoat because it is pouring rain. You have called and said you'll pick me up. You take me to your house. I'm a mess—fat, crumpled, awkward, incapacitated. You are completely collected. I ride in the backseat. I am so uncomfortable. I want to disappear. I feel tearful, at odds with everything.
>
> We go to your house, a different one from my previous dreams. As we approach, I say, "I've been here before." We go upstairs to your bedroom. You are showing me jewels. It seems you have access to a special source. We are looking at a pair of earrings, square, gold and silver. You give them to me to wear. I say, "They are too heavy." I'm uncomfortable with the "raincoat Carmina." You push them into my hands, and then you kiss my hand. I panic. I don't want this to happen. I remember the first dream I had about you running your hands down my back, the sexual danger. Here too it is dangerous.

There were literally hundreds of dreams between Carmina's initial dream in therapy in which she feared our intimacy and this dream four years later. Yet the unconscious was following the same purpose. Carmina remembered her initial dream within this dream and recognized the development of our relationship that was necessary for her development. Her sponsor, or Ideal Woman, in the guise of me, is pushing her a step further, insisting that she accept the earrings, that she take on her role as initiate.

Like the Kinaaldá girl, she has to wear the jewelry that belongs to the older women who have already been initiated. She needed to assume responsibility for her own maturation. This dream helped Carmina to counteract the feeling that she was unworthy of the initiate's role. It went against the "raincoat Carmina" complex. In spite of her fear of being overwhelmed, the feeling for her about the dream was one of welcome acceptance and a sense of being honored.

This dream accomplished a step in the initiation, because Carmina had both a strong relationship to her unconscious and a strong bond to me as analyst. She said, "I have always loved your jewelry. You are the link for me; you are married to a man." The earrings were silver and gold, female and male, moon and sun metals. For Carmina, my being married gave her hope that she would be able to overcome her fear and become capable of intimacy with men. Carmina feared men/the father/the patriarchy, and she had a deep capacity for intimacy with women. She wanted to find with men the closeness and understanding that she had previously experienced with women so that she could honor her sexual attraction to them.

In the course of psychologically identifying with me, her symbolic sponsor, Carmina continued to separate from her personal mother. Three months later she dreamed:

> There is a spiky silver necklace made of hollow pods. The necklace
> is taken away from me. Children fill each bead with something. My
> mother takes it. I take it back and say it's mine. It's heavy and warm.

Carmina's relationship to clothes, her blonde shadow, and her separation from her mother were intertwined in the following dream:

> I'm in an ancient city built on a steep hill that goes down to the
> water. There are stone buildings, Assyrian style, baked dry, and stony.
> I'm walking through the streets on a journey, looking down the cliffs to
> the water lapping at the bottom. I see one promontory and head for it.
> It looks like a fort. I get there, and suddenly I'm with a girl, my com-
> plete opposite, small, blonde. We're supposed to be going to a party.
> She has all the right clothes; I don't. I feel big, awkward, underdressed,
> wearing jeans but with a silk shirt that's almost passable.
> Then my mother is saying to me, "You're not going to wear that
> leotard to teach in, are you?" I say, "If I were teaching a dance class, I
> would."

Carmina's association to this dream was that the previous session I had said to her, "It's nice to see you." She said, "It's hard for me to believe that." At this point Carmina's negative self-image prevented her from accepting my appreciation of her. Her self-esteem was all in the blonde shadow figure in her unconscious.

Feeling thwarted in her desire to express herself, Carmina made a trip to Barcelona to study Catalan and look at art. She was drawn back to Spain because she had been named after her Catalan great-grandmother. She wanted to return to Barcelona, site of her menarche and first spiritual crisis as a girl; she hoped to reclaim the language and the place as a woman. While she was there, her immersion in the lively artistic and intellectual atmosphere of the old city both subtly reconnected her with her matrilinear heritage and reawakened her artistic inclination. When she returned seven months later, her descent into the unconscious deepened. The recurrent theme of searching for her feminine value as symbolized by jewelry came up in dreams. Six months after her return she dreamed:

> I am sorting through my jewelry. I can't seem to find anything that
> I want to wear. Everything is too plain or too cheap or doesn't match
> what I am wearing. Where is *my* jewelry?

Carmina said, "I feel like the awkward teenager I once was. I rejected my mother and in so doing rejected myself." Carmina was naming the psychological legacy of many women in our culture whose mothers, victimized by the patriarchal system, could not offer them the guidance, modeling, and transforming rituals that Navajo girls inherit by birth.[24] If a girl does not find her own value in her mother, she must go on an inner quest for the feminine. Woman-to-woman therapy is a place where the value of the feminine can be reclaimed.

One of the strands in this process for Carmina was freeing herself from the powerful self-hating complex that had kept her defended against intimacy with me and others. A year later she dreamed:

> I'm wearing a necklace of beads around my neck, orange and yel-
> low, associated with my childhood. You come up and break it off my
> neck. I'm shocked at the violence. I say, "You've been wanting to do
> that for a long time!" You say, "Yes, I just couldn't stand it anymore."
> Then I'm dreaming about your two children, who are unearthly beings,
> silvery. I'm put off that they're not real children.

Carmina said, "Who am I going to be when I am finished with this process? I'm envious of those magical, ethereal children. I feel alienated from them as people and from your life away from here. I'm afraid to tell you these dreams, afraid you're going to see something that will make you hate me, that you'll get frustrated with me because I'm so frustrated with myself." Feelings of self-hatred came up most frequently when Carmina was premenstrual. She had twenty-one-day menstrual cycles, so she was often subjected to the intense anxiety and depression induced by this self-destructive complex. The frequency of her bleeding also contributed to her fear that something was fundamentally wrong with her, that she was infertile. Whenever the bleeding began, however, her mood shifted, and the power of the complexes to annihilate her diminished. Slowly and painfully, Carmina had to learn to trust her changing body, her changing nature.

The magical children in the dream referred to the work that Carmina and I were generating between us. Breaking a regressive childhood bond, symbolized by the necklace, created new possibilities in her psyche. This motif is an inversion of the Ideal Woman adorning the Kinaaldá girl with necklaces. That the children were mine and difficult for Carmina to know suggested that her potential was still largely projected into me. Projection is a necessary element of depth psychotherapy.

In psychotherapy or analysis there is a period when the container of the work and the relationship to the therapist take precedence over everything else in a woman's life. At this juncture—when dependence on therapy is most intense—her therapeutic progress usually causes disruption in her outer relationships. This peculiar situation can be both exhilarating and frightening, but if both women can embrace, or at least allow, the merging, the process between them will naturally turn toward differentiation from the therapist. As a woman individuates, her feminine ego will emerge from the unconscious. The dependency will lift. The projections will be withdrawn, and the work will begin to influence her external life in constructive ways. After her immersion in the unconscious, however, the woman always retains the sense of her inner life flowing along beneath her daily concerns. This parallels the way in which the Kinaaldá girl retains the power of Changing Woman after the puberty ceremony.

The dream of the silvery children evoked a new feeling in Carmina. Unexpectedly, she began to feel a sense of responsibility for her own life that included taking her art seriously. When she had given up painting she had sacrificed something of her essence. The loss of her creativity tormented her; it was as if her hands were paralyzed when she could not paint. She began to realize that art was her vocation, that the call came from within, from her soul, and that she had to answer that call.

The initiatory themes of bodily adornment also appeared in SARAH's dreams during therapy. The importance of a woman's hair was portrayed in her dreams of me, where my reddish brown hair became more red and flowing than in reality, symbolizing the power of the feminine for her. She associated the intense redness with Jezebel or Mary Magdalene. Unconsciously, she was projecting into me some of the aspects of the feminine that are denied in our culture: power, sexuality, and nonconformity or individuality. These were the aspects that she had repressed as a good Catholic girl. Sarah had long, thick hair but wore it in a restrained fashion. Early in our work she had the following dream:

I have a vision of myself in the midst of other people. I am going
bald. The top of my head is bald. In the front and the back there is still
hair.

Sarah associated her hair with femininity and losing it with revealing
the shadow. During this period in psychotherapy she was suffering the sacrifice of her "good girl" image as she related to me many incidents in her
past of which she was ashamed. All her childhood sins, like tattling on boys
or cheating in algebra, were recounted. It was a time of catharsis, of purification, in which she honestly and willingly faced her own shadow. On another level, the loss of hair in the dream was a psychic picture of the lack of
feminine power that existed because Sarah was father-identified. Living in
accord with masculine values at the expense of her own instincts and desires, she was going bald.

Sarah's relationship to her mother contributed to her inability to define
herself as a woman. At the age of thirty-two, although she had rebelled
against her mother's "control," she still let her mother choose her clothes
for her. Early in our work she dreamed:

I am in a chapel dressed almost like a nun. The principal says I
can't come into the chapel because I don't have one piece.

I am going to rob a bank, but I have to change clothes in order to
do it. I am uncomfortable because I am not dressed right. There are
other women there.

Sarah said, "My mother usually has a hand in picking my clothes; she
buys them from secondhand stores. She knows my taste, but it does bring
up my control issues with her." Sarah dresses as a nun in the dream. Nuns
were her authority figures as a girl. They represented a different ideal from
her own mother. In a sense Sarah's first Ideal Woman was her favorite nun,
whom she respected for her wittiness, intelligence, and dedication to her
chosen path. The fantasy of being a nun functioned psychologically to keep
Sarah her father's daughter: being celibate and related only to God. Although becoming a nun was not Sarah's path, she did split her ego from her
shadow. She retained an ego-identification with the nun, "Daddy's good
girl," while sexuality and other elements that didn't fit with the ideal were
relegated to the shadow.

The second dream revealed how far apart Sarah's ego and shadow had
been. She is going to rob a bank, commit a crime, and has to change
clothes in order to do it, has to assume a different ego-image. Criminality
appeared because she had thoroughly repressed her own capacity to do anything wrong. The unconscious presented a lawless image to compensate for
the ideal image of the nun in the first dream.

Three years later Sarah's unconscious displayed another variation of her ego-image, which was moving toward an integration of feminine opposites, in the following dream:

> I see you outside the therapy context wearing an old-fashioned tight skirt. You are flamboyantly, provocatively dressed, projecting a very sexual image. Then I am in a fashion show modeling a gown. I don't feel part of this elegant affair. There are spiral staircases and velvet drapes. I am wearing an elegant formal. Some friends see me and ask me about it. I tell them the show must be over, because I am the last one to walk downstairs. I dismiss their questions because I am embarrassed.

Sarah said, "I was uncomfortable with who you were in the dream. That is a side of me I do not show. If I do try to dress more provocatively, I'm afraid my husband will laugh at me or ignore me. My friend gave me a sexy bra for my birthday. I was embarrassed when I opened it; my mother gave me a flannel nightgown. In high school I used to wear formals." Sarah returned, as Carmina did, to her adolescence, when she first dealt with her sexuality as reflected in how she wanted to present herself. She was uncomfortable both with the flamboyant shadow image that she projected on me and with the fashion model presentation that she made in high school. Instead of a duality between perfection and sin, a feminine duality emerged, depicted in dress, between the sexual woman and the formal, virginal adolescent. Sarah has projected her Mary Magdalene shadow on me. These two aspects of the feminine are capable of integrating; the nun and the criminal are not.

Some months later, Sarah talked about buying a new dress, instead of a secondhand one, at a time when she felt depressed. She said, "I was drawn to it, but my reason was against it. I almost didn't buy it, and I still feel guilty about the cost. But I love it, and I feel wonderful wearing it." Sarah could afford the dress, but she believed that doing anything nice for herself was self-indulgent, vain, trivial, and selfish. She had always secretly criticized other women for caring about their appearance. She was inhibited from spending any time on herself by her *paternal* primary ego value of achievement in the world supported by her *maternal* sacrificial propensity toward taking care of others. It was difficult for her to feel and embrace a healthy feminine narcissism that would allow her to uncover the value of self-care and to hear her own voice. For her, buying a pretty new dress was a beginning.

The conflict between her patriarchally driven external life and her relationship to her feminine nature was expressed in the following dream two years later:

I am working with an ambulance crew. We pick up a young boy whose mother decides not to go with him. I get in back instead. We have to go across the bay. I see a huge stadium where I know my husband is at a meeting. I see his car illegally parked. I jump out and run over to the car. Next to the car on the ground is a diamond from my wedding ring. I pick it up. I haven't noticed it is missing. Later we go to visit his parents. His mother is sick with cancer, but she has a huge burst of energy to study for the board exams. When I have a chance, I tell his mother the story of the ambulance and the diamond.

After this dream Sarah was amazed to realize that the four rings she currently wore were given to her by women—her mother, her mother-in-law, and two aunts. She had lost a stone from her wedding ring years before and had never had it replaced, so the ring from her beloved Aunt Maisie served as a wedding ring. In the dream her crisis work, responding to the immediate needs of her job as a physician, prevents her from noticing the feminine value she has lost. She also lauds the mother-in-law's capacity to be achievement-oriented even while severely ill. This was Sarah's attitude: she denied her own limitations, physically and emotionally.

In a dream just a week later, the women have become inner figures with different agendas in the maze of the unconscious.

I am working as a spy in the underground. I have managed to get into the castle to overhear a phone conversation. It is mazelike with arches and pillars. I can see people, but they can't see me. When I try to find my way out, another woman from the underground comes to help me. She guides me to a rough part of London, where we meet two other women. The three of them go up the stairs. Two big, tough street women come in and start to accost me. First, one grabs my silver-and-onyx necklace. I lie and say, "It's my grandmother's, leave it alone!" I call for help from upstairs after trying to fend them off by acting tough myself. Others come down. The two women take off.

There was much unresolved conflict between different female energies in this dream. Sarah was divided in her therapeutic work. Her ego felt like a spy in the labyrinth, where she was completely involved in her dream incubation. Her feminine identity was at odds with itself. In one of Sarah's associations to this dream, she recognized that, although she feared the controlling aspects of her mother's personality, she also feared giving up that matriarchal power herself. She was well aware of her own controlling patterns in relation to her husband and other people in her life. That week, she had experienced problems relating to her husband on the telephone; his work as a lawyer had taken him to another city so they were living separately, commuting on weekends.

The necklace in the dream had been a gift from her mother, an ornate Victorian trinket. In the dream she attributes it instead to her grandmother, implying the value that accrues through women from one generation to another. She knew unconsciously that her feminine value was dependent on her heritage, that in separating from her mother, she had to keep alive the enduring value from her grandmother. The dream said she had to lie, accept her shadow, in order to accomplish that end. Although Sarah could intellectually see this lost value and her denial of the shadow, I continued to carry her feeling for these tasks for many years.

Unlike Sarah, who had many women relatives in her life, BEATRICE had none. Severed from her mother and grandmother at the age of seven, she had bonded with her stepmother only for survival. Her loss was dramatically reflected in her initiatory dreams about her hair and jewelry. In an early dream her archetypal Self figure appears for the first time.

> I am holding a cellophane package. In the package is a long silver hairpin with Kuan Yin's face and sleeves. I put it in my hair.

Beatrice said she prayed to the Chinese goddess of compassion, Kuan Yin, whenever she felt troubled. She had derived a connection to the goddess from her mother, who kept a small altar to Kuan Yin in their room in Shanghai. In the dream, the goddess's face and sleeves adorn a pin for Beatrice's hair. The image shows Kuan Yin as an integral part of Beatrice's femininity, in that She could be called on as part of a daily feminine ritual. The appearance of this goddess gave me hope that a central Self structure had survived the adverse circumstances of her life. Beatrice's only personal memory to do with her hair being groomed was that her grandmother had always pulled her hair very tight when she braided it. The feeling of harshness in this memory was compensated in the dream by the graceful protective image of Kuan Yin's face and sleeves.

Beatrice's capacity to engage with me immediately in a strong, positive way seemed to spring from some hidden source of which she was unaware. At the outset of therapy, she intuitively connected to the psychological meaning of her own development and was able to make appropriate applications of insight to her daily life. This capacity to utilize therapeutic work was contradictory to the defensive system she had developed for survival over twenty-five years. I believe the spontaneous energy and motivation derived from the underlying archetypal relationship that sprang from her core affinity for a compassionate and merciful Holy Mother. "In Buddhism, Kuan Yin is the goddess who hears the cry of the world and sacrifices her Buddhahood for the sake of the suffering world."[25] In our relationship, Beatrice found the perfect fit for her projection in my lifelong devotion to the Virgin Mary as the core of my intensely feminine spiritual life. Beatrice's devotion to Kuan Yin found its way to that figure in my unconscious. I felt compassionate toward Beatrice as a child lost in the world, grateful that she allowed me to take her in.

A few years later Beatrice had the following pair of dreams:

> I can see strands of my hair and a pair of hands tying it up into granny knots. I feel great anxiety.

> We have two robberies in the house. In the first, someone steals the decorations off the Christmas tree and breaks the tree into twigs. In the second, they steal the pearl necklace that my stepmother gave me on my twenty-first birthday and my old wedding and engagement rings. I look to see if a freshwater pearl necklace I bought is gone too, but it is still there. That provides minor relief amidst feelings of great loss.

Beatrice was desperately worried about money at this time. In addition, the traumas of Vietnam were beginning to resurface after a hiatus during which she had experienced no nightmares. Neither a personal mother nor the archetypal figure of Kuan Yin is present in the first dream. She is being tended by a pair of disembodied hands. This referred to her defensive capacity to split off from the reality around her and function mechanically in her life. Beatrice said that initially she had been a "nervous wreck" in Vietnam. Then she had developed the trick of seeing everything happening around her as if through the lens of a camera in order to protect herself from the horror of what she witnessed. This picture is the inverse of the Kinaaldá girl's experience of being surrounded by beauty and harmony, the sacred path of her people. I believe the self-protective splitting in Beatrice began much earlier, during her childhood experience of abandonment and abuse.

Beatrice felt that the robberies in the dream had to do with a necessary separation from the past: that if she did not accomplish this within herself, it would be forcibly accomplished. The destruction of the Christmas tree reflected her depression about having no money to celebrate the holiday. That the stolen items had been given to her in the past by her stepmother and ex-husband, while what remained was something she bought for herself, suggested she had to form her sense of value independently of them. In addition to suffering post-traumatic stress from her terrible experiences, Beatrice struggled with her complex of pleasing men in the day-to-day unfolding of her relationship with her lover. The psychotherapeutic container was the first place she had found since her mother had left her in which she was safe to reflect on herself and her life.

All three women made a symbolic return to menarche during therapy that found expression in part through the imagery of hair, jewelry, and clothes. For BEATRICE, the return was fraught with the fear she had experienced when she thought her bleeding meant that she was dying. In the absence of a personal mother to contain her developing femininity, her psyche reached into the archetypal world to present the caring spirit of Kuan Yin. Feelings of anxiety and loss predominated in her dreams about her hair and jewelry. Without a mother to care for her, physically or emotionally, Beatrice had never learned to care for herself. Although she had wonderful taste in clothes, she often looked like a neglected child, slightly disheveled, uncombed, and tattered. On rare occasions when touched by Kuan Yin's spirit, she would appear in a new dress, hair freshly washed, with a glow of self-appreciation that was lovely to see. Her psyche slowly provided the needed self-valuing that could be expressed in this archetypally feminine way.

For SARAH, the symbolic return in therapy meant bringing to consciousness all the feminine mystery that had been repressed when her menarche was ignored. She had denied her feminine body, beauty, and sexuality; those had been relegated to a dark, denigrated shadow. The dreams revealed her unconscious merger with her mother, reflected in her mother's still choosing her clothes for her. Sarah projected her feminine shadow aspects on me—her Ideal Woman or sponsor—through images of women's hair and clothing. But as she developed psychologically, Sarah began to feel womanly and to find her own feminine style. Throughout her subtle changing, the interplay between her ego and her shadow was played out in her choice of dress.

CARMINA's symbolic return to initiatory age also brought up the task of separating from her mother in a new way. Though she had asserted herself in terms of hairstyle and clothing as a teenager, Carmina needed to define her own individual identity as an adult and realize her feminine power. In an intangible way, her relationship to her mother kept her alienated from men. Through the imagery of hair, clothing, and jewelry, the dreams revealed her blonde double, suggesting White Shell Woman, who held the positive power and asserted the value of the woman-to-woman therapy for the initiation process.

The Kinaaldá girl awakens to a sense of her own feminine divinity when her people ceremonially endow her with symbolic items of jewelry, clothing, and song; a woman in analysis first experiences the numinous nature of the feminine archetype in an individual way through her own unconscious. Then she looks for external concrete forms with which to manifest her new inner Self in the outer world.

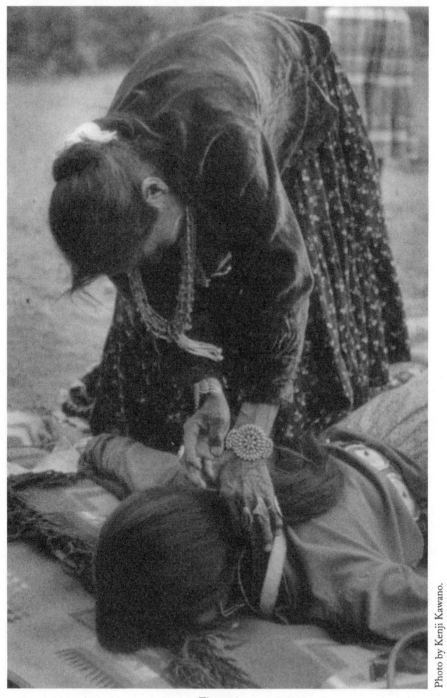

Figure 6.
The Ideal Woman Molding/Massaging the Initiate in the
Navajo Girl's Puberty Ceremony.

3

Molding a Woman

Although the initiatory archetype always originates from the same feminine ground, each woman's path in psychotherapy is different. While her conscious goal at the outset is to resolve a conflict or disturbance, she may find, as the work progresses, that her deeper nature demands a submission that she had not envisioned. In the Kinaaldá ceremony, the girl knows that through the hair washing and combing, the adorning with clothes, jewelry, and song, she is being re-created as Changing Woman. The woman in psychotherapy knows only that she is profoundly changing. Who she will become and the order of her change cannot be outlined or imagined in advance. Her old mental constructs begin to crumble and dissolve; she begins to doubt her assumptions, attitudes, and ideas. During this process of disintegration, she finds herself in a state of extreme vulnerability. Dissolution of old patterns and vulnerability accompany all the biological and psychological stages in a woman's life—menarche, menstruation, defloration, pregnancy, childbirth, menopause.

The ritual reflection of the vulnerability that precedes the formation of a new identity is found in the molding ceremony of the Kinaaldá (figure 6). The Navajo believe that at the time of menarche, a girl's body becomes soft again, as it was at birth.[1] She is therefore susceptible to being reshaped, molded and massaged, into the cultural ideal of womanhood. The girl is also considered to be psychically susceptible, so she is given continuous instruction during her tasks throughout the four-day ritual.[2]

After the dressing and ornamenting on the first day of the ceremony, the re-formation is enacted. The girl lies on a pile of blankets in front of the hogan, with her head facing west. Guests and family members lend her their prized blankets so that the initiate's touch will bless them. The Ideal Woman ties the girl's hair back and then massages the girl's body from toe to head.[3] The sponsor is thought to have Changing Woman's power to reshape the girl in Her image.[4] The molding is accomplished by one of "the best loved, sacred songs"[5] from the Blessingway complex, sung by the Ideal Woman. When the Ideal Woman sings, massages the initiate, and helps her to dress and comb her hair, it is said that "she is being adorned with a song." [6]

A woman is being formed.
With turquoise shoes she is being formed . . .
With turquoise leggings she is being formed.
With turquoise visible all over her body, she is being
     formed . . .
With turquoise shirt, she is being formed.
With turquoise beads on her body she is being formed.
With turquoise clothes, she is being formed . . .
With turquoise bracelet, she is being formed.
With turquoise neck piece, she is being formed . . .
With her face being turquoise, she is being formed.
With her voice being turquoise, she is being formed.
With a perfect turquoise on the top of her head, she is
     being formed.
With a turquoise headplume, she is being formed, at its tip
     a very beautiful female cornbeetle appears, she is
     being formed.
As her words are brought forth her voice is beautiful, she
     is being formed.
With turquoise, in blessing she is being formed.
With white shell, in blessing she is being formed.
With various jewels, in blessing she is being formed.
With various fabrics, in blessing she is being formed.
With these ever increasing, never decreasing, she is being
     formed.
With long life-happiness, she is being formed.
Behind her it is blessed, she is being formed.
Before her it is blessed, she is being formed.[7]

In this song, the girl is being re-created by means of the sacred stone, turquoise. Changing Woman was said to have been formed from a piece of turquoise.[8] Turquoise is thought to enhance and strengthen eyesight. The repetition in the song serves to emphasize the girl's jewel-like, sacred nature, as her vision becomes that of Changing Woman. The sponsor or Ideal Woman touches the Kinaaldá girl in order to mold her into a woman. With her touching she imparts some of her female wisdom and power to the pubescent initiate. This motif was inversely reflected in CARMINA's first dream when my touching her turned me into someone ugly. Carmina feared being hurt or hurting me. But the dream also acknowledged the archetype of initiation inherent in the changing effect of touch. The therapeutic path would involve not only Carmina's mind but also her body and soul. Through the efforts of the Ideal Woman, the girl is molded into her new womanly form modeled on Changing Woman. By the end of the ceremony, symbolically, the girl has *become* Changing Woman. And by ornamenting, dressing, and massaging the initiate, the older woman has renewed her own relationship with Changing Woman's divine energy.

The molding or massaging motif in therapy is an expression of a woman's physical, nonsexual relationship to another woman. Six years into our work together, Carmina dreamed:

> I am talking to you. Your face keeps changing, the proportions changing. I ask, "Why do you do what you do?" You say, "I do it to get my heart back." The color green is somehow important. Then suddenly you get really old, wrinkled, aged. Your face cracks as if it were made of dried mud. I'm shocked awake, then fall asleep again quickly. I say that I am not close enough to you. We are standing with bellies touching, facing. You are much younger, my age. How could you have been so old?

Here is Changing Woman powerfully alive in the feminine mystery: the woman who grows old and then young again with the turn of the seasons. Changing Woman is Earth.[9] Green is the color of renewal, the color of spring, life, new growth. In the dream, my face is like dried mud, the earth in winter. Carmina and I are standing with our bellies touching. She is not afraid of our physical contact in this dream. The archetype of the feminine deity is constellated and the purpose of our intimacy revealed. Carmina had been looking at an old family photograph album in which she saw pictures of her mother as a girl and as a twenty-six-year-old (Carmina's current age) pregnant with Carmina; pictures of Carmina's High Episcopal church rites, baptism, Holy Communion, and confirmation; and pictures of Carmina with her maternal grandmother attired in a frivolous fashion. The photograph of her pregnant mother gave Carmina the impression of a fertility figure—isolated, stiff, and costumed. In the dream, Carmina's matrilineal female energy was brought into the woman-to-woman container of therapy where Carmina could access the fundamental potential in her own heritage. In the dream I, as her therapist-sponsor, become Changing Woman as I move from old age to maturity to young girl—touching her all the while. The touching imbued Carmina with the inner rhythms of feminine changing.

Carmina often felt as if her heart was stony or frozen. She said she needed to reclaim her feeling. In her dream I said, "I do my work to get my heart back." In order for Carmina to be initiated into her own womanhood, I had to have an equally meaningful investment in the work we were doing. My heart had to be in it. I had to be with her in her purpose.

Two years later, Carmina dreamed:

> I am lying next to you, and we are talking. Suddenly I am horrified to realize that my hand has been resting on your breast. I pull my hand away in alarm, but you stop me and ask why I am so upset. I explain that I have unconsciously done something inexcusable and that I'm embarrassed. You assure me that there is nothing to be embarrassed about. You are not disturbed.

Carmina said, "You are sanguine. I'm afraid of myself." This was another eros-laden image that actively involved Carmina's body in relation to my body as the sponsor for the sake of her development. As her trust in me grew, it brought her closer to me, therefore closer to her Self in therapeutic process. With increasing intimacy, however, came her fear of retreating into a sexual relationship and drowning once again.

In the Kinaaldá, after the molding and massaging comes the stretching ritual, in which the initiate stands on the pile of blankets and stretches the young children. She moves her hands upward from each child's waist to the tip of his or her head. The stretching is said to mimic the growth of a plant, from the sowing of a seed to its flowering at maturity. The girl lifts upward, bestowing the blessing of healthy growth on the children of the tribe.[10]

The symbolism in the stretching ritual again shows the power of touching to communicate the renewing energy that the girl dispenses to others during the ceremony. In woman-to-woman therapy the intimacy of the sponsor-initiate dyad results in a mutual initiatory experience, both of us undergoing different changes. Carmina and I were subtly influenced by each other's development all along.

For the Navajo, the pubescent girl's transformation into womanhood has the power to affect anyone she touches. In deep psychotherapy, the woman undergoing change at times observes her own inductive effect on other people in her life. The power of her unconscious activation may push her friends and family toward greater consciousness themselves. This inductive effect may be experienced positively or negatively. Carmina perceived that some of her friends were more drawn to her, while others wanted to avoid her. During the darkest part of her journey, she often felt lonely and isolated. She had no way of sharing the initiatory descent outside the therapeutic container. By contrast, the Kinaaldá girl has the understanding, participation, and support of the whole community during her transformation.

Twice a day for four days, the Kinaaldá girl leaves the hogan to run a race in a prescribed pattern: she runs eastward from the hogan toward the sun, makes a clockwise turn and returns westward to the hogan. Other children or adults may participate in the races, but they are forbidden "to compete with or outdistance the initiate." Violating these restrictions is said to result in premature aging and death. The girl and her companions run to a place the girl chooses as the end of the first race. There she circles a young bush or plant in a clockwise direction.[11]

The race follows the sun's course.[12] In the creation myth, Changing Woman, Earth, became pregnant by Sun and by Dripping Water and gave birth to twins.[13] In a variation of the myth, Turquoise Woman conceives by Sun, White Shell Woman by Dripping Water, and each gives birth to a boy.[14] The double and triple aspects of the feminine are given shape here. The initiate's runs are accompanied by racing songs like the following:

Black Jewel Girl,
     the breeze coming from her as she runs is beautiful,
Her black jewel moccasins,
     the breeze coming from her as she runs is beautiful . . .
Her black jewel leggings,
     the breeze coming from her as she runs is beautiful . . .
Her black jewel skirt,
     the breeze coming from her as she runs is beautiful . . .
Her black jewel clothes,
     the breeze coming from her as she runs is beautiful . . .
Her black jewel bracelet,
     the breeze coming from her as she runs is beautiful . . .
Her black jewel ear pendant, now she has put it on her forehead,
     the breeze coming from her as she runs is beautiful . . .

All kinds of horses lead up to her and go beyond,
     the breeze coming from her as she runs is beautiful,
All kinds of sheep lead up to her and go beyond,
     the breeze coming from her as she runs is beautiful,
All kinds of wild game lead up to her and go beyond,
     the breeze coming from her as she runs is beautiful,
All kinds of vegetation lead up to her and go beyond,
     the breeze coming from her as she runs is beautiful . . .

In long life, in everlasting beauty,
     the breeze coming from her as she runs is beautiful . . .

Before, behind, it is blessed,
the breeze coming from her as she runs is beautiful.[15]

The running ceremony entails and instills endurance and strength.[16] The initiate is expected to challenge herself by running a little farther each race. As the song shows, physical prowess and bodily adornment combine in *hozho*, beauty. The girl is at the center of a sacred, beautiful, and harmonious world: before, behind, below, above her it is blessed. In her running, the energy and vitality of her body interact with nature. During the molding and massaging, the initiate is receptive; she is being formed. In the race she becomes active, comes alive.

A year before terminating her psychotherapeutic work, Carmina had the following dream, in which the themes of a special dress and running a race were juxtaposed:

> I have a dress, Italian, old, antique, feminine, cotton with white lace. It is a shirtdress for summer. I bought it at a flea market. My paternal grandfather scrunches it up and says he has the right to take it because it was his mother's so rightfully his now. I say, "No, I bought it." But I get confused. Maybe it is his?
>
> Then I'm with a group of women. We're running a race somewhere in the mountains. A big, rude woman pushes past us all. At one point we've collapsed on the ground. I get into an altercation with her because I don't like her. I say, "Your spitting on the ground spreads germs. I don't like it." It is a big risk, because I am not sure I am right. Two women, one on either side of me, put their hands on my arms in a gesture of solidarity. I feel it was right to confront her.
>
> I see a group of women runners, Amazons. They have a red piece of cloth held as a banner in front of them. A coach, a man, arrives. My group is still sitting on the ground, collapsed. He says, "We need another group of women to run like them." I am the first one to volunteer. And I think I can't do it, but I *do* it!

Carmina was reducing her therapy hours to every other week at this point, and she expressed regret at beginning to separate from me. Currently, her priority was to fight her negative, undermining voices and to revitalize small, nurturing rituals that made her feel good about herself. In the first part of the dream, she doubted her body-image self in the face of the patriarchal voice claiming it/her for his own. She needed to claim her matriarchal heritage. The white dress alluded to White Shell Woman again. In the second part of the dream, Carmina is running. She had learned that running grounded her psyche in her body and gave her a feeling of health and well-being. Running suggested the initiating motif of the Kinaaldá rite. She takes her rude shadow to task and feels good about being supported by other women for her act. This shadow figure was the self-denigrating one in league with the patriarchal voice who told her she was worthless. But the feminine aspects of herself consolidate, and she is able to accept the challenge of the coach to run another race, to run like an Amazon. She is the first to volunteer. Still doubting her capability, she succeeds. In this situation, the heroinic attempt was in the service of her increasing strength, autonomy, and independence from me and the therapy.

During the first two days of the Kinaaldá ceremony, the girl also has the task of roasting and grinding whole-kernel corn into meal with ancient stone tools.[17] The cornmeal is to be used for the ceremonial cake, or *alkaan*. The girl "is said to have soft bones which will be strengthened by corn-grinding."[18] Grinding corn and running races are the active physical ordeals that serve to prepare the girl for her life as a woman. They contrast to the receptive rituals of hair combing and washing, and adorning with jewelry and clothes. Similarly, a woman in psychotherapy receives transforming energy from her therapist in intangible ways—knowledge, encouragement, support, amplification, or interpretation. But she must also actively engage with her own psyche and take up the challenge of initiation in her outer life.

All the girl's labor in the Kinaaldá is directed toward re-forming her character as well as her body. In this way she is re-created.[19] Throughout her domestic activities, she is instructed by her elders in the cultural taboos that surround the rite, which include food, water, sleep, actions, and attitudes. For example, she is told not to eat candy or sugar, otherwise her teeth will rot. And she is told to be careful not to eat food while it is still hot, or she will scald the bone of her teeth. She is warned to stay away from evil places and to watch closely over her jewelry, taking special care not to break a necklace or to lose anything.[20] These restrictions stress her physical and emotional vulnerability during this time. Attitudes of kindness, generosity, and cooperation are repeatedly modeled for her and emphasized in her teaching.[21]

On the morning of the third day, one woman and a few men dig the circular earthen pit, in which to bake a ceremonial cake.[22] The diameter of the cake may be several feet to accommodate thirty pounds of cornmeal. When the cornmeal grinding has been completed, the initiate grinds a white crystalline stone, aragonite. With its fine powder she silently blesses the ground meal, letting the powder fall over the cone-shaped pile.[23]

The afternoon is devoted to mixing the cornmeal batter, which is stirred with ceremonial sticks. The tied bundle of seven smoothed, dark greasewood branches is considered one of a woman's most valued possessions. The initiate and her women helpers then line the baking pit with corn husks.[24]

After the batter is poured into the heated pit, the initiate prepares for the cake blessing by meditating over her ceremonial basket, which is filled with corn pollen. The girl makes the pollen offering by forming a cross on the cake, sprinkling it from the four directions, around the circumference and over the top. The participants make a similar offering from the initiate's ceremonial basket with an accompanying prayer.[25]

On the evening of the third day the hogan is arranged for the all-night sing. The initiate sits at the west end of the hogan with the medicine man or chief singer opposite her. Between them is a blanket with ceremonial goods. The women sit on the north side, the men on the south side. In the hogan's center are a fire that has been kept kindled for the four days, a mound of earth, and a pail of water representing three essential elements.[26] "The east is left open; the doorway to the hogan is located there; at dawn the first rays of the Sun will enter through this door, just as Sun came to Changing Woman through her hogan's eastern door at the beginning of time."[27]

The Ideal Woman or the chief singer blesses the initiate with sacred pollen preparatory to the sing. There is a strict order to the blessing of her body, beginning with the soles of her feet and finishing with the top of her head. The singing begins with the Hogan Songs and progresses with the night into the Dawn Songs. The initiate is expected to stay awake all night.[28] The songs continue the transformation of the initiate into Changing Woman.

At dawn Washing Songs are sung while the jewelry and hair of the girl are again washed. She is adorned with her jewelry while it is still wet and leaves the hogan for her final race.[29] After the singing has finished, the participants gather at the pit in which the cake has been baking all night. From the heart of the cake a tiny ball is pinched and buried at the center of the pit as an offering of thanks to Mother Earth.[30] The center cut of the corn cake is given by the initiate to the chief singer as his or her fee for doing the sing. The Kinaaldá girl is forbidden to taste her cake but serves it to the others. In this way she demonstrates her increased maturity as a result of the ceremony.[31]

Sacred corn represents life for the Navajo. The cake is a symbolic cluster. Round, yellow, and fire-baked, it evokes a solar, masculine image, but it is baked in a subterranean pit, within the feminine body of the earth. Both men and women cooperate to make it. The placement of the corn-husk crosses provides a sacred orientation to the six directions. Sharing and eating the ceremonial cake on the fourth day of the Kinaaldá is a communion for the participants both with the Holy People, the gods, and with one another. Unity and balance are restored to the tribe.[32]

I have presented the ritual of making and blessing the cornmeal cake in detail because it elevates the providing of food—feminine nurturing—to a sacrament. Changing Woman is identified with the earth and its fruits. The art of cooking includes the archetype of feminine eros that women enjoy when cooking together. I have experienced this alchemical process with my own mother continuing into my adulthood and her old age. One of our favorite recipes is cornbread, which resembles the *alkaan* in color, shape, and texture. We have shared intimate and treasured moments in the kitchen, often preparing for a ritual feast. I have participated in this transformative life of the kitchen in Greece, southern Italy, and El Salvador. In Navajo or Pueblo homes, women are highly respected for the meals and the nurturing that they provide. In psychotherapy, images of preparation of food, baking and cooking, and the sharing of meals come up in modern women's dreams only in fragmented form. Carmina did dream of baking bread at moments when she felt her creativity bubbling up from within. But nurturing has been denigrated and even pathologized in our culture even though men expect to be nurtured by women. Women do not feel proud and affirmed in that role. And the collaborative effort of women cooking together in the kitchen that is featured in the Kinaaldá is almost completely lost in a society based on the nuclear family. Cooking has become a chore for the already-burdened woman, and the meal has lost its sacred quality.

In the Kinaaldá, after sharing the cake and the morning meal, the initiate returns to the hogan for her final hair combing accompanied by a Combing Song:

> White Shell Girl, they gaze on her,
> Her white shell moccasins, they gaze on her . . .
> Her white shell leggings, they gaze on her . . .
> Her white shell skirt, it gazes on her . . .
> Her white shell clothes, they gaze on her . . .
> Her white shell bracelet, it gazes on her,
> Her white shell ear pendant, it gazes on her . . .
>
> With all kinds of horses following her in a line, they gaze
>   on her,
> With all kinds of sheep following her in a line, they gaze
>   on her,
> With all kinds of vegetation following her in a line,
>   they gaze on her. . .
> With her it spreads out; with her, it increases without a
>   blemish, it gazes on her.
> Now the girl of long life and everlasting beauty,
>   they gaze on her.
>
> Before her, it is beautiful; they gaze on her,
> Behind her it is beautiful; they gaze on her. . . .[33]

In this song the girl is identified with the White Shell aspect of Changing Woman. During this combing, the initiate's hairstyle is changed. On the first day of the ceremony her bangs were left hanging over her eyes and she was instructed not to touch them. On the last day, her bangs are pulled up and back with the rest of her hair.[34] The initiate's final adornment in the ritual is white clay paint. The Ideal Woman applies it to the girl's body, from toes to head, using an upward motion.[35] A last massaging and molding completes the initiate's transformation into beautiful womanhood.[36] During the course of the initiation she has absorbed elements from all aspects of Changing Woman, turquoise, white shell, jet, red abalone.

Through the ritual the girl has become Changing Woman, has become the Goddess, the power of change and fecundity in all things. Her womb and the earth's womb are now seen as one. The qualities of long life, happiness, and blessedness, reiterated in the songs, now emanate from her as they have always emanated from Changing Woman.[37]

I am here; I am White Shell Woman, I am here.
Now on the top of Gobernador Knob, I am here.
In the center of my white shell hogan I am here.
Right on the white shell spread I am here.
Right on the fabric spread I am here.
Right at the end of the rainbow I am here.
As a child of a white coyote robe I am here.
As a child of a white robe I am here.
As a child of tanned buckskin I am here.
As a child of dark tanned buckskin I am here.
As a child of white spotted fabric I am here.
As a child of a dark robe I am here.
As a child of footwear I am here.
As a child of skirt fringes I am here.
As a child of big white deer I am here.
As a child of a beautiful doe I am here.
As a child of white shell I am here.
As a child of turquoise I am here.
As a child of abalone I am here.
As a child of jet I am here.
As a child of slender white shell I am here.
As a child of long strings of valuable stones I am here.
As a child of perfect things I am here.
As a child of ear pendants I am here.
As a child of slender beads I am here.
As a child of braided beads I am here.
As a child of big beads I am here.

As a child of red beads I am here.
As a child of mountain lion I am here.
As a child of black bow I am here.
As a child of an eagle-tail-feathered arrow I am here.
As a child of various fabrics I am here.
As a child of various jewels I am here.
At the corner of my hogan made of fabrics I am here.
Protecting the knowledge of my fabrics I am here.
Now it increases, never decreases, I am here.
Now I, I am long life, now happiness, I am here.
Before me it is blessed, I am here.
Behind me it is blessed, I am here.[38]

The initiate who has "walked into beauty" is entrusted to hold Changing Woman's power as sacred. For four days after the ceremony she remains adorned in her ceremonial clothing and jewelry and quietly reflects on her own changed state. Then she is expected to assume increased initiative and independence and is accorded a new respect.[39]

In order to accomplish her transformation, the initiate transcends the historical moment in which she lives and enters the archetypal world of myth. She becomes a symbol, an instrument and source of rebirth for her culture. Those who participate in her initiation are also re-created. To the extent that the Kinaaldá girl retains her sense of oneness with Changing Woman beyond the context of the ritual, she continues to draw on a divine source for her womanhood.[40]

Likewise, the woman initiated in a deep psychotherapeutic process also retains its effects beyond the context of the therapy and continues to draw on the deeper source of the unconscious for her womanhood. That source may at times be symbolized by a divine feminine figure, by relationship to her own matrilineal wisdom, or by the dialogue that she has succeeded in creating between her inner and outer lives. It may also bear fruit in a sense of renewed kinship with other women. Having come to appreciate her own feminine nature, she can now admire other women instead of seeing them as competitors for men or beauty or goods. She can regard other women as sisters struggling with variations of the same issues she has struggled with in changing. She can feel them as potential allies in the ever-present undertaking to assert a woman's place in our patriarchal culture. Through her initiation, a woman can, like the Kinaaldá girl, become an instrument of rebirth for her culture.

In the Kinaaldá ceremony, the container for the girl's experience is almost exclusively female. The main role is played by the chosen sponsor or Ideal Woman. The girl's mother and other female relatives are also directly involved. All other women of the tribe participate in some way. The chief singer for the all-night sing may be either a medicine woman or medicine man. The men's participation is peripheral. Men help dig the pit for the cake and carry and pour the batter into the pit, and they join in the singing. The girl's father can lend a helping hand at key moments, helping her demarcate the bush to designate the length of the run, taking a turn stirring the cake batter, robing her in the wool shawl before she blesses the cake. Her grandfather can keep the fire burning under the cake.[41] Both his functions and those of the other men are supportive to the girl and her sponsor and to the women of the tribe whose ceremony this truly is.

As we have seen, the ritual acts focusing on hair combing and adorning and ornamenting the Kinaaldá girl's body, the tasks of grinding corn and helping with domestic chores, are also exclusively feminine in the Navajo culture. Running races is an activity of both men and women. The cake as a solar symbol brings the divine masculine fertilizing element to the ceremony. But the girl is nowhere asked to engage with male figures or with the role maleness will have in her life. The emphasis in the ritual is one of matrilineal connectedness from the origin of the Navajo people in Changing Woman from grandmother to mother to daughter through time and into the future. And the overall feeling is one of strong caring, appreciation, and gentleness toward the girl as she moves from receptivity to actively assuming her identity as an adult woman.

In the case of the Festa das Moças Novas, the Festival of the New Maiden, currently performed by the Tukuna people in the Northwest Amazon, the young initiate experiences violent confrontation with male powers during her initiation and is subjected to painful hair pulling at the culmination of the event.[42] The girl is thus prepared for her relationship to male forces as a woman. Unlike that of the Kinaaldá girl, the Tukuna girl's ritual begins immediately when she sees her first blood. At that moment she removes her necklaces and ornaments and hangs them on the cross beam in the family's house, or *maloca*, where her mother will find them. Then she goes into the forest and hides. Her mother discovers the ornaments and searches for her daughter, who calls her with the sounds of tapping two small sticks together.[43]

Psychologically, this part of the Tukuna ritual represents the daughter's choice to leave the mother, dictated by the change in her own body, the blood that presages her womanhood and her own potential motherhood. This parallels Persephone leaving Demeter at least partially by choice in her elopement with Hades. In the Tukuna culture the separation is symbolized in ritual form, the search in the forest, before mother and daughter reunite for the greater part of the ceremony.

The Tukuna mother brings her daughter back to a small round seclusion hut, where she stays alone, seeing only an aunt, until the culminating feast. The preparations for this feast may take up to three months. Celestial designs—sun, moon, and star—painted on the exterior walls of the hut represent heaven, one of many realms into which the Tukuna world is divided. The name of the seclusion chamber, *nãpi i,* means "to go into the underworld."[44] The initiate or *vorëki,* is believed particularly susceptible to the demonic Noo of the underworld, as well as to celestial beings, during menarche. The chamber provides a place where she actively enters the Noo's realm, invites danger, and endures a descent. The Noo assault her there, and "the slightest breach of ritual precaution will permit them to kill her, suck the viscera from her body and carry her empty body to their domain."[45] Celestial beings may also appear to the girl, to counsel, comfort, instruct, or even to take her up to their heavenly abode.[46]

The moment at which a woman actively chooses to follow the pull from her unconscious and undergo a descent is the moment at which she enters the seclusion chamber of psychotherapy. This moment may not coincide with her first therapy session or with her first therapist, but when it does happen, the change is unmistakable. Two of CARMINA's dreams after eight years of psychotherapy reveal the dark realm of the underworld:

> I'm in one place. I move with someone into another place, cross over some sort of boundary. The place I move into is associated with death, gray, black and white. Ghosts. I am afraid, but I am taken there by this person.

> I am on a trip or voyage. I may be on a ship. I can trust no one. People become "the demon" without warning. I am afraid but alert and willing to persist. I try to keep my eyes open for danger, looking for real people among the dangerous demons.

Carmina said, "I am trying out being dead." Like the Tukuna woman, she had entered the chamber and was assaulted by ghosts. Suffering her demons of self-doubt, inadequacy, and insecurity, she struggled to maintain a sense of personal identity. Her external life had lost all color at this point. The analytic process was paramount, and its aspect was deathlike. She was wandering afraid in the unconscious, led by me as guide. In Tukuna terms she had moved from the realm of earth's surface to that of the underworld. This is an extraordinarily difficult time in analysis. It is a time when nothing seems possible; nothing seems to have been gained; nothing positive in the future can be imagined. One has gone from a state of relative adjustment, with undercurrents of distress or conflict, into a process of change that feels like death. No landmarks exist. The Tukuna girl is allowed one female human contact while she encounters the demonic and the celestial worlds; in like fashion, Carmina was enclosed in the chamber of psychotherapy with me as her only companion.

This descent into the underworld is also an experience of many women before or during their monthly menstruation. Carmina's demons were most destructive at that time. Each menstruation to some extent returns a woman to the original vulnerability that she experienced at menarche. Seen in this way, each menstruation is an opportunity for a psychological re-formation or re-molding as menarche was the original molding and formation. The dark pole of this experience is demonic; the light pole, celestial.

Another dream of Carmina's from the same period highlighted the celestial dimension of her enclosure:

> I am in a chamber below the ground. The walls come up to ground level. It is a rectangle, and in the middle there is a concrete pillar. I'm walking around looking up at the sun through subaquatic light. I'm getting ready for work, and I like the way I look. There are three mirrors. The front mirror reflects on the outside, the middle mirror reflects my back, and the third my front. I am wearing white, and my hair is in pigtails.

The activity in the chamber or container of therapy is similar to alchemical transformation as it took place in the alchemist's vessel.[47] One stage of the process for Carmina is reflecting on herself from many different angles through an odd, watery light. It was the beginning of the self-reflection and self-absorption that would eventually result in a complete transformation of psychological perspective. The light is a kind of grace that descends in the privacy of the moment, "I like the way I look." This self-appreciation was rare and absolutely crucial for Carmina. Wearing white, with her hair in pigtails, she returns to a girlish, premenarche, Kore-like self-containment. The white dress and the watery light also suggested her light double and White Shell Woman. One reason White Shell Woman is associated with water is that she is said to be "in charge of female rain."[48]

For the Tukuna girl, the battle with the demons is finally acted out at the three-day climax of the ceremony, which begins with a full or new moon. A corral is built outside the *maloca*, adjoining the *vorëki's* seclusion chamber. Intoxicating drinks and smoked meat and fish are prepared while guests arrive by canoe. The guests drink, dance, and make rhythmic music with ordinary instruments—turtle shell drums, bamboo horns, and stamping tubes—to ward off the Noo. The spirits' voices, made by ghostly sounding wind instruments, respond. The Noo are present wearing grotesque barkcloth masks and costumes. Some demons have large phalli, others bloody decorative masks to indicate their consumption of human flesh.[49]

The masks reflect a Tukuna myth with a theme of revenge upon those who upset the balance of life. The heroine of this myth is the first of three mythic heroines that the initiate, *vorëki,* has to identify with in the course of her ceremony. The first heroine is a new mother who saves herself, her husband, and their infant child from death because she observes proper food taboos following birth. Other tribesmen who ate the flesh of the animal without observing the proper hunting rituals were killed by the Noo. For the initiate, this wife and mother is the model of female fertility combined with a respect for life of all other species.[50] "Like the mother in the story, the *vorëki* faces danger from the Noo which she has to overcome if she is to attain maturity."[51]

The second heroine with whom the *vorëki* must identify is Ariana, a mythic girl who ascends to heaven as a bird. There she has the nerve to pluck one lock of red hair and one of blue from the sun. The sun tosses her down into the Tukuna underworld. When Ariana returns from the underworld she brings the gift of maize for the Tukuna. Like Ariana, the initiate must undergo an ordeal in which she wins something of value for her people.[52]

Inside the seclusion hut, the girl is painted with black and red dye from head to toe to protect her from the Noo. Outside, the masked demons maniacally dash around, swinging clubs, breaking things, assaulting the people and the chamber. The initiate is dressed in ornate ceremonial clothes decorated with feathers, beads, and tassels. Her red-feathered crown is pulled down over her eyes so that she will not see the sun.[53] Early on the third day of the ceremony, designated women together with an uncle enter the chamber and cut it open "like a cocoon." They move out holding the girl firmly to protect her against the assault of the Noo that peaks at this moment. They all dance until dawn, warding off constant attacks by the demons.[54]

As in the Tukuna ritual, the demons that a woman has to struggle with in her psychotherapeutic process often take male form. Psychologically, woman's woundedness is inextricably bound up with male woundedness. Changing woman involves changing man; men and women share the wounds of our cultural heritage. The shared wound was dramatically defined in a series of Carmina's nightmares after two years of psychotherapy. She was then twenty-one years old.

> I am living in an apartment with a woman friend who is in love with a man. She has the stereotypical, perfect Barbie and Ken attitude.
> I'm sitting in a window seat, cross-legged with her. Two men walk by, gross men, fraternity types, drinking beer. I hate them, flip them off. My friend says, "That's not good; you're going to cause problems." They come in, offended. A big fight ensues, screaming, hassling. A man is standing against the wall. I take a beer bottle and throw it. It hits his head and splits his head open. At the same moment the identical wound appears on my head, but my wound doesn't hurt. Then he is

going to kill me. I go down on my hands and knees and say, "Please don't kill me; don't rape me," knowing I hate him and hating myself for apologizing.

Carmina associated the dream with her feminist philosophy, which included much anti-male vengeance. She also had a memory of splitting her head open in a pool as a little girl when she jumped into the shallow end. But on a deeper level she said it felt like the wound from her father. "I experience no pain, but it is there." At this time, Carmina was experiencing her suffering in projection, in uncontrollable anger toward men, although she was still able to feel love for her father and brothers. This capacity to suffer the wounds inflicted and still love men is heroinic. I have seen the capacity to hold these opposite feelings in many women; it reflects the strength women have to continue to find value in relationships even where they themselves are experiencing devaluation. It is not masochism but a profound capacity for relationship under almost any circumstances.

Carmina and the macho man in the dream formed a picture of the extreme roles of patriarchal male and victim female. When Carmina acts out her hatred toward the man, both of their wounds are revealed. That revelation was the beginning of her finding a way across the gulf that separated her from men. Carmina said, "I'm becoming a superior lesbian bitch, intelligent and political. I think I have an invisible shield around me. I don't have to think about men, so I don't have to think about what I eat, how much I weigh, or what I wear. I've always thought I was abnormally ugly." These comments reflected the deep nature of the wound in Carmina. She had to deny her attraction to men to counteract her intensely negative self-image. She had internalized this feeling of self-denigration from her experience of her mother's and father's respective gender roles. At this period in her psychotherapy she was denying her beauty in order to protect herself from men. She cut her hair short, wore clothes that disguised her body, and made herself as unattractive as possible. I felt sad for her during this period but respected her willingness to break with the cultural expectation that women dress and act according to male standards. Psychologically Carmina needed to manifest how she felt inside—angry, neutered, damaged—instead of living with the discrepancy of looking beautiful and feeling terrible.

A person possesses an innate sexual orientation that often manifests itself at a young age. Nevertheless, at times an individual can confuse a true orientation with a psychological defense. Such a defense is usually based on a child's negative experiences with family members that distort his or her view of either men or women. At this point in her life, Carmina was in flight from her father, and it was unclear to what degree this reaction was influencing her sexual identity.

The problem of male aggression toward women in our society is multi-layered. Rape and violence against women are on the rise. Attractive women have always been considered "fair game" for men from the patriarchal point of view. Diminishing her beauty did provide Carmina with a protection from men by avoiding their attention. Personally, Carmina had experienced her mother's struggle with weight and appearance in relation to the cultural emphasis on being thin. Carmina's mother was kind, supportive, and intelligent, but the stress of having a child with a congenital handicap and a lack of positive feminine value from her own mother made it impossible for her to model this value for Carmina.

Carmina also grew up in the midst of a battle between her parents that took the form of reason versus feeling; her father argued, and her mother cried. Neither could bridge the gap. Many years later, Carmina's parents sought therapy themselves to work on their own issues. Carmina had set an example by her own dedicated work. Like that of the Kinaaldá girl, Carmina's initiation generated renewal in those around her.

Carmina said to me about this dream, "I'm angry at you for not being more political." I continually refocused the work in our sessions on inner psychological issues and refused to engage in political debate about gender issues with her. At this time in my life I was nursing an eight-month-old baby boy, my first child. My experience of the masculine energy in my life was positive, encompassing as it did both my nurturing, supportive husband and our delightful infant son. I was quite removed from cultural gender battles during that early period of motherhood. But during our sessions, while I was concentrating on Carmina's psychological dynamics, I felt as if she were teaching me, bringing me into a lesbian world where an important feminist movement was taking place.

Gender questions became critical in my professional development as my analytic training progressed, and lesbian feminist writers like Judy Grahn and Audre Lorde helped me understand what I was experiencing. I often think of statements Carmina made during those years and appreciate her as having dramatically raised my awareness about many feminist issues.

Six years later, after Carmina had resolved many of her conflicts relating to her father, she had the following dream, which again took up the theme of the wounds:

> I am meeting in a training group with my man lover. Our trainer has a list of words and comes to each of us asking questions. We are supposed to use the word list to answer. It is difficult. Not many people are getting it right. When it is my lover's turn, he is belligerent, sure he is right, and gives a wrong answer. *When it is my turn, I invent my own process.* The questioner says, "They were having a rendezvous . . . they

traveled over . . . ?" I choose the word *egg* and continue "its smooth ovular surface." The questioner says, "No, no, it's wrong." I say, "Of course it's right; there is no right answer to your question."

My lover gets defensive on my behalf. The male questioner kisses him on the mouth by way of defusing it. My lover slugs him. A fight ensues. I can't relate to it. My lover picks up a flail, an Egyptian whip. His opponent is unarmed. The crowd starts chanting, "Give him a whip, give him a whip," until the opponent gets one of his own. I back off, back into a square hole in the ground, and watch them brutally beating each other bloody. I'm numb, crying. Someone comes over to comfort me, a pale, fleshy man, nonthreatening, repulsive. He is wearing an elaborate ancient toga and strange metal ornaments. I'm so upset that I kiss him. I'm very aroused by this kiss. Then I fall asleep. When I wake up I feel blood on my face, and I see that I have the same wound on my face that my lover has from the fight. My beauty is hopelessly scarred. I see the pale, repulsive man near my lover's body, guarding it. The phone rings. I think it is you.

The wounds men inflict on one another through aggression and battle also affect a woman, even when she avoids confrontation. The dream dramatized a problem that Carmina encountered with her father: his argumentative intellect, always tinged with hostility. She learned to argue with him at a very early age. Related to this combativeness is the competition between the two men in the dream. Carmina sidesteps the interrogative game by saying there is no right answer. With the image of the egg she asserts her own feminine reality. The men settle the problem with battle; through her relationship to her lover, not her enemy, Carmina once again participates in the wound. The end of the dream recalled her to our therapeutic relationship, which held the possibility for healing the wound.

Two months later, the next dream showed the collective nature of the wound among women:

I arrive late at your house and office for an appointment. I am angry; you are frustrated with me. There is a police car outside the house. A Polynesian woman with her baby girl is hurt, bleeding. Inside there is a group of Polynesian women. You are one of them. You also have been hit in the head with a rock and are bleeding. Another woman has the same wound. But you are in control, walking around. I feel awkward, intrusive. I can't figure out what I am doing there. One woman says in reference to the criminal, "The silly fool, knowing the legend that whatever you throw will come back to you, he thought to throw a stone into her purse so that the stone would fly back to him with her money." I think maybe I should leave, not stay for my appointment, but you stop me. Somehow it is all right for me to be there.

Carmina said, "I resent having to feel outside, left out. Theoretically I have every right to be as successful as you are. I always smash any hope." She was very angry with me during this time. The dream showed me and other women sharing Carmina's psychological wound. The Polynesian culture may allude to island myths of maiden descent like that of Hainuwele, an Indonesian "coconut maiden," that parallel the Greek Demeter and Persephone story. In such equatorial cultures, a girl was sacrificed for the fertility of the land.[55] The dream had a leveling effect on the relationship between Carmina and me. It diminished her idealization of me and made us more equal. I became the wounded healer.[56] As the medicine woman in our dyad, I had also taken on her pain in order to help her work it through in the analysis.

I told her that I felt her self-destructive complex was trying to smash my belief in her. I firmly trusted her potential and her intact core. I did not feel that she was fundamentally damaged; rather, I saw her as tremendously creative, intelligent, energetic, and capable of breaking with this complex. I persisted in encouraging her hope that she would find her way through the nightmare she was living in her therapy. In the face of her ongoing depression and external life difficulties, I experienced purpose and meaning in the evolution of her unconscious imagery. I could not predict the outcome or what concrete form her emergence would take; I could only repeat in session after session what I knew intuitively to be true, "It will change, I don't know when or how, but eventually the depression will lift." This mantra reflected my own extended experience with the dark descent. It was a belief I had to carry until she could feel it herself. She acknowledged that "there is a whole choir of complexes who want to prove you wrong."

Carmina's demon complex took the form of an ogre in the next dream:

> I'm in a country occupied by a tyrant, a male ogre. I'm one of a
> group of women, a cavalry, who are prisoner to the tyrant. We have
> been tested for who can ride the fastest because we're trying to oust the
> tyrant and reclaim the territory. At one point I'm flying pell-mell down
> a hill. The tyrant's familiar, an enormous, horrible black dog, tears
> down the hill and takes a big bite out of my horse's flank. We are next
> to a mailbox. I see the mailman and know there is something for me. I
> can't get to him. A childhood friend is there in a purple dress.

Here again there is a cultural element to the complex. The whole country is enslaved by the tyrant. A group of women are fighting to free themselves and their land by ousting the despot from power. In dreams like this one, Carmina became the valiant cultural heroine. Like the Tukuna girl, she confronted the demon, the ogre.

Two weeks later, the core of Carmina's personal demon complex appeared in the following dream:

> I'm with my family, although my mother is not present. My brother and father are there. My brother is helplessly vomiting over and over again. He is wearing a rubber bib that is horrible and clinical, like an artificial limb. My father is trying to take care of him over and over. I am standing there watching, repulsed and angry.

Carmina said, "I still feel angry. I'm depressed. Why am I not getting better? I can't have compassion for myself or my brother. I feel like a twisted, deformed rock." I told Carmina that I thought her brother came between her and herself and that this bound her to him in hatred as well as in love. "I am linked to him like a ball and chain," she said. Struggling with both inner and outer demons, Carmina nonetheless persevered in trying to resolve her alienation from herself and from men in the midst of assault.

For SARAH, who strongly identified with the patriarchy, the demons took other forms. Having earned her father's favor by achieving in the world, she frequently found herself allied with the male power structure. This alliance gave her a heady sense of inflation that was very seductive. Once she dreamed that "I am walking with God through long corridors." In medical school she found in the doctors a perfect fit for her godlike projections on men and received much gratification from being the efficient handmaiden to certain male teachers. But in her psychotherapeutic work she continually expressed the fatigue and diminishment of her core self as she compulsively persisted in these old behavior patterns.

The wound that manifested in her dreams about fifteen months into therapy was the following:

> I have gone to a woman in a castle, with stone buildings and ramps, seeking help. Next, I am going to an elderly pope in the Vatican to get help for a family eye disease. I am staying with King Lear in a room next to the laundry. I am trying to set up a donor system for eyes. Initially, the Pope supports my cause. But then I find him bundled up in pontifical robes in a tall wheelchair. His crown is tipped to one side like that of a caricature or figurehead. He is surrounded by his cabinet. The members of his cabinet are trying to kill me, so perhaps they have injured him.

An eye disease suggested that there was a problem with vision, with the way Sarah was seeing. Like a woman of ancient Greece who sought healing in the labyrinth, Sarah was undergoing a dream incubation in psychotherapy. But the woman from whom she seeks help, the woman she identified with me, is less present and powerful than she was in the castle dream. Although her vision was changing, Sarah's allegiance is still with the Pope, the leader of Catholicism, and with Shakespeare's King Lear, the patriarch who, possessed by blind greed, forfeits the true love of his daughter Cordelia and brings about his own fall. Sarah tries again to find healing in the patriarchal structure she has trusted all her life. The dream shows the Pope to be at the mercy of the men in his cabinet, who apparently have a vendetta against her. She is a cultural heroine here: she wants to set up a donor system for eyes; she wants to help change the way the feminine is viewed in many people. But she can't depend on the men in power to help. For every man who is willing to help, there are several men who would injure him (and her) in order to keep her down. Sarah had to shift her vision to the chamber of her own analysis, where the woman-to-woman relationship could strengthen the Queen in herself who needed to reign. It was through the Queen's eyes that she had to see, not the Pope's.

More than a year later, Sarah dreamed:

> I am at work and come downstairs to meet a doctor friend in the lobby. When I see him, he has his hair cut and dyed bright red at the roots. He has a dark brownish mark on his forehead like a birthmark or burn scar. We are discussing a case. Another woman physician is there. I feel as if I have to defend my competence and my friendship with the man to her. There is a confrontation in which I lie about my experience. She leaves. I ask the man if the mark on his forehead will go away. He says, "Yes."

Sarah was actually flirting with this male doctor in the hospital. But she was embarrassed about her sexual feelings for him. She felt she was projecting the "mark" on him as she did with her husband by withholding herself, not offering her intuition, sensitivity, and femininity. Like the power and the glory in the earlier dreams, Sarah saw the wound in projection. She didn't feel the pain or scars herself. She saw the problem in the men. Her competitive and dishonest shadow came up again here. She had to lie to maintain her persona as the best doctor to the other woman. The "other woman" shadow was experienced as negative by Sarah's ego, but the shadow's questioning would bring a shift in consciousness or vision. Sarah's competence needed to be questioned within her psychic structure because she was using it to ally herself with the dominant male point of view.

Four years later, at the age of thirty-six, still struggling with demons of overwork, exhaustion, and drivenness, Sarah dreamed:

> I am looking through a window. I see a man lying down in a meat market. He looks dead, eaten by a shark. He still has the teeth of the shark in him. The mouth of the shark is still attached. He looks dead, like a piece of meat, but his head is still on, and he is still alive.

Then there is an image of an incestuous relationship between brother and sister. I am involved.

Sarah identified with the half-dead man. She felt frightened about the implications of this dream. Intuitively, she knew that it referred to the driven way in which she performed at the clinic, neglecting herself and her husband. The second dream suggested that her compulsive dedication to healing might be, in part, an attempt to atone for the sexual play with her older brother. Sarah was an excellent doctor. In her work she brought to bear all her skills, including her sensitivity and aspects of her new feminine perspective. But she felt like a man, and the shark, a cold destructive force from the unconscious, attacked her. Her refusal to respond to her body and her feelings led to increasingly violent compensations from the unconscious. She had done herself violence. The bloody faces of the Noo in the Tukuna ritual carry this kind of unconscious energy.

For BEATRICE, the demons in the early weeks of therapy took the form of her traumatic war experience in Vietnam. She reported recurring nightmares about her life there and the death of her lover:

> Sometimes my lover's head is intact. Sometimes he is putting the gun to his own head, smiling and saying, "This is how to do it." Sometimes his head just explodes. He is willing it to do so. His voice is always saying, "You did this to me." His stomach is always hanging out.
>
> I am being held down, and cockroaches are crawling all over me. I can't open my mouth to call for help or else they will climb in. They are in my ears and on my eyes.
>
> Rats are eating me.

Beatrice described her nightmares as "a form of punishment, my just desserts." She felt guilty because she had insisted on accompanying her lover on the dangerous mission to take pictures of the Chinese coming over the Cambodian border that led to his death. She said she had behaved like a child, threatening to go back on heroin if he did not let her go with him. And because her safety was important to him, she knew she had delayed him; he had protected her at his own expense when they were attacked. In her repetitive nightmares, she relived the hours when he lay wounded and her own firing of the bullet that took his life.

In Vietnam, Beatrice had been plagued by flying cockroaches; now her apartment in San Francisco was being fumigated for cockroaches. She had once camped near a river in Vietnam with her lover and awakened in the night to find a rat gnawing at her ankle; she bore a scar from that bite. In telling me these stories, she experienced a catharsis of her horror in a safe feminine container. This was the first time she had been contained since she had left Hong Kong and her mother. Beatrice bravely engaged with her psyche in the work of sorting out her past. A month later she told me the following dream:

> I am in England walking along Brighton beach. It is dawn; I am out after curfew. When I see an ambulance and teams of stretcher bearers engaged in secret activity, I hide between the kiosk and some sand dunes. The stretchers are painted bright blue. They are large, with room for two or three people on them. I watch the ambulance going along with the bearers. They come to a body and roll him over— I wonder if I will recognize him. I think it might be somebody I knew in Vietnam. But they go to the next body and put a mask over the face before I can see him. The mask is iron and robotlike. They are going at a very slow pace, as if they have all the time in the world. Only the bodies near me have masks. Usually in dreams I can walk around and see the faces of the dead, but not this time. I am not afraid; as long as I stay hidden, I will be all right.

The dead had haunted Beatrice in her nightmares during the twelve years since she had left Vietnam. In this dream, however, a ritual burial is taking place. She can no longer recognize individuals as people she had actually seen wounded or dead; the trauma retreated to the archetypal realm. The burial rite put a temporary end to the recurring night terrors in which she relived the horror and atrocity she had witnessed. She stopped dreaming about Vietnam and her dead lover for over a year. Beatrice spoke again about blocking her feelings by looking at things through the lens of a camera. "I still do it now. Psychologically, I sit with a camera to separate and divide me from what is happening." In our hours I experienced her capacity to distance herself from her own emotions. It was an automatic aspect of her personality. As a naturally introspective woman she could at times describe her feelings, but without a trace of affect. The temporary cessation of the nightmares gave Beatrice a respite in which to examine some of the behavior patterns she had developed as a result of being forced from an early age to be responsible for her own survival.

All three women—Carmina, Sarah, and Beatrice—were struggling with internal and external demons that reflect the patriarchal culture in which we live. Carmina was trying to heal her wounded relationship to the father/brother maleness in her psyche as well as to connect with a real man in the world and to find her own vocation. Sarah was trying to uncover her feminine identity beneath her father/career identification at the same time that she negotiated the unequal relationships with male colleagues and with her husband. Beatrice was trying to heal the post-traumatic stress she suffered as a result of having witnessed the murder of men, women, and children during the Vietnam War. The war experience overlay the child-hood wounds from her mother's abandonment. Each woman was conscientiously dedicating herself to her own individual development in the context of the patriarchal culture she and her foremothers have had to endure. Each fought for feminine values in her own way.

In the Tukuna ceremony the power of the demons or ghosts is ritually broken at sunrise when the girl throws a firebrand, a solar weapon, at the Noo of the underworld. She dares to borrow the sun's power as the mythic heroine Ariana did. But unlike the Kinaaldá girl, for the *vorëki*, bodily mutation comes about in a violent way. Instead of the gentle hair combing, washing, and adorning of the Navajo ceremony, in the Tukuna ceremony, at midday the dancing is interrupted by the girl's paternal uncle, who grabs a lock of the girl's hair and pulls it out. Next, a group of women sit around her and pull all her hair out. The last lock, dyed red, is pulled out by her uncle. She puts her feather crown back on, and the wild dancing begins again. The *vorëki* endured the pain, and her baldness is now the sign of her transformation.[57] At the initiatory level, Sarah's early dream of going bald suggested her psychotherapeutic transformation.

Bodily mutation in the female initiation practices of the Tiv tribe of Central Nigeria also involves pain. Whereas the changes in the Navajo ceremony are addressed with massaging, molding, and painting, the Tiv girl has to undergo incisions in her skin, scarification, to produce a pattern that she displays for the rest of her life.[58] For both Tiv and Tukuna girls, their transformation involves visible permanent physical alteration. In one of CARMINA's dreams eight years into therapy, the image of female skin appears affected by disease and by ritual bodily mutation:

> I am being worked on. I have these crustaceous barnacle-like things on me, a disease. Part of the work is getting rid of these things. The other woman has black-and-white designs on her nude body. The designs are symbolic of something she has accomplished. I envy her her exotic body. She is going through a similar process.

Carmina and the other woman, her shadow/me, are undergoing a cleansing or purification of the skin. Again the woman-to-woman relationship involved body and psyche. The designs inscribed on a Tiv girl's body beginning at menarche are three concentric circles around her navel and a vertical line running from throat to navel. Subsequently, the pattern is elaborated throughout her life.[59] According to Lincoln, the woman's navel represents the present, the point of nurturance for future generations, both part of the scarification and not, since it is naturally there from birth. "At puberty, however, it takes on new significance as the vital center where life will be formed, and at that moment it becomes the center and starting point for the symbolic design that makes a girl into a woman."[60] The scars are said to promote human and agricultural fertility.[61] In the dream, Carmina recognized the black-and-white designs on the other woman's body as a sign of initiated womanhood.

After the hair-pulling rite in the Tukuna ceremony, the masqueraders remove their costumes and pile them around the *vorëki;* she accepts them as an offering. The transformation of the girl into a woman also results in the demons being humanized. By eating smoked meat, instead of raw, the guests become civilized again and can once again participate in furthering the initiate toward womanhood.[62]

Following the feast, the community concentrates its protective powers on the girl. The initiate has moved from the underworld of the chamber to the earth of her *maloca* to the sun outside and to earth again. Now she is carried on a tapir skin to the river to go underwater where the aquatic monsters, the Dyëvaë, live. Women remove her ornaments and clothes while the shamans stick an arrow in the water to ward off the monsters. The girl kneels naked in the water, bathed by the shamans, who pass the water from her feet to her head. She swims around the magic arrow and through a shaman's legs, diving deeper into the water. Then she returns to shore and is dressed again.[63]

Mother of Timbo is the prototypical initiate the *vorëki* is emulating in the bath. This woman gave birth to a son by the spirit of the plant called *timbó*. When the mother noticed that her son's bathing caused fish to die, she limited his swimming to allow the fish population to increase. Tiv men use *timbó*, a fish poison, in moderation to kill fish for the tribe to eat. "Each girl wins the gift of timbo, as Ariana won the gift of maize."[64]

The girl is taken to a fishing spot, where she is given a second bath with *timbó*. A *timbó* bath is thought to make a woman temporarily sterile. The first bath by the shamans may represent the sacrifice of a part of the girl's fertility to benefit the world of nature. But she also makes it possible for her people to have an increased supply of fish by becoming Mother of Timbo. Through her journey through the worlds, the girl has been prepared for the *timbó* bath and for the responsible use of contraception.[65]

As the Tukuna girl identifies with the three mythic heroines, she herself becomes a cultural heroine. Each woman in psychotherapy becomes a cultural heroine through her individual initiation. In the course of becoming a woman-identified woman, she courageously takes up the work of confronting the internal and external demons that plague her instead of passively acquiescing to the patriarchal system. In this way she lights a lamp as Psyche does in the Greek myth.[66] Psyche dares to risk her husband's loss in order to know him and herself in a different way. In one early account of Changing Woman, Turquoise Woman and White Shell Woman are called on to be "light-bringers."[67] Each woman in psychotherapy who dares the descent brings back a gift to all of us, a gift of consciousness; every woman and man whom Carmina, Sarah, and Beatrice encounter in their lives is touched by their light.

The interrelationship between the welfare of the tribe and the individual fertility of each woman in the tribe is beautifully portrayed in the Tukuna girl's rite. At the height of celebrating her fertility, she ritually dedicates herself to reproduction and ceremonially enacts the means of contraception. For these three women, psychotherapeutic initiates, menarche held no such wisdom. Carmina said, "I came of age without any guidelines, rules, or context." Sarah said, "It was not a memorable occasion." And Beatrice said, "I thought I was dying." In the process of psychotherapy, each of them encountered unconscious conflicts about their own fertility and the use of contraception.

For most adolescent women in our culture, fertility is thought of in the negative terms of avoiding pregnancy. Fertility becomes an issue in a different way when a woman's desire to have a child awakens. Many shifts in awareness occur in this process. Years of fearing pregnancy create a strong psychological set that then conflicts with a woman's instinctual desire. She suddenly becomes more aware of her body as a vessel, of how she takes care of herself, of how she has neglected herself. She may realize that she has little knowledge of the side effects of the contraception she chose years earlier. She often experiences deep ambivalence about having a child. If she was deprived of mothering in any way, she wonders whether or not she can give a child what it will need. Fear and anxiety accompany the primordial longings to have a baby.

A woman awakening to the desire to bear children may dream about contraception or experience deep ambivalence about using contraception with her lover or husband. At the beginning of therapy, when CARMINA was only nineteen years old, she had a deep, irrational fear of being pregnant. This fear abated for a time, but it erupted in full force some months later after she had an intense, several-hour conversation with a man. The meaning of her fear revealed itself slowly in the labyrinthine twists of the unconscious. When she was sixteen she had thought she was pregnant and had had to confront her father with that possibility. This was a terribly shaming experience, fraught with fear and emotional violence. She had planned and strategized her approach and "argument." But it had traumatized her. Being pregnant includes open acknowledgment that one is a sexual being; it is also a manifestation of having been penetrated. Carmina was still afraid of being violated, of acknowledging relationship to a man, of losing her sense of being "one-in-herself," whole, intact. Being in relation to a man meant having to both accept and reject her father and maleness in new ways.

Seven years later, after Carmina had moved into relationships with men again and wished for children, the diaphragm, her chosen method of contraception, functioned as a symbolic barrier to accepting male fertilization.

> I am making love with a man. It is sexually and emotionally positive. Then twelve hours later I am making love with another man. I have a problem with my diaphragm, and I am terrified I am going to be pregnant.

The dual image of maleness in the dream referred to inner-outer male as well as to father-lover conflicts. Although she could feel her attraction to a man, Carmina had yet to become receptive to change, symbolized by pregnancy in the dream. She resisted taking the seed, allowing the maleness to have its effect. But six months later a dream revealed a dramatic psychological shift in Carmina's attitude toward intimacy with a man and/or her inner maleness.

> I am on a camping trip with my lover. I go into a barrackslike room where we are sleeping and begin to look through things on his bed. I find beautiful things that are meant to be gifts for me—silk things, jewelry. I am surprised, and I quickly cover it all up so that he won't know that I've seen anything. Later we want to make love, but my diaphragm is malfunctioning. My lover gets impatient. We eventually make love.

Here Carmina unexpectedly discovered that a man, her inner man, valued her, or the feminine, symbolized by his gifts of precious jewelry and clothing. Affirmed in these beautiful objects of adornment, when the diaphragm malfunctions, she is not prevented from making love, nor does she panic about becoming pregnant. The diaphragm was no longer symbolically functioning as her defense, her barrier to intimacy. Paradoxically, in positive relationship to her inner male, she found confirmation of her deepest feminine self. That internal confirmation would potentially be reflected in her relationships with the outer men in her life.

SARAH, who bore a child a year after she began therapy, experienced ambivalence and conflict about becoming pregnant again when her son was thirteen months old. Two years into psychotherapy, she dreamed:

> I am being raped. My husband is there but pushed into a closet or out of commission.

Sarah said, "I wanted to forget this dream. I am worried that I'm pregnant. I use the diaphragm, but one weekend we didn't use it. I don't want another baby now, but my husband does. I feel forced and violated in the dream." When she told her husband her feelings, he said it sounded as if she was threatening him with having an abortion. Sarah had simply wanted to be heard and felt "forced" to keep quiet about negative feelings in the relationship. "It's an invasion of who I am to act like everything is all right. I find myself willing to doubt myself when he disagrees with me. I want us to go into therapy together."

What Sarah expressed is what many, many women feel. Where a woman feels the patriarchal imbalance in her intimate relationship, where she feels her wholeness is not being respected, sexuality and pregnancy become an invasion, rather than a fulfillment of her femininity. Carmina felt the inequality in her family of origin as a child and young girl, which caused her to reject men as lovers and for a time to reject her own creative potential. Sarah coexisted with the domination by being her father's good girl and continuing to be father-identified in the world. As a professional woman, a doctor, she was able to express herself. In her marriage, however, she felt unheard, unrecognized as an individual and a woman. The inequality between men and women often deteriorates into a power struggle in a marriage or relationship.

This inequality is not only inequality in power, pay, and opportunity; it is the intrinsic cultural identity of women versus men that Riane Eisler has called the dominator versus the partnership model of society.[68] The effect of such cultural inequality in psychotherapy has been described by Jean Baker Miller, founder of the Stone Center Institute at Wellesley College. In an article "The Construction of Anger in Women and Men," Miller describes the effect on women of living in a male-centered and patriarchal society. She points out that the dominant group, men, tends to act destructively toward the subordinate group, women. Men restrict women's range of actions and their reactions to destructive treatment. They discourage women's full and free expression of their experience and characterize women falsely. And men describe this as normal—usually as natural, ordered and ordained by higher and better powers, ranging from God to biology.[69] Women are born into a hostile environment and are required to adapt to it cheerfully. With this as a given in our culture, Sarah's dream and feelings about her dream were completely understandable. She felt weak, unworthy, that she had "no right" or "no cause" to be angry. Her feelings reflected the attitude of the existing male power structure in our society, not pathology. Getting in touch with her right to be uncomfortable and angry was a healthy step in Sarah's development.

Unlike the Tukuna girl or the Kinaaldá girl, whose social, religious, and instinctual goals are ceremonially resolved for her, a modern woman has to find an individual solution to the multitude of impulses that clamor to be satisfied within and outside her. Ambivalence about having a child is not merely a neurotic disturbance. For some women, it reflects discontent with their subordination to the patriarchal system. For others, it reflects a consciousness—a consciousness of choice—that did not exist in prehistoric Çatal Hüyük and does not exist in rural cultures today where women are still completely engaged in the business of survival. A woman in our culture is confused by conflicting societal messages. She is educated in a system designed on a male model of the psyche in which she is exposed to many possible careers. In this context she sometimes has to misrepresent herself, her femininity, in order to achieve. Though a life of the mind is held out to her as an option, the subtle societal influences that keep a woman secondary begin to operate in her prepubescent years. As she becomes sexual, she feels the shift in attitude that puts her in a category lesser than men. She becomes aware of the denigration of domesticity and hears mothers blamed for their children's problems. As an adult she finds herself battling for a place in the work world at the same time that she battles her mate at home to share domestic responsibilities. This environment is disheartening for a woman considering making a lifelong commitment to children, who deserve intense energy and care for many years. A woman understandably hesitates to divide herself and take on more stress and more battles by becoming a mother. As a mother, not only will her time and energy be divided, but also, internally, her loyalties, her commitments, her priorities. Mothering brings a woman into the deepest aspects of her nature and into the powerful natural edge between life and death.

PART II

Transformation

Figure 7.
Mother/Maiden Goddess.

Photo by Mrs. M. A. Mellaart.

4

Knowing the Power of the Womb

*E*nclosed in the sanctuary of a woman-to-woman therapeutic container, a woman begins to distinguish among all the voices, emotions, thoughts, and desires that have been clamoring for attention inside her. Once she can trust the enclosure, she can give herself more fully to the transformation or metamorphosis that she is undergoing. Although transformation happens mostly in the dark, in the unconscious, there are moments in therapy or in between therapy of clarity, vision, elation, and realization. Her inner world, shifting and moving in her dreams and fantasies, slowly offers up the jewel—the form of her individual feminine identity. A woman's seemingly amorphous change is manifested in her changing attitudes and behavior in everyday life. For instance, she may suddenly find herself being assertive with a lover or husband in a way she never could before. Or she may start setting limits with her children that enable them and her to appreciate one another more. Or she may begin to challenge the patriarchal authority she encounters at work and consider changing her job or career. Whatever the external source of stress, the effect of the metamorphosis in woman-to-woman therapy is a new validation and definition of the woman from a feminine perspective, not a masculine one.

At the deepest level, change or transformation in therapy involves an experience of death and rebirth: the death or sacrifice of an old way of being that allows a new way to be born. This changing is embedded in a woman's womb, which sheds its lining and renews itself as the moon wanes and waxes. The womb is the vessel of death, transformation, and rebirth.

The image of birth erupts in a woman's dreams and fantasies. The desire to bear a child may be the desire for a literal child or a yearning for the lost femininity that she is trying to birth in herself. If she embraces the feeling, she opens herself to her own mystery and to a sublime initiation into the next stage of her development, whether that be motherhood or her own adult creativity. If she resists the process, often because of negative mothering in her own childhood, she can fall into an inferno of conflict. For her to come to a meaningful experience of the power in her own womb, intense therapeutic work may be necessary to illuminate and transform her personality.

Whether or not to have a child is a question many women face today. Though the bearing of children is a biological task, the existence of choice creates a new psychological constellation for women that includes both internal and external considerations. A woman who chooses not to have a child realizes her womanhood in other ways. I have worked with women who fulfilled their creativity in a career such as art, social work, counseling, or law. Sometimes a woman's path is religious or contemplative, her focus on the inner world. The painter Meinrad Craighead speaks of women's primary creativity in the text accompanying her painting entitled *Egg:* "I have never conceived, but whether or not a woman does conceive, she carries the germinative ocean within her, and the essential eggs. We have a spirituality full from within. Whether we are weaving tissue in the womb or pictures in the imagination, we create out of our bodies."[1]

Some women who fervently desire a child/motherhood are forced to come to terms with infertility. They may choose to adopt children or to redirect their energy to other endeavors. A woman without children generally develops relationships with other women and men to fulfill her need for intimacy. She may also be godmother or special aunt to nieces, nephews, or children of close friends. Or she may become involved in fostering other's children in such programs as Big Sisters. Frequently, a woman's path to choice is long and twisting, consisting as it does of an ever-changing interaction among her own individual inclination, her relationship choices, and her biological fertility.

Both my women therapists, Magda Proskauer and Barbara Hannah, chose not to bear children. Miss Hannah embraced a single life, a life of scholarship, analytic practice, teaching, and writing. Magda chose a married life and devoted herself to psychotherapeutic work. Both women fulfilled themselves creatively in their choices. My path proved to be different. After I realized my vocation of Jungian psychology, the desire to bear a child drew me into the heart of my femininity. I found deep fulfillment in bearing children. Over a period of six years while practicing psychotherapy, I had three pregnancies. Two of them were wonderful, healthy experiences that resulted in the births of my son and my daughter; the third, in between the two births, ended in a miscarriage at four and a half months. Being pregnant, working with pregnant women, and listening to women's dreams and fantasies about pregnancy led me to research ancient sites and rituals pertaining to the maternal archetype that are the source for themes, feelings, and images of fertility, pregnancy, and childbirth in women today.

While preparing a seminar for professionals, "Transference to the Pregnant Psychotherapist," I discovered Dorothy Cameron's monograph on the Neolithic town of Çatal Hüyük.[2] Cameron amplified the images of the birth-giving Goddess found at this site when she excavated there with Professor James Mellaart.[3] Reading her material deepened my understanding of the powerful imagery I had experienced in my own pregnancies and had perceived in women's psychotherapeutic work. Çatal Hüyük provides fascinating examples of the maternal archetype in our prehistoric heritage. Fertility, pregnancy, and birth were the core of spiritual worship in this Anatolian community. The mud brick honeycomb settlement contained multiple shrines, excavation of which revealed artifacts rich in symbolism of the Great Mother. The inhabitants were agricultural people for whom plant, animal, and human fertility were seen as interconnected. The Mother Goddess was responsible for all life and, in her underworld aspect, for death and rebirth.[4]

Archaeological material shows that women at Çatal Hüyük were responsible for the social and cultic life of the community as well as for the activities of weaving, pottery making, and other arts and crafts. The birth-giving Goddess, or "Goddess of Regeneration"[5] was the central deity of these people, the focus of spiritual life. The prehistoric precedents of the mother-daughter pair seen later in Greek friezes and paintings of Demeter and Persephone are vividly represented in this ancient town. In the shrines, red and black handprints evoke Her power working through the hands of her priestesses as midwives. Red was the color of blood and life; black was the color of mourning and death.[6]

Among the most cryptic images at Çatal Hüyük are a goddess giving birth to a bull or ram in the so-called "birth-giving posture": upraised arms, outstretched legs with feet upturned.[7] Twin goddesses, mother and daughter, older and younger, one larger, one smaller, one with breasts, one without, also appear, sometimes in birthing positions.[8] In one shrine three large bull's heads protrude over a row of plaster women's breasts, each of which contains the jaw of a boar.[9] This is an image of death in life. The wild boar is a scavenger like the vulture, which represents the Goddess in her death aspect. The pig was the sacred animal of Mother Earth for thousands of years.[10] Belonging to Demeter, it was the sacrificial animal in the Eleusinian mystery rites.

In another shrine the horns and head of an aurochs (a European wild ox, now extinct) take precedence. In the center there is a large bull's head. To the right is a pair of pendulous breasts with the skull of a griffin vulture in each. Each nipple is open at the end, painted red like the muzzle of the bull, the beak of the vulture protruding from each breast.[11] The breast is full of milk, nurturance, but also contains the vulture of death. Life contains death and the promise of rebirth.

A woman who gives up her baby for adoption may experience this "death in life" when the milk in her breasts lets down every time she thinks about the child she bore and lost. The giving up is a death to the *in utero* relationship and potential mother-child relationship. No matter how consciously such a choice is made or how right the decision may be, a woman to whom this happens is forced to experience herself as container of both life and death.

Cameron found the core of a transformation mystery in her observation that though some of the decorated bull's heads from the shrines have eyes and mouths, others do not. Cameron saw the uterus in the bull's head image. She postulated that the bull as the phallic principle symbolized power, and the womb, the container of the power women carry within their bodies. "If we accept that the extraordinary coincidence and similarity of the bull and the uterus shape was the basis for the sacredness of the bull, we can see how the worship of the Mother Goddess was strengthened by such a transformation mystery; perhaps indeed this could be the seed of the later flowering of the Mystery religions."[12] The bull/uterus image was a revelation to me. It made visible what I had felt in extended labor during childbirth: the tremendous power in my own womb. I wished that I could have had such imagery on the walls of the hospital room during labor; it would have given me strength for the ordeal of my initiation into motherhood. Instead, the prehistoric female birth imagery of Çatal Hüyük infused my preparations for the seminar with their regenerative power. I dreamed of my nearly three-year-old daughter:

> I am "teaching" two little girls: my daughter and her best friend. I am setting limits, chastising them, trying to prepare them for life. The setting is outside, parklike with green grass. The sun is shining on their precious heads. But, extraordinarily, the "teaching" is simultaneously putting together the handouts for the seminar, actively assembling them. When the packets are finished, they are silver and gold constructions, also reflecting the sun. The shining packets and the shining little girls are all of a piece, an intricate piece in the sunlight, allusively interrelated.

The twin girl children, mothering, and teaching are all magically intertwined in this dream. The power of the double and triple feminine and the beauty of creative work make a whole.

Pregnancy and birth images in a woman's dreams appear during the course of psychotherapeutic transformation. Sometimes the first dream or the presenting problem revolves around pregnancy. Incubation in the woman-to-woman container is often signified in a dream as a pregnancy. Sometimes the initial hidden spark of life, the fertile moment in a particular hour, manifests in a dream as conception. Carmina had a vision of a seed in the midst of her darkest period in analysis. The seed presence sustained her when all seemed lost. The embryonic processes of change and evolution manifest themselves as we go along. Metamorphosis is not linear, but always circular, spiral, or labyrinthine. Birth may precede conception; embryos may die, pregnancies evaporate, conceptions falter. Dreams of a healthy pregnancy may be followed by dreams of dead babies. When an old psychic structure is disintegrating there is often a reversal of the order, as if a woman has to regress back to conception in order to be reborn.[13] Death, the shadow of birth, inevitably accompanies transformation.

In the sixth year of her analysis, when CARMINA was truly in the depths of her process, she had the following dream:

> I am spinning, enclosed in an egg. All around me people are dying of a terrible disease, all unknown faces except one. A woman is giving birth to a baby. I have to make a moral decision about whether to risk myself and take the baby. She is going to die, but I can save the baby.

Carmina's body contained all the eggs of her potential children, actual or symbolic. Unlike the previous dream, in which she chose the word *egg* to assert her femininity in relation to the masculine, here the whole universe is an egg, reduced to the container of psychotherapy. She is completely enclosed in her work. The old order of her psyche, embodied in a pregnant woman, is giving birth at the same time that it is dying. The baby is the potential new state of being. But Carmina is afraid the baby will be contaminated by her old way of feeling. She said that this dream had the same feeling as her earlier dream of the earring-gift initiation with me. She was caught between separating from the old and taking on the new as her own.

To endure this place of tension between death and rebirth in psychotherapy requires tremendous courage. It is a terrifying process to feel all you have known and believed about yourself disintegrate. It feels as if nothing is left, as if everything you counted on, the very ground you stand on, is disintegrating. Even the container of therapy feels threatened. Carmina's negative shadow identification was dying and simultaneously struggling to give birth to a new Self image. Psychologically, birth and death were again intertwined. This was no intellectual process; Carmina's body and soul were profoundly involved. The Great Mother archetype is there in the background.

Dorothy Cameron suggested that the flowerlike ends of the fallopian tubes of the uterus, when viewed frontally, may have been the source of inspiration for the rosette symbol. The rosette has been an attribute of the Goddess since Neolithic times. SARAH had a dream about giving me red roses early in her therapy. The red rose originally represented female sexuality, creativity, and beauty, women's blood and genitals.[14] The white rose identified the virgin daughter; the red, the mother/Demeter. The red-and-white rose, the daughter within the mother, was appropriated by alchemists as a symbol of the sacred womb in which the alchemical child, the result of the work, would be born.[15] In a litany to the Virgin Mary, she is addressed as "Mystical Rose."[16] Meinrad Craighead evokes the power of this image in a painting entitled *Rosa Mystica*. In the accompanying text, Craighead presents the rose as enclosing the Virgin's devotee: "God speaks in these warmed cave temples. God says, Come into my enclosed garden. Come into my lap and sit in the center of your soul. Drink the living waters of memory and give birth to yourself. What you unearth will stun you. You will paint the walls of this cave in thanksgiving."[17] Sarah had sometimes tended the shrine of the Virgin Mary in the Catholic church growing up; we shared this knowledge of the Madonna. Now in the context of our concentrated work in the psychotherapeutic container, Sarah's symbolic gift had both sensual and spiritual overtones. The gift of the blood-colored rose acknowledged the female eros and creativity in our relationship. In her outer life, Sarah loved gardening, which allowed her a mystical identification with nature. Growing flowers became her feminine devotion in the years we worked together.

Images of rosette-type flowers recur in women's dreams, evoking beauty and a tribute to feminine sexuality and spirituality. CARMINA's dream of a familiar rose garden eight years into therapy brought an unexpected discovery:

> I am looking at terraced beds of flowers. I feel envious; they are not for me. Suddenly I am around the corner, looking up a steep hill. The earth on the hill is newly turned, being readied for planting. Some very old rose bushes are in bloom. The old-fashioned house has finally opened its windows to light, air, and the smell of roses. It is a place I know well; I've just never seen it from the back before. I start to cry and say, "Oh my Mother, oh my Mother . . . " I realize that she tried to give me these things, this place with the earth and the flowers.

In this dream Carmina both feels her loss of connection to the feminine and regains it in realizing that her mother had tried to provide her with the basic feminine ground that earth represents. Earth is also Changing Woman. The identification of the earth and its fruits with femininity is found in all agricultural societies. Carmina's psychic house is transformed, the ground of her psyche newly tilled. Old roses, her feminine heritage, still bloom within her. She saw her mother's legacy from a different perspective as she experienced her own transformation in the therapeutic process.

The horns of the bull at Çatal Hüyük are moon-shaped. The birth and death of the moon is reflected in a woman's monthly cycle. The fusion of moon, horn, and uterus is a potent generative symbol. At the Palace of Knossos in Crete, the palace walls and parapets were adorned with hundreds of horns of consecration.[18] When I was pregnant with my daughter I had a dream in which a voice said to me, "You are connected to the moon and the earth." And I thought, "Surely the moon, but the earth, doubtful." I had always felt connected to the ever-changing, cyclical quality of the lunar feminine, but I was still "grounded" in my mother. It took having my own daughter to bridge the connection for me.

Inverted triangles in patterns at Neolithic Çatal Hüyük symbolize the pubic triangle. The spot in the center is associated with conception. The number 3 is associated with generation: the male-female-child triad; the Great Goddess as bride, mother, and crone; and the three phases of the moon. The triple aspect of the feminine came up repeatedly in Carmina's work. Two years into our work together, she had the following dream, which evoked the feeling of the triple identity of Changing Woman, Turquoise Woman, and White Shell Woman:

> There are three images of me, standing face forward, side by side.
> One is shorter, one medium height, one taller—all me as I look now. I
> focus on the central figure, where the lines are becoming more refined.
> I have a sense of the power in women's spirituality after the dream—
> power, serenity, and happiness.

Carmina was becoming more involved with the lesbian community at this time and being exposed to positive feminist input both intellectually and spiritually. The central image in the dream is becoming more refined; Carmina is re-creating herself. She is walking into beauty. A few months earlier I had had a dream about my work with Carmina that also addressed the spiritual motive in her initiation:

> Carmina is coming to me with some deep religious question. I am
> trying to answer it by reference or analogy to a dream of mine in which
> pagan and Christian meaning fuse. The point I keep emphasizing is
> that the source has to be her unconscious, that the answer has to come
> from her.

My dream showed me that Carmina's ambivalence about her sexuality and her difficulties with her body- and self-image were part of a religious quest. The purpose of the analysis was a spiritual mystery. My own spiritual journey was important in my work with her. But ultimately, no matter what I could teach her, I, as she, had to trust her unconscious to reveal her path.

When Carmina reclaimed the spirit of her art and began painting again, her body- and self-image began to change dramatically. Her triadic nature came up again in a fascinating dream six years later:

> There are three me's; one more prominent than the others. I have arranged for the other me's to move into a house. It is falling down, with leaks in the roof. But I say to them, "If you clean it up, paint it, and fix it, it will be a really nice place to live." They go in and start the painting job. I come in to see how it's going. They are depressed. They say, "It's worse than we thought. You let us down." I say, "Well, all right, I'll paint it, I'll stay here." So I start painting all around the windowpanes. As I'm painting, my impression of the place improves dramatically. Then as I paint I'm no longer painting a wall, but I'm painting a picture of the window, and I'm also painting myself into the picture. It's a lovely, luminous picture of a woman. The other me's leave. As they leave, they call to me from outside the window, "You're beautiful; it's a self-portrait."

In this dream Carmina's psychic house, which she had previously devalued by feeling damaged, unworthy, and ugly, begins to have potential. It is not enough to assign the task of renovation to the shadow figures in her unconscious. Her ego has to assume power and take over the job. As she paints, the environment changes. Finally, as she paints herself into the picture, she *sees herself* as the beautiful woman she is for the first time. The form of her feminine identity emerges from her creativity. She is acting, not being acted upon. She defines her changing nature with her self-portrait.

Assuming responsibility that implies the power to act and effect change is difficult for many women. Women have been taught to diminish their power, hide their beauty, conform to male standards of propriety for women. To compensate for the sense of inferiority caused by the devaluation of the feminine, the unconscious often produces ancient female symbols of power. Two years earlier Carmina's struggle to affirm her femininity without losing herself in another woman was reflected in the following dream:

> I'm showing a woman friend my brooch. She says, "It looks really psychedelic." I say, "No, I bought it from this woman in New Mexico who made it. I love it. It reminds me of a labrys, perfectly balanced." I look at it and see that it is corroded and asymmetrical.

The labrys is the double ax of Minoan Crete with which priestesses sacrificed bulls in their ceremonies. Based on her observations at Çatal Hüyük, Cameron thought that the early double-ax symbol was derived from a gynecological context. Cameron pointed out that during the birth of a baby girl there is one moment as she emerges from the birth passage in which the embryonic pubic triangle of the daughter is opposite that of her mother, joining point to point. In an early diagram, the lower triangle is smaller than the upper one. The mother-daughter relationship and the pubic triangle are condensed into one image. A wall painting at Çatal Hüyük shows how the image has become a butterfly and henceforth becomes part of the Goddess transformation symbolism, which reached its high point in the Cretan labrys.[19]

Carmina persistently feared that anything belonging to her would turn negative, be corrupted, damaged, or destroyed. In the dream, at the very moment she asserts the personal meaning of the labrys-shaped pin, she sees it corrode in her hand. She could not yet hold and assert her own value without self-doubt. The labrys originates in the double-triangle, horn, moon, butterfly cluster of symbols. Multiple layers of meaning reinforce the power of both symbol and dream. The labrys was the instrument of sacrifice, of feminine religious power in ancient Crete. The dream emphasized Carmina's capacity for penetrating the mystery, for realizing her power and renewing her femininity.

In ancient Crete, whose famed labyrinth held the Minotaur, the bee and the butterfly were the manifestations of the bull-born Goddess of transformation and regeneration (an ancient mystery belief holds that bees are begotten of bulls):

> The ancients gave the name of *Melissae* ("bees") to the priestesses
> of Demeter who were initiates of the chthonian goddess; the name
> *Melitodes* to Kore (Persephone) herself: the moon (Artemis) too whose
> province it was to bring to birth, they called *Melissa*, because the moon
> being a bull and its ascension the bull, bees are begotten of bulls. And
> souls that pass to the earth are bull-begotten. (Porphyry)

> In Egypt if you bury the ox in certain places, so that only his horns
> project above the ground and then saw them off, they say that bees fly
> out; for the ox putrefies and is resolved into bees. (Antigonos)[20]

Carmina was led by her unconscious into the Cretan labyrinth through a series of bee dreams. The first took place seven years into therapy:

> I am a warrior with a companion. We are offered a choice of
> weapons, either the wind or the knife. I choose the wind and leap out

into space. Part of my job is protecting a sick young girl in trouble. I rescue her. We go to a loading dock behind a market. Cases of strange fruit have been delivered because of our ingenuity in rescuing the girl. We have green plastic tokens that work as theater tickets. We have enough left to go to the *théâtre vivant*. I can participate as one of the nudes, outside. As we're walking toward the site, we see strange, wonderful things in the grass. It's a park full of unicorns, goats, and other fantastical creatures, a joyful, sacred place. I see a swimming pool and run to jump into the water. I see too late that the entire surface of the pool is covered with bees. I dive through them and stay under water, afraid to be stung. I come up quickly and risk jumping out. I'm afraid I have bees in my hair. I go running to my mother, who is sitting there, and ask her to look for bees in my hair.

During this period of time Carmina had begun to paint again, and her spirit was coming alive through her actions. Archetypally, the bees represented the transformative energy of the Goddess at work in her psyche that took Carmina back to the relationship to her mother in a positive way. The wind motif suggested that Changing Woman's energy was activated. Carmina's fear of being stung was her fear of undertaking this momentous change. She had been unable to make art for years, and taking it up again meant acknowledging her own talent, power, and capability. Making art meant facing the critical voices in herself that she identified as male, the internal critics who told her, "Your work is worthless."

In the dream Carmina is again a woman warrior, acting on her own behalf. She is protecting the sick and troubled younger aspect of herself. That deed earns her access to the living theater of her rich internal and external life with both mundane and sacred dimensions. She is nude, proud of her body, not ashamed. Her reward is in fruits, fertility. She participates in a sacred rite that leads her into another dimension of her initiatory journey.

In the next dream the bee theme continued and was enlarged upon:

> There is another strange ritual that has to do with sacrifice. Three characters are participating: one, the bee person or beekeeper; two, a water carrier; three, someone wearing a mask with horns.

Here the allusion to sacrifice that was hinted at with the earlier labrys dream is named. The beekeeper, he who takes care of the hives, is involved; a water carrier, who reflects the waters of life and death that we see in the zigzag wavy lines at Çatal Hüyük; and the horned mask, alluding to the bull horns of Çatal Hüyük and Crete. The elements of bee, water, and horns have been combined in a ritual way to perform a sacrifice. What would the sacrifice mean for Carmina? It had to include giving up her dependence on the wounded little girl who could not have or find the power to deliver her creativity.

Identifying with being the victim of familial dysfunction gradually wanes in psychotherapy. This is a delicate process. Carmina had been wounded within the family constellation; she needed to regress during the psychotherapeutic process into her younger, weaker identity. Then in order for her to move on and become a woman, she had to emerge from the regression and assume an active role in relation to the demons of her unconscious. Like the Tukuna girl who throws the firebrand at the sun, she had to fight back. I understand this act as meaning to match the negative force with positive feminine energy. In the previous dream, Carmina chose the wind, a natural element with which she was comfortable, as a weapon. Accessing a powerful attribute of the divine feminine, Changing Woman, allowed her to rescue the young girl from death, to rescue herself from identification with her own wound.

Some months later Carmina talked about fighting the internal demons when doing her art. "In order to get away from the male critic's voice, I become an enormous female pot. Then he can't touch me. When I do my painting as a devotion, the image is off the record, and he can't reach me. I bypass him." Struck by the significance of the bee image in Carmina's psyche, I told her about June Rachuy Brindel's book *Ariadne,* in which the demise of the Minoan culture on Crete is dramatized. A few weeks later, she told me that the book had drawn her further into the devotional process of her art. There was one passage she found particularly calming when she read it as a meditation:

> I am standing in the apiary among the hives. The sun is warm and the earth fragrant. Bees are all around me. Their wings reflect the sun. I hear a voice from somewhere, though I see no one. It whispers, "Your body is pollen. The journey is forever. Be still." And then I am not sure whether it has been a voice or just the sound of the bees.
>
> It was as though a great light had grown in my eyes, increasing in intensity and size until it filled all the sky and the earth, the palace, the sea, everything. As if I had been drawn into the sun, hot and white, a constant noon absorbed my sight, and in my ears was the incessant buzzing of all the world's bees, not so much speaking to me as covering up a sound that I kept trying to hear.[21]

Carmina said, "I bypassed the critic again. My new painting is a meditation. I am doing my art with the attitude that this is my altar, my devotional work. The bee passage from *Ariadne* makes me feel potent and expansively rich." A month later she dreamed, "I am swimming in a swimming pool. A bee stings me on my foot." She said, "I made a cocoon in my painting one day, and spent the night in a gold beehive." With the bee sting, she becomes one with her own development; it is a sign of acceptance by the Goddess in her bee aspect: the initiatory sting or bite.

Implicit in Carmina's rapport with the bee is the transforming process of psychic rebirth. In the Red Shrine at Çatal Hüyük, progressively larger circles drawn on the wall resemble the stages of cervical dilation during labor.[22] Zigzag wavy lines denoting the "cosmic waters" (amniotic fluid) link the circles. The zigzag motif also represents the regenerative symbol of the snake. In Minoan Crete, the Goddess took anthropomorphic form as the snake goddess.[23] Other accoutrements in this shrine indicate that the architecture was designed to contain and reflect the woman's experience as she labored to give birth.

During the months of her apiary meditation Carmina dreamed about birth:

> An obese woman I know is pregnant and about to give birth. I am amazed that she can do this. She "disappears" in order to give birth to her baby. In her absence I experience her labor pain, as if I'm sampling it. I'm shocked; it is *so* painful. I never realized it could be that painful. I am impressed that this woman is able to go through with it. I see how far I have to go to reach that point. I think how fortunate I am that I live in this century, because I can ask for help when I give birth. Otherwise I would surely die.

Carmina's identity was developing as she resumed her art, but she still felt the pain of her laboring and feared death as she waited for rebirth. Here the pregnant shadow did not succumb to the pain but delivered new life. Carmina was growing into womanhood, painfully but surely. She had finally realized that she did not have to do it alone. She could "ask for help."

The obese pregnant woman in Carmina's dream is an image of female fecundity that is found in the sculptures of pregnant goddess figures at Çatal Hüyük. A woman in the Çatal Hüyük community must have felt her own personal connection to the fertility of her land and her people. She revered the power of the Goddess over plant life, in the form of a baked clay statue incarnating a plump, pregnant fertile woman with crosslike flower patterns etched into her body.[24] But Carmina had internalized our cultural neurosis that emphasizes thinness as the ideal for women. This obsession with being thin is part of the patriarchy's repression of women; men fear women's power. Carmina feared obesity, but the dream evoked fertility and strength in the powerful shadow's capacity to endure the pain of childbirth.

The Neolithic woman who lived at Çatal Hüyük probably participated in a fertility ritual evoking the interrelatedness between human survival and the earth's fertility. A small clay statue of the enthroned Goddess as Mistress of Animals was found in a grain bin.[25] This goddess is giving birth supported by two felines, her right foot resting on a human skull. She is the provider of game as well as grain. In these statues a Neolithic woman would have been able to see herself mirrored in the larger scheme of nature. She would have seen life, death, and rebirth as a whole. Her physical experience and her spiritual experience were meaningfully intertwined.

In our culture, artistic representations of a pregnant woman are rare. Their association with the divine is rarer yet. Under the patriarchy the art and religion that immortalize that sacred state have been hidden, not displayed. The Virgin Mary, usually represented delicately pregnant, is virtually the only one we have but for a few examples by modern women artists. A Neolithic woman saw female images with red concentric circles on their bellies, emphasizing their pregnant condition. She saw reflected in these figures the life that she felt stirring within her womb. The snake configuration on the pregnant belly, often in the form of double spirals, symbolizes birth, death, and regeneration.[26]

Carmina, as a modern woman initiate in psychotherapy, was psychologically experiencing these ancient birth rituals that reconnected her to her own maternal ground of being. That revitalization included the possibility of accepting her body as the source of her knowledge and the honored seat of her soul and mind. Dream images and actions are powerful; they affect a woman's conscious attitudes in strong ways. For days, weeks, sometimes months, a feeling will linger that infuses a woman with a different sense of herself. Carmina said, "There is an awareness coming to me, an awareness of myself. When I wake up, I feel it. Then I feel it several times a day. I think, 'I have a body, I drew the picture on the wall. This is my reality.' "

The twin goddess statue from Çatal Hüyük (figure 7) manifests the double aspect of the Great Goddess, mother and maiden with two heads, two pairs of breasts, and a single pair of arms. Psychologically, this image can be interpreted in several ways. As a picture of a woman's internal state of connectedness to both mother and maiden in herself, it renders in an exquisite way the dual nature of her psyche as well as the singularity of her identity in the world. With her hands she functions in life. Internally, she is always moderating her relationship to her own mother and daughter, her own older and younger parts. Externally she relates to mothers and daughters and other female friends who constellate aspects of the mother-maiden pair. The Neolithic woman was not asked to separate from her mother in order to fulfill her individual identity; her life depended on her mother and other women as well as on men of the clan. For modern women a liberation from domestic work and reproductive necessity has resulted in the call to individuation.

To become an individual, a woman in our culture must separate from her mother, who carries a patriarchal identification, and reconnect to a source of feminine value that exists in her mother's heritage. Paradoxically, completion of the second task often leads her to a reunion with her mother on different terms, different ground. Like Persephone, she brings a new identity back from the underworld, an identity revitalized by her feminine history. Potentially, in reunion with her mother, she infuses her mother with some of this vitality. Often, this task has to be accomplished in the face of a negative relationship back through the generations between her mother and her maternal grandmother and her great-grandmother. To begin to address this multigenerational woundedness requires tremendous courage, persistence, and patience. But it can be done.

The tension and paradox inherent in this task is evident in my interactions with Carmina about my pregnancy with my first child after two years of therapy. I told her when I was three months pregnant that I would be taking a four-month leave of absence to await the birth and care for my baby. She expressed joy and delight in the news:

> It's great that you're having a baby. In the midst of death, trauma, despair, and degeneration of my family problems, it's wonderful news. You are so nurturant. From the beginning I found a mother in you. In one way I could see that it's taking you away from me, but it takes nine months to make a baby. I have months to adjust to you going away.

Carmina was struggling with the intense pain of relating to her own mother at the time:

> The closeness with my mother is such that all she has to do is say one negative thing to me and I feel terrible pain, what a terrible person I am. It's as if she is intent on making me suffer some long-term deep suffering of her own. My mother is guilt-ridden, and I feel guilty when she bursts into tears because I say I'm only coming home for four days. I feel like a bad person. Then I want to make it better. But I don't want to go for longer, because I want my time to myself.

The intensity of Carmina's struggle was heightened during this period by her conflict about telling her parents she was having female lovers. She wanted to bring her lover home but was afraid to confront them. At one point during my pregnancy when she asked about how I was feeling, we chatted about my condition for a few minutes. She came in the next session, saying, "It was nice to talk about your having a baby. I was missing you. Everything for me is conflict-oriented and painful."

Carmina's comment "I was missing you" held a world of meaning in the psychotherapeutic process between two women. It showed that the relationship between us was very important for her development. A woman cannot develop or change in isolation. Traditional psychoanalytically oriented therapy has isolated the analyst from the "other person" in the room. A woman with such an orthodox therapist is always forced back on herself. The therapist withdraws from human connection; this is death to a woman's heart and soul. A woman needs to feel the *presence* of the therapist. She needs to hear from her, sometimes about her, in order to feel contained. This need is not always present; it may come up once every few months or once a year. Even if it never comes up overtly, it is a valid relationship need that enhances the work.

In our last hour before my maternity leave, Carmina said, "I always feel a sense of continuity with you even when not seeing you. I'm excited about your baby. I had a blowup with my mother. We need to separate from each other."

Carmina's feeling affirmed the continuity of our therapeutic relationship, which she felt even during the absences we had due to changes in her life. This was the first time in our relationship that a change in my life had caused the separation between us. She was happy for me about the impending birth of my child. In the same breath, her association to my pregnancy was her need to separate from psychological symbiosis with her mother. Though the fear of pregnancy for herself was an obsession at the beginning of therapy and was still synonymous with an invasive negative force, my pregnancy instead became the symbol of hope for her inner life. Pregnancy evokes hope and necessitates change. With my pregnancy, in the context of the therapeutic relationship, Carmina could maintain a positive sense of connection to her own potential and separate from her mother at the same time.

Birth imagery of a different sort also erupted at the outset of SARAH's therapeutic journey. Her issues around pregnancy and around her relationship to her mother came up immediately. When Sarah met with me for the first time, she had not used contraception for a year and had not become pregnant. Although her husband, established in his career as an attorney, wanted children right away, she was ambivalent about becoming pregnant, because medical school was so draining. Her underlying power struggle with her husband also contributed to her ambivalence about conceiving. Sarah's initial dream in therapy revealed her concern about having a child:

> I give birth to a mentally retarded child. I know at birth that it is
> retarded. I didn't even know I was pregnant.

On one level, Sarah was afraid of having a child because she had Crohn's disease. She feared both for herself and for the fetus she might carry. In her endocrinology training, she was adding to her storehouse of knowledge about pregnancy as illness. But psychologically, the dream symbolized her fear of the therapeutic process and her tremendous unconscious resistance to change. Her second dream continued this theme:

> I give birth to a tiny baby. I have it at the hospital and can put it in my pocket. I want to breast-feed the child, but the only way is to put a tube into my pocket.

A few months later, she dreamed:

> I have a child. The child is normal. But it does something abnormal like moving spastically. It breast-feeds normally sometimes, but sometimes it needs tubing, as in my earlier dream. I feel warm and loving but also vigilant, watching for abnormalities.

On a literal level, Sarah said that she had always perceived motherhood as "going backwards." Rebellious toward her mother's controlling nature, she feared that becoming a mother herself would bring her back under that control. Furthermore, she was committed to her work as a physician, thus felt conflict about how she would manage the early stage of mothering and practice her profession at the same time. Three months after beginning therapy, she found that she was pregnant and expressed some resentment at it having been her husband's "decision."

Sarah had chosen to stop using contraception the year before. Until that time she had always been conscientious about using her diaphragm. Unable to resolve her ambivalence about having a child, she had gone along with her husband's wishes but emotionally let him carry the weight of her desire for a baby, so she held it against him at first when she became pregnant. Sarah was able to acknowledge her responsibility and, early in the pregnancy, admit that she wanted their baby. It was as if she had to let herself be seduced into taking on motherhood because she feared falling under the control of her mother again, externally or internally. In the early months of pregnancy, she struggled with separating herself as mother-to-be from her own internal mother complex. Late in the pregnancy, when Sarah was preparing for the birth, her mother came to visit her, and she found her mother's presence surprisingly calming rather than competitive.

Psychologically, the last dream showed hope for Sarah's therapy. Although she is being vigilant for abnormalities, she does give birth to a normal child, a new Self. Internally, the abnormalities symbolized the shadow for Sarah. Her initial work in therapy revolved around guilt and shame for things about herself that she didn't like and finding acceptance both from me and within herself for not being perfect. In this way the potential rebirth image in the dream pointed to an identity that included both light and dark aspects. Because she had repressed anything negative, kept it shrouded in shame and discomfort, the shadow side of life appeared as abnormal in the unconscious. The unconscious was compensating for her one-sided view of herself as the good, dutiful daughter.

A few months after Sarah finished her endocrinology training, she delivered a healthy baby boy in a difficult vaginal birth after thirty-nine hours of labor. Although both she and the baby were in intensive care for a few hours after the delivery, they both emerged from the trauma well. Sarah loved mothering him from the beginning. A few months after the birth, the family relocated to another state where her husband's law firm had offered him an important position. Alone with her newborn in an unfamiliar city, Sarah said, "I'm stuck with myself and with the relationship. I'm alone for the first time. We have always been with other people." She and I continued her analysis with a combination of telephone sessions and letters. Sarah stayed home for the next year, devoted to her baby yet missing her identity in the world of physicians. In her diligent work during the first year of her son's life, she became aware of shadowy feelings of depression, of being trapped and without control. These feelings contrasted with her "Pollyanna" persona. Integrating dark emotions, she realized, "makes relationship more real and more powerful."

Sarah's identification with her father and the driven nature of her career performance had been reinforced by a two-year psychoanalytic experience with a traditional male Freudian analyst. Originally she had gone to him because she had trouble staying home for the two years when she had the flareup of Crohn's disease. She said the therapy had been problem-oriented and stayed on the surface. Although the analyst said little in the course of their work, there were two things she felt she learned from him: "One, that my husband will never comfort me when I cry; two, that I will never be the loving mother I want to be." Both these statements, apparently reiterated in the course of their work, only served to reinforce Sarah's inability to gain access to her own feminine nature.

Sarah had always had trouble expressing her emotional needs to her husband; she didn't trust her feelings, because she saw them as weaknesses. She tried to rationalize everything from her husband's point of view before letting herself feel directly out of her own experience. Often she didn't know how she felt, because she could always see a problem from all sides. This ability served her well as a doctor, but it kept her from taking a feeling stance with her husband. Her work with the male psychoanalyst reinforced her hidden sense of shame about emotional needs. The implication was that her wishes to change the relationship, to have her husband respond to her tears, were wrong. She was expecting too much, or it was neurotic of her. The message was, "Tears are manipulative and bad, so of course a man won't respond to them. You are wrong to feel you want a response."

The psychoanalytic work had been equally undermining on the issue of mothering. Sarah already felt leery of falling into what she perceived as her mother's overcontrolling mode by becoming a mother herself. Although love is the redeeming value in the face of such fear, her previous therapeutic work made her doubt her capacity to feel love as a mother. When she did have her child, she gave him consummate love and care. She was naturally disposed to maternity; she found nursing her son satisfying and delighted in watching his developmental steps. Love and care came easily to her as a mother. What was more difficult was caring for herself and temporarily giving up her profession. She felt depressed and missed her more ego-oriented life at work.

When her son was a year old, Sarah and her family moved back to the Bay Area, where she assumed a position at a clinic specializing in endocrinology. Back at work, she encountered the awesome task of trying to mesh her achievement-oriented career goals with the less defined, less focused, nonlinear needs of being with a young child. Motivated by her alliance with the medical model, she struggled with a compulsive need to overextend herself at the clinic, even at the expense of her health and time spent with her toddler.

Near the time she went back to work, I told her I was pregnant with my first child. She congratulated me and said, "I was wondering if you and your husband were going to have children." Sarah knew that six months after she had begun working with me, I had married. It was a relief to her when I told her that I was pregnant, in that it brought me across a threshold she had already crossed. My sense was that Sarah unconsciously wished that I would develop as she did so that I could continue to understand and engage with the new challenges she was encountering as a parent.

The first challenge for me was that of the change in my state of being that began in the first trimester of pregnancy. I suddenly found all my usual biological patterns disrupted, subordinated to the new life growing inside me. As my energy began to turn inward, my desire for certain foods and more sleep and my social needs changed according to the developing embryo's demands. A slight queasiness attended me. As my body reorganized itself for the purpose of nurturing the fetus, my psyche too began to reorganize itself, subtly initiating changes in my perceptions and my attitudes. One manifestation of this changing was increased permeability between my conscious and unconscious life. There was also a thinning in the membrane between inner and outer life. The distinction between my dream state and my waking state was not as sharp. A dream of mine brought up the genetic concerns that Sarah's dreams had revealed in a different form:

I come into my kitchen to find that it is overrun with animals—cats, dogs, snakes—all of whom have come in through the cat door. They are wallowing and invading. I want to let them out, but none of them will budge, and I realize, on closer inspection, that some of them, if not all, are subtly genetically altered. For instance, there is no natural animosity between the different species. They are all obliviously lumped together. One fat animal, a cat, is stuck in the cat door; the sight sickens me. A snake suddenly emerges from my pocket. Something is also different about it. It is flat and pale yellow, almost translucent, and moves slowly with no life force.

This dream reflected the common biological ground of all life, the undifferentiated state of nature. With this unseen life process going on within me, I had no idea what would manifest at term. I had listened to the process of Sarah's pregnancy with total absorption. But now I was gestating and understanding it more fully. After the first three months, I felt stabilized in this incubatory state and began to prepare myself and my patients for the change in my practice that this pregnancy would bring.

The session after I told Sarah about my pregnancy, she dreamed:

I am giving a party for a woman who is pregnant. She is eight months along, almost ready to deliver. I have invited a lot of people. I want to have a baby there. I feel this woman should have a chance to be with a baby. I find a four-week-old and put a candle in the baby's mouth. The pregnant woman is to blow it out. I am worried about the baby. I think about giving it a cookie or cracker instead. It is important to me to do this ceremony.

Sarah said, "The woman in the dream was you. I feel like giving you a party." Sarah rightfully felt that she could be the initiating female sponsor for me in this rite of passage. She was already a mother, and she wanted me to have hands-on experience with an infant before I had my own. In the dream I am eight months pregnant instead of three, which suggested that she was eager for this threshold to be crossed, for me to join her in motherhood. The candle in the baby's mouth was puzzling from a literal point of view, but in terms of Sarah's psychotherapy, it pointed to the theme of rebirth for her. The candle is a symbol of the light of consciousness. Sarah's relationship to me was based on a symbolic process of furthering her individuating journey. So the four-week-old baby she wanted to bring to the party was her newly developing self. Four weeks previously she had reported the rape dream that she associated to fearing that she was pregnant. The dream had enabled her to make conscious and verbalize repressed feelings about her relationship to her husband. Sarah had found her own voice, her own self-expression. That therapy hour had birthed a consciousness that was now included in the ritual for me. Her newly developing therapeutic child and my pregnancy coexisted and interacted in meaningful ways.

By the time I took my maternity leave, Sarah was back at work, overwhelmed with fatigue, worried about her son, who was suffering with chronic diarrhea, and experiencing hostility and tension with her husband. Curiously, she talked about this state with an odd passivity, an acceptance that prevented her from seriously thinking about changing the pattern. In fleeing from her own mother, she had fallen into being the martyr in a different arena; at work she was giving of herself in a kind of limitless mothering. She acknowledged she had a secret pride in her own heroics, in choosing to overwork herself.

In one session she expressed concern that she might disturb me by talking about a patient of hers who had delivered a stillborn child. Sarah's tears for this woman came easily, as did her empathy for my vulnerability in pregnancy. But empathy for herself that could move her to set limits at work was not evident. She was distraught about her son's obvious need for more attention from her, but she could not yet motivate herself to change on his behalf. She and her husband, however, were seeking conjoint counseling during my forthcoming absence.

Sarah was accepting of my leave and the baby, although she felt she would miss me and our work together. She asked, "May I write you? It would help me feel the continuity. But I wouldn't want you to feel that you have to write back." I was happy to grant that request; I also felt it would give a sense of continuity to our work. Again, I marveled at how sensitive she was to me in contrast to her ignoring of her own limits and needs.

After the first trimester of disorientation, I had felt wonderful with my pregnancy. Carrying new life in my womb made me feel absolutely whole. I was able to continue my practice until three weeks before my baby's due date without any sense of stress. My life felt completely in balance. While I was consciously absorbed with becoming a mother, a dream took me back to Zurich to visit Barbara Hannah, my psychological grandmother:

> An older woman friend has taken me to Zurich for this visit. Miss Hannah is bursting with energy, exuding vitality as she talks to me. She wants to give me something of herself, of her abundant energy. She pulls out some beautiful stationery, heavy parchment, pale sand colored, and thrusts it at me. I don't know whether to eat it or use it for writing. I nibble on it and think it is like a communion wafer in that it dissolves on my tongue, but the texture is rough and ancient. Later I notice that it is gone.
>
> Meanwhile Miss Hannah has pulled out several more boxes and laid them on the bed in her room. Each is filled with a different wonderful stationery but none so special as the first. One is tissue-thin in brilliant orange and yellow colors. My woman companion seems con-

cerned that I have more of the parchment type and looks around for it. I feel that Miss Hannah's special state of relating to me, immediate and extroverted, rather then archetypal and otherworldly, has something to do with supporting my work, that she is pouring energy and feeling into me for the next stage of my analytic training.

This beautiful dream emphasized my psychological path as an individual while I was becoming a mother. It also reflected the spiritual aspect of my work with Miss Hannah. She was the archetypal grandmother offering me communion, as she had offered her wisdom in my analysis with her. My lifework is dedicated to the word, spirit, and meaning incarnated in relationship. Writing is alluded to in the dream: the communion wafer is also stationery. Stationery specifically implies writing letters and was to be the means of communicating with Sarah and other patients during my leave.

My involvement with Sarah did not stop after our last session before my leave. During the next few weeks, before my labor began, I had two dreams about our work:

I am at Sarah's house dressing for work. The house is huge and modern. I can't get on with my dressing, because Sarah needs to talk about various problems with her parents and family. There are several people wandering around who look emotionally disturbed or mentally retarded. Sarah identifies them as members of the family. I also tell her that I had a dream about her. But we never really get to her hour, and I am confused that I am still working.

I am walking with Sarah to my supervisor's office in order to have a therapy hour. We go up hill and down dale but never arrive. I feel frustrated.

I had moved out of my therapy office and arranged to relocate my practice after my leave. Without an office, I had no container for therapy with Sarah. The dreams show me first in her home, then en route to my supervisor's office, looking for a place to see her. My psyche had not disengaged with Sarah's. I was still honoring the need for our relationship to have a form. The transition to her writing me had yet to take place. My commitment to the therapeutic relationship was as authentic as my commitment to the child I was carrying. Psychologically, Sarah and I were incubating new life together. A psychological child is as important as the actual child in the womb. If the symbolic value of the birth is not honored, it is death to the therapeutic relationship. The fine edge between the death and rebirth of the psychic structure in deep psychotherapy or analysis parallels the duality of life and death that a woman feels when she is actually pregnant with a child.

Figure 8.
Childbirth.

5

Encountering the Goddess of Death

A pregnant woman encounters the Goddess in her death aspect when she has to face abortion, miscarriage, fear of death in childbirth, or fear of genetic damage to her child. The vulture shrine at Çatal Hüyük celebrates the Goddess as the receiver of the dead. The walls of the shrine are covered with paintings of vultures in both red and black. In one alcove, a bull's head/uterus decorated with the zigzag water of life design is enshrined opposite a human skull.[1] A woman with young children sees the cold eye of the vulture fixing her with its gaze when she or her children are seriously ill. In being responsible to life, she also becomes responsible to death. Psychologically, a woman may experience the goddess of death in her fear of being devoured or being abandoned by her own mother or by the Goddess in her life-giving aspect. In psychotherapy, the goddess of death manifests in the ego's experience of being compelled to give up control to the larger design of the Self.

Vultures were sacred birds because they are scavengers; they do not eat live animals.[2] In Çatal Hüyük, the corpses of the dead were placed outside for the vultures to clean. The bones were collected and temporarily buried under the floor of the person's sleeping place. Once a year a collective funerary rite was enacted in which priestesses dressed in voluminous vulture robes gathered the bones of the dead and ceremonially buried them in common ground.[3] Eventually the vulture or death aspect of the Goddess became abstracted to the bird's eye only. Today in Greece and Turkey small blue beads are still hung on a baby's cradle "to keep the evil eye away."

With that act, a mother both invokes the Goddess as protectress in her powerful life-giving aspect and wards off her opposite death-dealing side. By acknowledging the duality, a mother hopes to magically secure protection for her infant. Prehistoric bird-goddess figurines of mother and daughter exhibit large, staring eyes.[4]

At the beginning of therapy, BEATRICE, who had suffered her mother's abandonment and encountered the goddess of death rampaging in the Vietnam War, dreamed:

> I am pregnant. I am in a room in my house. My girlfriend is visiting. We are chatting. The baby keeps sticking its elbow out; I see it, and I hold my left hand to my stomach to keep the elbow in. Then I'm still talking with my friend, but it's a gathering in a crowded room. There are two children, my lover's children, twelve or thirteen years old, one with a haircut like mine, the other a drooling idiot who mutely wants me to love him. And I can't. He silently stands there with a pleading look. I feel so guilty because I can't love him. They are both my sons.

Beatrice said that she wanted to have children, but she had been diagnosed as infertile as a result of her past heroin addiction. In Vietnam she had had a miscarriage, after a long interval of amenorrhea. She commented about her addiction, "I didn't like myself; I was rebelling against a father figure; I was angry that I didn't have parents of my own to rebel against." Three weeks after she had this dream, she was shocked to discover that she was pregnant. She had not been using contraception for many years due to her medical diagnosis and had never conceived.

The first part of the dream, in which she pushes the baby's elbow in, pointed to her repressing the fact of her pregnancy. Symbolically, it referred to her ego's attempt to deny the power of the therapeutic process, which already had a life of its own. The two older boys, her and her lover's sons, presented a more cryptic image. But it was my impression that this masculine pair represented two aspects of her own *yang*, or masculine energy.[5] As a professional in the world, she was extraordinarily competent, well-adapted, and highly intelligent. But her emotional woundedness was represented by the youth who was genetically impaired, with no possibility for improvement. Given the absence of any male figure in her life until she was seven, and then the succession of abusive men, it made sense that she would be drastically wounded in relation to men and maleness. In terms of her prognosis for therapy the impaired child indicated that there might be a place in her that could not be healed. But if it was her capacity to love that was impaired, and if she could come to love the "idiot," could that transform him/her?

Beatrice and her lover, a musician, had been together only a few months. Although she found herself wanting the baby with all her heart, she could not imagine continuing the pregnancy without his support and commitment. Her lover found it impossible to commit himself to marry and have a child on such short acquaintance with her. Beatrice had an abortion at six weeks and felt overwhelming grief. The week after the abortion she reported "a terrifying dream about my mother." The abortion released a memory in Beatrice of her mother being especially attentive to her in Hong Kong before she sent her away and saying, "I'll miss you, but we aren't going to be parted for that long; before you were born, you wouldn't go away." In her grief over the loss of the embryonic life within her, Beatrice realized that her mother probably had tried to abort her. Many half-formed impressions and feelings crystallized in this realization. One of them was a pervasive sense that she should never have been born. Her grief intensified, but simultaneously she had an equally intense and opposite reaction. She said, "But I did give birth; I gave birth to me. I have a new security. I know what I want now." To me, it felt as if the sacrifice of the actual child had produced a revitalization of the life force in her on a spiritual level. There was a subtle change in her personality, a feeling of having been brought to earth, in dramatic contrast to our initial meeting, in which she had been in a state of terror because a man she had been involved with had threatened to kill her.

Unbeknownst to Beatrice, I was also newly pregnant when she began seeing me. Feeling my own joy at bearing life again made the agony of Beatrice's forced choice to terminate her pregnancy acutely painful for me. A month after her abortion, I told her about my pregnancy, now three months along, and expressed my sorrow at having to confront her with my possession of what she had lost. I knew it had to hurt her, but she said, "That's wonderful. I still wish I were pregnant. Is it just to keep a part of my lover? He's all the things I'm not—energetic, creative, decisive—and he encourages me to be the same. At work I'm confident, precise, think on my feet, but otherwise I'm tongue-tied, lethargic, struck dumb sometimes." The image of being dumb was reminiscent of the mute boy in Beatrice's first dream. After that session she always asked at the end of the hour as she walked to the door, "How do you feel?" referring to my pregnancy.

Six weeks later, at four and a half months, I had a miscarriage and found myself in a state of deep grieving similar to Beatrice's. When I called to tell her that I had miscarried and would be taking a week off from work, she said, "I'm sorry. I know it must feel terrible. I *chose* to abort, and it still felt terrible." I did feel bereft, but I had some comfort knowing that nature had taken care of a nonviable embryo. During this pregnancy I had felt oddly unwell, unlike when I was carrying my son. I had also had nightmares that had caused me to worry about something being wrong. My first dream was about the Great Goddess in her death aspect:

> I am on the street with an old crazy lady who is clutching my arm and talking obsessively. It is as if she has a hook for a hand. I somehow know her "craziness" is murdering children, either directly or in a "remote" way. For example, I see her glance at a little boy about six years old. She catches him with a beady eye, witchlike, and terrorizes him so that he loses his balance and falls backward down long stairs to his death.

The crazy old lady in the dream has the beady eye of the death goddess in the vulture shrine at Çatal Hüyük. I had seen the blue glass beads used to ward her off on babies' cradles in Greece. Now she had taken my child from my womb, and I felt her clutching at me in a very disturbing way.

My second dream had an internal, organic quality of disturbance:

> I am walking along some shop fronts. I encounter a large lizard, heavy and slow-moving but tenacious. It is a dark orangy red color. The man in charge of the lizard doesn't keep it away from me. It scratches my foot once or twice and clings to me as if I were a tree. I scream at the man at one point to keep it away. A young attractive Mexican woman comes along with a baby. I warn her about the lizard.

The orange-colored lizard reminded me of a developing embryo. The fact that this primitive creature was attacking me felt like the symptoms of unwellness that I experienced during the pregnancy. Its clinging to me as if I were a tree suggested the unhealthy embryo draining my life energy. In these dreams the lizard and the crazy lady both clung to me. The physical symbiosis identified me with the disintegrating, dying fetus. It felt as if something were attacking me. Although losing my baby distressed me, the miscarriage confirmed my intuitive sense that something was intrinsically wrong.

Five days after the miscarriage I dreamed:

> I am standing in my kitchen. A crabapple bonsai is growing in a pot on the counter. I'm breaking off a dry piece and lighting it with a match. I'm trying to light the greener pieces of the plant, or perhaps the early fruit, and making small objects with them intended as ceremonial pieces. They are to be used to propitiate the gods and ensure fertility.

With this dream, my unconscious was creating a ritual that both marked the sacrifice of the dead fruit of my womb and used it symbolically to seek fertility for the next child. The fruit-bearing tree is analogous to a woman's body. A crabapple bonsai grew in the garden outside my analyst's office, and I watched it flower, bear fruit, and lose its leaves every season for years. The little tree further carried the meaningful weight of my own analytic ritual. A few days later I had another dream:

> My husband and I are on the verge of remarrying, having another wedding or other relationship ritual, perhaps another baby. The priest who married us performs an abortion on me at his home. He tells me that he has noticed a strange odor to my body and found strange, starfish-shaped worms in my body that must be eliminated.

This dream made me realize how interwoven Beatrice and I were through our recent losses. It took me back to memories of the abortion I had had as a girl of twenty-one. In the mid-sixties, before *Roe* v. *Wade,* when abortion was illegal in the United States, I became pregnant. Deeply involved with university studies, I could not envision continuing if I became a mother. I made the choice to go to Mexico with my boyfriend to obtain an abortion.

As I mourned the loss of my miscarried child sixteen years later, I relived my earlier abortion and mourned that child too. I remembered how single-minded I had been in arranging the complicated trip to Mexico. I remembered how excruciatingly painful the crude dilation and curettage procedure had been. I remembered the nurse leaning over me, her long, black hair brushing my arm and face as she tried to comfort me while I cried and writhed in pain. Afterward, I had been nauseated and doubled over with cramps, bleeding copiously. She had given me a handful of pills to swallow and sent me out to dress and leave. Reunited with my boyfriend, I had sobbed the whole way back to the border. But once across, I had felt an intense relief, a giddy joy at being freed from the burden of that embryonic life, free to go on with my own life. Back in my college apartment, my sense of relief and of the rightness of my action had prevailed. And my love for the man had endured, although we did not, ultimately, make a life together.

Looking back on all this as a mature woman and a mother, I was amazed that as a young woman I had felt no fear. I had been oblivious to possible impairment of my future fertility or danger to my life. A sense of basic trust, grounded in my relationship to my mother, had led me simply to act on my feelings, believing that everything would turn out all right. I had been acutely aware of the discrepancy between my feeling of rightness about choosing to have an abortion and my revulsion for the sordid circumstances and doctors both in the United States and in Mexico that I was forced to submit to in order to exercise my choice.

Faced now with Beatrice's suffering, I could at least be thankful that she had not had to risk herself through the same kind of dangerous abortion. Reliving the experience of my abortion with conscious consideration to the body and soul implications of what my choice had meant, I realized that at twenty-one I had chosen to nurture my own psychological development rather than to nurture a new life. Beatrice, too, was reaping the psychological benefit of having had to terminate the pregnancy. She had the container of psychotherapy in which to deal with her experience in a meaningful way. The near-simultaneity of Beatrice's abortion and my miscarriage intensified our therapeutic bond. We had shared an experience of the death aspect of the Goddess. With her new sense of groundedness, Beatrice continued to engage with her psyche in the work of sorting out her traumatic past.

Nightmares about having gone against her desire to keep the baby continued to plague Beatrice:

> I am seeing inside my own womb. It seems like a universe. There are all these children shrieking inside me, hundreds of faces inside my womb, cowering in terror from my looking. They are not born, and they are never going to be born. The womb is a place of death, not life.

The dream manifests the Goddess as receiver of the dead. "The womb is a place of death, not life"—an image of the fusion of womb and tomb depicted at Çatal Hüyük. It is also an inversion of the image of Kuan Yin, who appeared in Beatrice's earlier dream adorning a pin for her hair; Kuan Yin is the goddess who perpetually contemplates the golden vial of her own womb, which produced the entire world. Here again, it seemed that the figure of Kuan Yin, the manifestation of the feminine in pure form, held the healing power for this woman. Beatrice had to let her urge to bear a child find expression; the abortion had gone against a profound spiritual need in her.

Beatrice's associations to this dream revolved around her stepmother, who was bombarding her with abusive letters and phone calls saying that Beatrice wasn't writing frequently enough. The stepmother derided her for being ungrateful and cast aspersions on Beatrice's origins, engaging in diatribes against her Chinese mother. Beatrice was feeling an instinct toward nesting and an increased longing for a child; her guilt about the abortion continued. Her stepmother's unerring destructiveness toward her seemed to cast a curse on Beatrice's capacity for creating new life, actual or symbolic. Her relationship to her stepmother—who epitomized the archetype of the cruel stepmother—endured out of the primitive need she had to belong somewhere. Guilty and fear-ridden, Beatrice remained attached to this woman in spite of the woman's evil conduct toward her. Perhaps it was here that the presence of the "drooling idiot" in Beatrice's dream "who mutely wants love" was revealed. The "idiot child" could not choose to leave a cruel stepmother. She would not have the *yang* energy necessary to effect separation and differentiation of emotion. She could only mutely yearn for love. At the orphanage, Beatrice had stopped speaking and retreated to an inner place where she mutely waited and yearned for her mother's return.

In our culture Beatrice found no ritual form except psychotherapy in which to mark her grief and loss. From her life in Asia, however, Beatrice was aware of ceremonies to help women ritually acknowledge the pain of losing a baby through an abortion. In Japan, where Buddhism recognizes abortion as inevitably conflictual, Beatrice knew that a woman could place a small statue in remembrance of her baby as part of a special ceremony done for aborted fetuses and their parents. This statue represents Jizo, a compassionate Buddha who nurtures and protects beings as they are born and as they die.[6] Beatrice remembered seeing dozens of these statues commemorating dead fetuses in garden shrines and on mountainsides. Beatrice's commemoration of her lost child took place instead within the analytic hour.

Seven years after Beatrice's abortion, two years after she terminated therapy with me and moved away, Sue Nathanson's book *Soul Crisis: One Woman's Journey Through Abortion to Renewal* was published. It would have helped Beatrice during her grief to read Sue's heartrending story of her own painful choice to abort her fourth child. In the book, she eloquently chronicles her struggle to come to terms with a woman's capacity to both give life and withhold life. Her dramatic suffering and dark descent in the aftermath of the abortion eventually transformed her from a well-adapted father's daughter into a woman-identified woman. The culmination of her healing process is dramatized in a ritual created for her by three women friends.

A few years after the publication of Sue's book, Yvonne Rand, a Zen Buddhist priest who has studied in Japan, began conducting rituals at the Zen Center at Green Gulch in Northern California for mothers of babies who had been aborted or miscarried. In these ceremonies, a woman joins other women sitting in a circle to sew a tiny red bib or apron commemorating her lost child. As she sews, each woman can speak or be silent as she chooses. At the conclusion of the ceremony, Yvonne asks for safe passage for the souls of the children, and the women hang their bibs around the neck of the Jizo figures assembled for this purpose.[7]

The power of women's blood sacrifice is also honored in the Tiv culture, where scarification is practiced for pubescent girls. The fertility of the land and the people is periodically renewed with the blood of a miscarriage or abortion, potential life. This is accomplished by means of a ritual for the great sacred object of the Tiv, a bone "owl pipe." The pipe is made from a human tibia, carved and embellished to resemble a woman. A hole bored in the center creates a navel. The statue is decorated with a design that mirrors the scarification patterns etched on the girl's body at puberty. Considered to be a relic of their primeval ancestors, the object is guarded by the Tiv as a secret mystery that holds life for the future of the tribe.[8]

The priests renew the "owl pipe" by pouring the sacrificial blood into the central hole or "navel." The pipe is then used to scatter the blood on fields and drip it in wells. The source of the blood is a miscarriage or abortion obtained from a woman who has not had any children. A woman who has lost her child to this purpose is said to be "specially favored by God" and is expected to become pregnant again at once and bear healthy children.[9]

The energy from the sacrifice that Beatrice made in giving up her baby was directed psychologically into facing her own tormented past and her uncertain present. A few weeks after my miscarriage, she dreamed:

> I am walking around my neighborhood. People on the side streets
> all have their backs to me. The houses are all alike, with windows shut,
> shutters bolted. I am walking and walking. I look up, asking to be let in.
> I know the houses can see me, but they are blind, turning their backs to
> me. I need sleep, and I am not allowed to go in and go to sleep.

This dream reflected her anguish as she struggled with ambivalence about her love relationship and deep mourning of the pregnancy. The content revealed her intrinsic sense of hopelessness about being homeless. Beatrice seemed cursed, unable to join in normal life. Since the abortion three months before, her depression had been intensified by her experiencing pregnancy symptoms during the second half of each subsequent menstrual cycle.

During this period, even as she longed for a child, primal evil and despair reasserted itself in the following dream:

> The scene has the look of the final scenes of the movie *Moby Dick*.
> I am standing on a small island, all on my own. The seas are rough. I
> can smell the "thing" that appears, the "thrortax," a mound, whalelike
> creature with rotting, putrid flesh. People are living on it, castaway
> fashion. They are clinging to the masts sticking out of it, calling out,
> "Save me, save us." It's an old thing that is rotting away. It won't come
> near me. I know it is going to dive down to the bottom of the ocean.
> Most people won't survive. I know I once lived on it and have managed
> to get off.

The scene reminded Beatrice of Gregory Peck in the film *Moby Dick,* all tangled up in ropes and debris around the whale. She said she hated the book and the movie because she loved whales. Many of Beatrice's immediate anxieties converged on her in this month. She did not have a job and felt on the brink of disaster. Her misery reflected deep insecurity when she was not "ruling the roost" by generating the financial resources and her enormous fear of dependence. She was also anticipating October 5, the beginning of the Festival of the Dead in Asia, to which she associated a feeling of morbidity and guilt about the abortion.

In the dream Beatrice was once doomed like all the rest but has managed to get off the creature. She is barely off, however, and is stranded now on an island. The island represented her ego state at the time—a tenuous place to perch in the face of much destructive energy being aroused in the unconscious. The "thrortax" creature would not come near her, so her status as survivor was not threatened. She had distanced herself from this decaying instrument of evil. Beatrice said that whenever she was depressed she always sought a solitary place with light and fresh air. She had learned to read and write in a secluded gazebo at the back of the orphanage property. The gazebo had been her island of peace away from the continual reminders of her abandoned state. Kuan Yin makes her presence felt in this dream: she lives on an island in the sea, whose name means "Kuan Yin's Paradise."[10] Changing Woman too has an island home "floating on the western ocean."[11] The archetypal goddess-power of the woman-to-woman container was having a transforming effect.

The name of the creature Beatrice associated to the thorax or chest. I thought it signified the wound to her heart at having been betrayed by her mother. She described her feelings at the time of this dream as panicked and out of control. The creature could also refer to the emotional wreckage of a refugee. Beatrice said, "The scene was not unfamiliar to me. I remembered the ocean . . . the bad smell . . . it had a very old, beginning-of-time quality." On a deeper level the dream was an ancestral memory of the casualties of generations of refugee life. Beatrice's mother and grandmother had been refugees from Russia, who went overland to China. Beatrice and her mother were refugees from Shanghai to Hong Kong; and Beatrice a refugee to England, then an émigré from there to the United States. Beatrice carried the wounds of her heritage.

The archetypal aspect of our therapeutic relationship was manifested at this deeper level of the wound. The sense of timelessness in this dream corresponds to Jung's definition of "the peculiar dimension of *time*," which exists in the mother-daughter relationship. The psychological sense of time between two women transcends the moment and permeates backward, forward, and down into intimate layers of the psyche. In an intangible way, Beatrice's relation to Kuan Yin and mine to the Virgin Mary, as well as the biological synchronicities[12] of our abortive pregnancies, engendered a therapeutic state in which time was suspended and healing could assert itself at a deep level.

Beatrice had experienced the bloody atrocities and "sacrifice" of lives inflicted by men in the Vietnam War. She had seen men, women, and children massacred by being machine-gunned or run through with bayonets. She had learned to view these atrocities as if through the eye of a camera in order to distance herself from the horror. She had drugged herself to numb the pain that inevitably crept in. She had been forced to help her lover die when he was mortally wounded in one of these battles. As a silent observer she was implicated in the destruction. Now she was coming to terms with her own capacity to destroy the life in her womb. It was almost too much for her to bear.

Beatrice's ability to endure her deep suffering was reinforced by the fact that I was sharing it in ways we could never have expected. Not only was I mourning the death of my own baby and of hers, but I was also familiar with the atrocities of war. My father had been an air force pilot, decorated for bravery in flying the dangerous Ploesti raids in World War II. His plane was shot down over Romania. Following the military code of honor, he bailed out last, but everyone else in his crew was killed. He survived and was captured and imprisoned for nearly a year. As commanding officer in the prisoner of war camp, he was the liaison between the prisoners and the officials in charge. The conditions in the prison were despicable and the treatment of prisoners degrading. All the prisoners were suddenly released when the Romanians were told that the Germans were invading. My father made his way back to Allied forces on foot.

My father's survivor guilt was repressed until many years later. I had grown up on war stories, on my father's heroic intoxication with living on the edge between life and death in both World War II and the Korean War. I had heard in these stories about war's glory and its destructiveness. I had seen the incredible emotional and psychological toll that it had taken on my father. Eventually, those wounds led to his taking his own life in a carefully planned suicide. My relationship with my father enhanced my understanding of Beatrice's suffering. The work with her felt fated from the beginning by the synchronicities of our abortive pregnancies, our devotion to two compassionate female deities, Kuan Yin and the Virgin Mary, and our different but deep knowledge of the experience of war.

As a doctor, SARAH experienced the death aspect of the Goddess in a synchronistic field of inner and outer events. Several life-threatening illnesses and deaths occurred in her extended family and in her patients' families in the course of a few months at the same time that her psyche took up the theme of inner death and rebirth. My unconscious responded to this field with warnings about her. When Sarah's son was twenty months old, I had the following dream:

Sarah invites me to have tea with her in a tea shop. We meet there for her hour, but she keeps leaving to do unfinished work at the clinic. We schedule another meeting. She again leaves the hour, to correct a mistake she made. I begin to leave after waiting forty-five minutes. She arrives and is immediately "in therapy," so I stay half an hour for her. Later, we are at her house with her son, visiting over tea. She is talking about wanting to be pregnant again.

It is time for me to leave. Suddenly there is a tidal wave that throws her son to the ground, his hand bleeding. But his chest is fine. There is a frightening moment before he moves, but he is breathing. Then all is well.

The dream addressed my fear for Sarah's son in the context of the pressures she was enduring as a full-time physician. Her husband had been traveling much of the time for the past year; in his absence, she had had to function as a single parent. Often she failed to eat, and she deprived herself of sleep, getting up an hour before her son awakened to work on clinic charts. She said, "I'm being the martyr like my mother." She was physically drained, and she was struggling psychologically with her good girl complex. It seemed she had to live out the complex by pleasing the older physicians in her clinic until she reached her physical limits. The pattern of ignoring her bodily welfare was impairing her once again. I worried for her, and I worried for the effect of this stress on her toddler. In the dream she was talking about another baby, seemingly ignoring the danger to the child she already had.

Therapeutically, the dream reflected Sarah's renewed resistance to change, which she was acting out by coming late to her therapy hours and avoiding issues she was afraid to face. When her mother was suddenly diagnosed with breast cancer, Sarah felt both that she wanted to be alone with her grief and that she simply had to forge ahead. Consistent with her pattern, she forged ahead. Her mother's illness brought Sarah back into the mother-daughter relationship in new and old ways. Seeing her mother in the hospital after surgery, diminished and pale, Sarah felt how much of her mother's former power she herself now wielded. She wondered whether her own power orientation at work, where she always found herself the favorite of her boss/"father," was the shadow of her ego ideal of Catholic goodness. She had been taught that evil was only the absence of good, not an entity in itself. She had never taken the shadow seriously.

Sarah told me that she also had trouble feeling responsible for the shadow aspects of her personality in relation to her inner process and to me in therapy. Instead she thought, "I'll do this 'good,' work on this problem, for you as the therapist." In this way she was treating me as a nun or teacher whom she had to please and perform tasks for in order to receive praise and feel "good." This was the critical fulcrum of the therapeutic relationship.

Until she could shift into feeling the weight of her shadow, Sarah would never find the deep motivation for her initiatory journey.

A month after her mother's mastectomy, Sarah had the following dream:

> I deliver a second baby at home, upstairs at my mother's house. I don't look to see if it is a boy or a girl. I leave the baby sleeping on the bed and go downstairs to tell my husband and others about the birth. Then I run back upstairs to check on the baby. I notice it is a girl. I don't try to take care of her or breast-feed her. I cover her with a blanket and go downstairs again. When I go up to check on her again, she isn't on the bed. I hear water running in my mother's bathroom. I go in, and my son and the baby are in the sink. The baby is dead, floating. My son is all right. I try to resuscitate the baby but to no avail.

Sarah's associations to the dream had to do with wanting another child, a girl, and with the memory of the traumatic birth of her son. "I wouldn't have been alive if I had delivered my son at home. He was too big. We needed the intensive care nursery," Sarah told me. She said she had been fantasizing about names for girl babies. The dream spoke to the many demands on her time and to the difficulty of keeping a new baby and a toddler safe. The Goddess in her death aspect threatened: "My mother's cancer brings death near. She is suddenly so vulnerable." Sarah saw her own vulnerability reflected in her mother's. The desire for a baby girl came up in the face of the possibility that Sarah's mother might die.

In the imagery of this dream, her mother's illness and Sarah's growing psychological awareness converged. Sarah's ambivalence about mothering the child in the dream spoke to her difficulty with mothering herself and with nurturing her own psychological process. The girl baby was her newly developing feminine self, about which she had expressed so much ambivalence a few weeks before. Doing the therapeutic work for me instead of for herself was like delivering a baby in her mother's house. That is, her attitude was one of being an obedient child in relation to me, a symbolic mother whom she was unconsciously resisting. Her identification with her father and with patriarchal values supported this resistance to the mother. In therapy her continued resistance would doom her initiatory process to failure. In bringing to light her ambivalence with me in the earlier session, the resistance had dissipated. She became conscious of the old pattern of obedient student to her nun/teacher that she had been reenacting.

Sarah made a valiant new attempt to accept responsibility for her therapeutic change and for her physical limitations. But the experience of being in a synchronistic field of death persisted for months. She said, "I keep hav-

ing fantasies of newspaper headlines that say I died in an automobile acci-
dent." She had two dreams that she was pregnant during a week in which
she attended conferences on death and dying every day. The student-
teacher dynamic with me reappeared in the following dream:

> I arrive at the board exam to find that it has already started. You are
> giving the exam. I am called out for an important reason. I leave and
> come back. I have missed a lot of time and think you will give me extra
> time to make it up. When the time is up, you say I can continue to
> work on it but that I have to go somewhere else. You go with me. The
> second room is not like the exam room, but more like your office.

Sarah was actually preparing for her specialty board examination at this
time. She said, "You are the person in my life who encourages me to be myself. I take advantage of those close to me." On one level, the dream referred both to her sense of having to pass a test in the therapeutic work in
order to satisfy an external authority and to her pattern of being late to
therapy, preoccupied with professional matters that took precedence over
her inner work. The expectation in the dream is that I will accommodate
her overextended needs. This was also Sarah's expectation of her own family, who, as she once put it, "has to do somersaults to support my perfect
persona in the world." This dream revealed another piece of the relationship puzzle between us and helped free her to be more herself. On a deeper
level, the dream suggested that the answers lay not in the external world of
achievement but in the container of her own analysis. It showed the beginning of a new initiatory attempt on the part of the unconscious. It showed
me, as her therapeutic sponsor, encouraging and allowing her to go at her
own pace, to create her own time frame.

At this point Sarah began to talk about feeling as if she were falling
apart. She associated not eating or sleeping and overscheduling herself with
her father's dictums: "Never say die" or "Heroism with ease." She said, "You
are the positive mother. I always feel better after I see you, but it doesn't
change my long-range father goals." At this session I told Sarah that I
thought she was in danger, psychologically and/or physically. She looked
eaten up by her work, drained and exhausted. Although she found this up-
setting, she was not yet able to extricate herself from her own compulsive
self-destructive pattern and from the pattern of life she had established.

During the next six weeks I told Sarah first about my pregnancy and
then about my late miscarriage. She expressed both joy and sadness in related ways on each occasion. And she said again that she was feeling positive about having another child herself. About a month later, she had the
following dream:

I am in an American Indian village. Many women in the village are pregnant. One woman comes to stay with me. She has fever and bleeding because she has been raped. They are looking for the man who did it. She and I have to stay in a little hut with a window. We have a fast food menu. Another woman is brought into the village on a horse sling. Her husband is walking beside the horse. This woman says she is having a second miscarriage after a second rape. They are also looking for the man. She says it won't help her if they find him. I picture the hut filling up with women all lying next to one another. I am worried about some of us being pregnant, some sick. Will we all catch the same disease, like rubella or chicken pox?

Sarah was struggling with her anger about her husband's law firm, which now threatened to request him to transfer again. She did not want to leave her position at the clinic, nor her friends and family in the Bay Area. She had difficulty with the conflict between saying she did not want to move and being supportive of her husband. She opted for suppressing her own feeling but found herself angry beneath the surface. The dream seemed to manifest both her individual problem and the cultural problem of women in the patriarchy. The feminine is being raped, and the resulting children are miscarried while mothers are injured and ill from the oppression. Although I do not appear specifically in the dream, I believe my second pregnancy and subsequent miscarriage influenced Sarah's psyche. It opened her to the cultural dimension of what she was experiencing as a personal father problem. Though I was not suffering the same inner compulsions Sarah was, I did have a marriage, a child, and a career, all of which needed careful attention to stay in balance. And as a woman in our culture, I was subject to the same patriarchal pressures that Sarah felt so intensely.

About a month after this dream, Sarah had a vivid image of herself as a child holding out her hand and not getting what she wanted. She told me that she had observed her mother's pattern of redirecting what her grandson wanted without acknowledging his initial request and had realized that her mother had done this with her, too. Sarah said, "As a result, I often don't know what I want." This inability to feel or name her own desires drastically interfered with her capacity to set priorities for her time and energy. She reacted to demands instead of orchestrating her life from within. She felt at the mercy of whomever claimed her attention most strongly. Sarah was paralyzed by the combination of beliefs that self-care was vanity, that martyrdom was a positive feminine value, and that achievement was the highest goal. Her own desires were smothered beneath these injunctions.

In our relationship, Sarah projected her self-negation on me. She told me her fantasy, saying, "I imagine that you don't spend any time on yourself either, that you are just like me." I told her that her fantasy was not true, that I relished time for myself, that drinking from my own wellspring allowed me to modulate the balance between myself, my family, and my work. This exchange had a startling consequence; it broke her paralysis. In the week following our session, Sarah had her ears pierced and bought a leotard and joined a dance class. She also cut her work time to 80 percent and conveyed to her husband her strong feelings about not wanting to move away. On the basis of her feelings, he was motivated to negotiate remaining in the Bay Area. The whirlwind energy of the Goddess of change, changing Sarah, was evident here.

How could my brief revelation bring about so much change in Sarah? Five years of participation in the ritual of once- or twice-weekly psychotherapy had prepared the ground for this transformation. In the few months leading up to this hour, Sarah had accessed her childhood feeling of not having her wishes acknowledged and had renewed her attempt to deal with her father complex. She and I had carefully worked through many of the feelings she had about me that kept her passive in the therapy. My puncturing her fantasy that I too was a martyr seemed to be the final catalyst that liberated her energy to act on her own behalf. In those months Sarah had also shared the experience of my loss of a child, which brought us closer as women. It was as if at the moment I revealed myself as *living* the feminine values that I was advocating to Sarah, I, as her Ideal Woman, touched her with the transforming energy of Changing Woman. The authentication for Sarah came in my defining myself as embodying those values.

The act of having her ears pierced symbolized a long-delayed initiatory ritual into Sarah's own feminine-identified self. In subsequent weeks, she told me that she felt better about herself, more in touch with her own needs and with making decisions for herself, instead of compulsively for others or for work. She was making choices, buying new clothes, and spending money on herself in ways she had never felt free to do before. And she and her family were able to consolidate their life by buying a home.

Just at this juncture in her work, Sarah forgot to arrange an important meeting for her supervisor, the male doctor in charge of the clinic. She was mortified. We both realized that her father complex was loosening its hold. In real life she was trying to work less hard. Something was finally moving in her psyche. Paradoxically, when she stopped adhering to the false heroics of the power-dominated patriarchal model, she could begin to be a true heroine through bringing feminine values to the men and women around her. She began to shine with a new light.

CARMINA's relationship to the Goddess in her death aspect had been influenced by her brother's genetic affliction. Her fear of pregnancy and of bearing a child who would be similarly affected derived from her identification with the deformed body of her brother. She felt it was unfair that she had had to suffer through childhood with him. During the years we worked together, her fear and mistrust of men was compounded by two terrible events: an aged aunt being raped and murdered in her apartment and her grandmother being raped and robbed in her home. The real violence toward women in our society reinforces a woman's patriarchal complex.

Carmina said, "I want a child or children some day. I'm embarrassed about not knowing about men. My father was inaccessible, my brother damaged. I have the fantasy that anything that grew inside me would be twisted, damaged. My cycle is all screwed up. I feel I'm about to encounter something terrible and ugly. I feel it in the air." Carmina feared death in life as a result of her woundedness.

A series of Carmina's dreams in the seventh and eighth year of her therapy took up the issue of her fear and mistrust of men and its relationship to her brother:

> I'm only a few months pregnant. I look down at my belly, feel the baby move, and realize that I'm going to give birth prematurely. I don't remember any emotion. Miraculously, it is a healthy tiny baby. But its neck is oddly floppy like my brother's.

> I'm lying on my back watching a movie. A man is sitting behind me. He reaches out and touches my face. I think I should push his hand away and tell him to get lost. But then I feel like I don't know the rules. I'm not sure how to invite him to join me, but I manage. There is a shadow of intimacy, but it fades out.

> I am with my mother. For some reason I am having a baby taken out of me. It is either a dilation and curettage procedure or a cesarean section. It is like an abortion. A friend is implementing this process.

> I'm on the beach at the ocean. Dolphins and whales are swimming by. At one point I'm in the water, not afraid. Then a dolphin comes up underneath me, and we swim away. I'm riding him.

At this point in therapy Carmina was very depressed and angry. "I feel like I am going to explode, that everything is my fault. I'm guilty and depressed. Why am I not getting better? I can't have compassion for myself or my brother. I feel like a twisted, deformed rock." Because her brother's image came between Carmina and herself, she found it difficult to maintain her creative flow. She felt afflicted as he was. The dreams showed her consistently trying to rid herself of some contamination. Her underlying fear of infertility continued to be aggravated by worry about her short menstrual cycle.

In the dolphin dream, however, Carmina frees herself of her personal burden when she enters the sea, the collective unconscious. This is reminiscent of the dream two years earlier in which she sought a cleansing ritual at the sea. She and her pregnant double have become one. She is alone and finds herself lifted up by a playful dolphin who swims away with her. This contact with carefree new life temporarily broke the iron hold of the complex. In some Chinese representations, Kuan Yin is depicted riding on a dolphin.[13] In the next dream new life appeared again:

> I have just discovered that I am pregnant. No sooner have I begun
> to get acquainted with the idea than I feel the water breaking, running
> down my legs. On the one hand, I am excited about the prospect of
> giving birth, but on the other, it is too fast, premature. Something is
> wrong. I go out somewhere and see my mother. I say, "Look at this,
> my belly is too small." She says, "No, it's fine, it's big enough; you can
> go ahead and have this baby."

Although Carmina said, "I still feel the anger," she also told me that she had felt a wonderful sensual awareness of her body over the weekend. She was feeling a shift in self-perception, moving away from a feeling of wrongness to a feeling of rightness. In the dream, her internal mother is reassuring her that the birth of these new feelings, as small and subtle as they might be, are enough for now and represent the beginning of being able to carry a baby to term.

The night before the session in which Carmina told me her dream of being pregnant, I had led a group birthing ritual for a woman named Leah whose baby was due in a month. I told Carmina the story of the ritual. We gathered at Leah's home to honor her. Of the eight women in the group, three were pregnant; two did not have children; the rest of us had babies or toddlers at home. A few women prepared an herbal infusion of rose petals, thyme, rosemary, and verbena on the kitchen stove for Leah's bath. In the candle-lit bathroom, they poured the steaming preparation into the tub. Other women arranged a simple meal of bread, fruit, and cheese on the dining room table. While Leah bathed, we chanted songs to her from the Navajo Blessingway ceremonial. After the bath we formed a circle to tell our birthing stories for the mother-to-be. Following the story telling, each woman gave Leah a tiny gift. The gifts were placed in a pouch that one of the women had sewn to be taken into the delivery room. As each woman presented her offering, she told us why she had chosen it. Each item symbolized an element of feminine strength or intuition that Leah could call on during her labor. The intent was to mobilize Leah's inner resources for the birth of her first child with the support of the other women in the group. It was a powerful experience of feminine sharing, and it felt wonderful to tell Carmina about it as an amplification of her dream. In the midst of her anguish and fear of the Goddess as receiver of the dead, the birth-giving face of the Goddess appeared between us.

Figure 9.
Hecate: Triple Moon Goddess.

6

Divining the Dark

A woman's encounter with the dark Goddess deepens the mystery of her existence. Confrontation with her bears fruit in an added dimension of gravity to the inner mother-maiden dyad. The dark Goddess is at home in the hidden labyrinth of the unconscious. If a woman knows her, she is able to divine the darkness of her own depths. The Greek moon goddess who personifies the dark moon is Hecate-the-Three-Headed, or Hecate Triformis (figure 9). Selene is the full moon and Artemis the crescent moon, but Hecate's power reigns supreme. The moon's growing or waxing phase is the generative aspect of heavenly power; the waning phase is the power of destruction and death.[1] But Hecate is also "Giver of Vision."[2] Magic, inspiration, and intuition belong to her realm. In the Homeric Hymn to Demeter, Hecate tells Demeter that she heard Kore's cries.[3] Then Hecate accompanies Demeter to the Sun, seeking help in identifying Kore's abductor. After Kore becomes Persephone, queen of the underworld, a dark goddess, Hecate becomes her companion. Psychologically, after her descent, innocent Persephone rejoins her mother, her earth ground, but also gains the dark, her shadow. A woman in psychotherapy who endures a descent likewise gains the fruit of the dark and becomes more whole.

Hecate is goddess of the crossroads, always there at transitions.[4] Her festival day is August 13. During the feast, the Greek people beseeched the goddess of destruction to forestall the storms until the harvest was brought in. The Catholic church chose the date of August 15 to celebrate the feast of the Assumption of the Blessed Virgin, and the prayers addressed to the Virgin Mary also ask her to delay the rains until the harvest is completed.[5]

In Greece today, the Assumption of the Virgin Mary is still a national holy day in the Orthodox church. One summer while living in Greece, I celebrated this feast day and experienced the mystery of the dark goddesses Hecate and Persephone immanent in the Virgin Mary. In the morning, almost everyone in the small coastal village where I was living embarked in fishing boats to a nearby island where the festival was to be held. There, a one-room, whitewashed church dedicated to the Virgin Mary stood high on a hill. The island was uninhabited except for the old priest and his wife who tended the shrine. As the bells tolled and prayers were said, we worshipers congregated on the beach in the hot sun. We built fires to cook our freshly caught fish. Using lemons and bay laurel from the surrounding trees, along with olive oil, for seasoning, we made fish stew. Fresh bread and retsina, the local wine, completed our communion feast. As part of my ritual observance, I climbed the hill to the church. Entering its dark cool interior, I gazed at the Byzantine icons of the Madonna. There in the darkness with the hot sun blazing outside and the sound of celebrants dimly in the background, I felt myself at one with the ancient past, with the present, and with my own soul. Later, as the moon rose, we sailed back across the water to our homes, guided by the light of the Goddess.

Years later, I received a visitation from Hecate and learned about her power in the realm of childbirth a week before I delivered my first child. Selene, the full moon, bestows fertility. Artemis is the midwife, Opener of the Womb. But Hecate knows the dark side of the birth process; a mother needs to ask Hecate for an easy delivery.[6] In the danger and pain of childbirth, it is she whose presence is mandated. The "dread" goddess, in her darkness, has the power to give a woman the strength to survive the ordeal of delivery.

I had experienced pregnancy as a blessed state. Morning sickness and physical discomfort had seemed insignificant beside the miracle of carrying new life within me. I felt wholly at one with myself and the universe and welcomed the surrender of my body and ego to the new life. Six days before my son's birth, I dreamed that my analyst, who was a grandfather himself, had had a dream about me:

> A young woman is learning something from an older woman to do with cooking or another nourishing activity.

When I went to see my analyst, he told me that he thought the older woman was Hecate and that she was the one who should be present at my birth to help me in my darkest moments. Meditating on Hecate's dark aspect proved to be lifesaving for me. Labor began with my water breaking and persisted with great difficulty over a twenty-four-hour period. My son was in an occipital-posterior position, which meant that my contractions were not helped by correct pressure from his head; the dilation of my cervix proceeded slowly and painfully. By the time I got to the pushing stage, I was exhausted and in excruciating pain, which every contraction heightened. Through the waves of pain—some long and thin, some shorter, some rising to higher and higher crescendos of intensity—whenever I felt like giving up, I called on Hecate to give me strength. By "drawing down the dark moon,"[7] I ritually invoked her magic powers as the ancient Greeks had done. With Hecate's aid, I was able to persist and finally see my healthy seven-and-a-half-pound son spill out of me in the ultimate miracle, his beauty and life the golden shadow of my agonizing ordeal. In the aftermath of this internal earthquake, I was profoundly grateful for Hecate's dark support.

During my son's birth I also experienced how instinct and archetype are volcanically fused in the birth process. As a woman in childbirth, the energy of my body, soul, and spirit crystallized into one creative endeavor. From the moment the baby was born, I knew I was forever changed. Something in me died and was reborn in his gestation and birth: death to the maiden, birth to the mother. I had a sense of pride and of power in having undergone the trial and triumphed. The initiatory labor endowed me with an irrevocable inner authority. I felt totally grounded in maternal feminine life as I put his head to my breast.

The nursing relationship with my son initiated me further into the revolution in my life that becoming a mother entailed. At my core I felt calm and solid—a burning flame of steadiness in mothering and caring for the baby despite the fragmentation of the rest of my life. The experience of permeability between conscious and unconscious continued, induced by lack of sleep and the flowing milk bond, with its attendant need for peace and quiet. The baby's intermittent frustrated tears and discomforts concentrated the steadiness of my being into responding to his needs. From the beginning, his needs called on all the impulses in me that I had previously been unable to satisfy, that I could find no object for. Mothering him allowed me to give and love unconditionally. And as he drank my milk, I drank in his being, his numinous participation in the Self.

The inner maternal authority that was birthed with the successful completion of labor grew as my mothering grew and my son developed. Internally, I found it counteracting my own self-repressive masculine voices; I began to live into my own feminine power. Returning to work, I found myself to be more natural and spontaneous. I enjoyed the balance between my work and my child. Gradually, my motherhood and my identity as a psychotherapist synthesized into a new pattern, a new identity.

Being pregnant brought my personal life into the dialogue of my therapeutic work. Life swelled within me; my body changed every week. Even before I announced it to my patients, some of the women I saw intuited the change. A male psychiatrist who supervised a group in which I was a participant asked me, "Why do you tell your patients that you are pregnant? Why not let them notice, ask you about it, and get them to tell you their fantasies before you acknowledge the reality?" Shocked at the suggestion, I remember responding, "Because that would be against relationship." Out of respect for myself and the deep processes that the people I worked with were engaged in, I wanted to give them time to respond, negatively or positively, to this monumental life change for me that was bound to affect them in ways neither I nor they could know until it happened. In my subsequent work with women therapists who had been pregnant while working, my sense of rightness about the value of relationship that came to the fore around this issue was reinforced. Some therapists chose not to tell because of their own ambivalence about motherhood and wanting to feel on firm ground before having to encounter potentially negative reactions. Others simply abided by the psychoanalytic model they had been taught, to let the patient carry the burden of the obvious without acknowledging participation in the process by the therapist. When a therapist decided to wait until the patient brought up the issue, she often saw her pregnancy manifested in her patients' dreams, fantasies, or play therapy. Other patients were too embarrassed or ashamed to ask about the therapist's growing belly but were increasingly disturbed in the therapeutic process. Uniformly, what such withholding accomplished was to evoke anger in patients, who felt deceived and unworthy of being treated honestly and respectfully with regard to such an important issue.

Although my awareness of Hecate retreated to the archetypal realm after the delivery of my son, my dramatic experience of the dark side of the moon gave me a new psychological weight. I felt the fullness of the feminine trinity within me. I met my patient BEATRICE when my son was eighteen months old. My identity as a mother, including as it did this dark moon aspect, unconsciously supported my understanding of the synchronistic field between Beatrice and me around her abortion and my miscarriage. A month after my miscarriage, Hecate appeared to me in another dream:

> From my house, which is high on a hill, I look down into a valley. I
> see an old woman with a broom handle trying to knock off a giant
> mushroom, growing at least fifty feet into the air on a stalk. It is a
> beautiful mushroom, and I am amazed that she is trying to destroy it.
> My husband and I are both watching. I rush down the hill and into her
> yard to try to stop her. I find, however, that she has clippers in hand

ready to cut it down. When I realize that she is not capable of appreciating it and leaving it intact, I offer to cut it for her in order to preserve it. I do this and discover the remarkably small pot of flowers out of which the mushroom grew. The flowers look like a bunch of sweet peas. I extricate the mushroom stalk and shake the flowers in their soil to straighten them. I tell the old woman I would be glad to take some of them to plant in my garden because I love the mushrooms that grow from them. She says, "No, I'll keep them now that the threatening mushroom is no longer here."

I understood this dream to allude to the miscarriage, the beautiful mushroom that had had to be sacrificed, the embryo at the end of the umbilical cord. Mushrooms grow in dark, secret, hidden places; they are soul food, underworld food. This one has grown as if from a magic seed. The old woman with the broomstick is dark, possibly Asian. She is the witch, Hecate in her destructive aspect, the grim reaper, simply doing her job. The pot from which the mushroom grew is small and filled with sweet peas that have a vulvalike form. The potential for another seed egg to miraculously produce a baby is still there, in spite of my sense of loss. And the moon goddess retains the power of future fertility.

Beatrice had had to sacrifice her baby, too, and she continued to suffer and endure her grief. In the same month that she had the thrortax dream, she told me another dream that expressed the potentially positive side of her desire to have a child with her lover:

My lover is drawing, concentrating on his work. He asks me to look at what he has done. He is pleased. It is a delightful drawing of a child in black-and-white done in fine pencil lines.

By this time Beatrice and her lover had consolidated their relationship and moved in together. Her association to the dream was that he had not been withdrawing from conversations about a baby lately.

Four months after the miscarriage, the moon goddess blessed me with fertility again. I became pregnant; two months later, Beatrice realized that she too was pregnant again, in spite of using contraception. This time her lover responded with a commitment to fatherhood and marriage. The next few months found them immersed in the transition from lovers to potential parents.

Initially, Beatrice was anxious about her pregnancy both biologically and psychologically. She bled heavily for a few weeks after receiving the positive result of her pregnancy test. In spite of the doctor's reassurance, she worried about the possibility of miscarriage. My own miscarriage and her continued guilt about the abortion contributed to her fears. At this early stage, she had a series of anxiety-ridden dreams one week:

I am standing at the top of a rickety wooden staircase with no handrail on a fire escape outside a building. I need to go down. I sit on my fanny and inch my way down, frightened.

A man is threatening me. I need to protect myself and the child.

My lover and I are in the middle of a haystack, naked. We have our arms and legs wrapped around each other. This image looks like a tarot card.

I have my hair cut in a short, curly style. I'm excited about it but afraid my lover won't recognize me. I'm afraid I have changed everything about me.

In another tarot card image I am lying down naked. There is a protector figure lying on his back, turned to one side. My belly slips to the side, and underneath is a round, iridescent, moonlike thing. I am patting it and stroking it. I can't see a fetus in it.

Beatrice said, "I do feel a need to protect myself and the child. I am always nervous about staircases because I don't have good depth vision." These dreams revealed her disorientation during early pregnancy with a first child. A feeling of self-preservation was suddenly awakening in Beatrice. As the vessel of embryonic life she felt more vulnerable.

In the third dream is the archetypal image, signified by the tarot card, of the *coniunctio,* the union of man and woman that engendered the new life. The earliest known representation of the *coniunctio* comes from Çatal Hüyük. This is a small sculpture depicting a man and woman embracing on the left side and a mother holding a child on the right.[8] From such figurines, it is thought that the man's role in conception was known as early as 6500 B.C. In woman-to-woman therapy, pregnancy of either woman overtly brings her partner, lover, or husband, the male fertilizing element, into the therapeutic process. When I became pregnant with my first child, many women in my practice suddenly began to dream about my husband.

In Beatrice's fourth dream, she is having her hair cut. This pointed to the change in body image and ego image that had happened to her since conception. The initiatory motif of bodily mutation spontaneously arises during the passage from one stage of a woman's development to another. Beatrice felt disoriented and overwhelmed by the all-encompassing nature of her transformation. Everything she knew about herself was changing. And she worried about her fiancé's response to that change.

The final dream, again at an archetypal level, referred to the moon goddess who had come into her life with the pregnancy. The roundness suggested Selene's aspect, the full moon of fertility; Beatrice's fertility had been more potent than the diaphragm she had used as contraception. In the dream she is already caressing herself and her child, emanating love. There is also a positive male protector figure in the dream. But she is still worried about not seeing the fetus. Her worry was reinforced by the results of a test revealing her blood to be Rh-negative, a condition that carries the potential for antibodies in the mother's blood to attack the fetus. Beatrice's pregnancy required close monitoring, because during her miscarriage in Vietnam she had already developed antibodies that could be harmful to her child.

About the same time as Beatrice struggled with fears while her pregnancy stabilized, I had a nightmare about giving birth:

A pregnant coyote is walking the streets of a city "jungle." Men have given her a strange drug to alter the gestation process. The effect of the drug is to change her scent and cause her to give birth prematurely. Other predatory animals will be attracted by this scent when she delivers her pups. Now she is looking for a place to deliver. Another coyote-like creature is following her, presumably with destructive intent. She finds a manger with straw in the corner of the parking lot. The other coyote helps pull a pup out with its mouth. Oddly, the mother refuses to have anything to do with it. The other animal also ignores it. I am worrying about her not nursing. I wonder if I should try feeding the cub with a bottle, but I know I can't. I hear my husband's voice say, "It doesn't look good. It will probably die, but we have to let nature take its course." The mother seems completely indifferent. I think maybe she doesn't have any milk because of the drug she was given. I'm very disturbed.

I was in my fourth month of pregnancy when I had this dream. I was ill with a bacterial infection for which I had to take antibiotics and was worried about the medicine's effect on my baby. I had also had an amniocentesis, which I experienced as intrusive and disturbing. Although the results had shown that I was carrying a healthy baby girl, the intrusion of rational, male-dominated medicine on my feminine process lingered for weeks. In the dream the coyote, a creature of the desert, is in the wrong place to bear her young. In the city she is subjected to the perversions of modern life; drugs are not found in the wild. The intrusion on the coyote's birthing process comes from the interaction of civilization and nature. The dream told me to stay in touch with my wildness, my instinctual nature. I experienced a strong introverted pull during my pregnancy.

Coyotes relate to the moon. In one Hopi story Coyote howls at the moon because the moon is his lost mother.[9] Hecate flies through the night followed by her baying hounds.[10] The main thrust of the dream was that Nature, my nature, had to take Her course, that I could not intervene. This may also have referred to Beatrice's psychological development having to take its own course. Beatrice had always experienced herself as a loner. One of the reasons she longed for a child was that she had no other blood relatives. She, too, was undergoing invasive medical procedures in an attempt to support her pregnancy. Her previous heroin addiction made drugs particularly worrisome for her. My dream, then, also said that I could not save her baby. Interestingly, it was my husband in the dream who made this clear and differentiated my responsibility for me.

During the early stage of pregnancy, Beatrice's psyche returned to memories of her mother and her own childhood. She remembered always being hungry as a child and having to stand in rice lines. She suspected that her mother had been malnourished when she was pregnant with Beatrice. "My mother used to say, 'The day when I leave rice on my plate, I will be truly wealthy.' So whenever I'm anxious, I eat something especially nice." Beatrice found herself becoming highly emotional. She anticipated stopping work when her baby was born but was obsessed with fear that her lover's income as a musician would not be adequate to support herself and her child. She also worried about his feeling for her apart from the baby and whether he really wanted to marry her. She had a dream about the orphanage, which brought back the memory of the resident child psychiatrist pointing to her habit of fiddling with her hands. He had said, "You worry too much. You have an exaggerated sense of loyalty. You won't allow a mother substitute." The memory of the psychiatrist's insensitivity renewed her old sense of loss at her mother's abandonment.

When Beatrice first heard her baby's heartbeat at two and a half months, she was thrilled and felt more secure about the pregnancy. She began to prepare for her wedding. A few weeks later, she had the following dream:

> I have died. My coffin is sitting there. They want me to get into
> the coffin; I don't want to. They are placing photographs of everyone I
> have known in and on the coffin. I realize I am both in the coffin,
> about to be buried, and also standing beside it saying, "Please, no." I
> am sad. My lover is standing beside me. I am saying good-bye to my-
> self. I wake up crying.

Beatrice said her death felt sad; that marriage would be forever. She said she had already buried much of her self. The shroud was white, as for a wedding. She had a fear of being buried but not of death. Death had been important and natural to her until she went to Vietnam, then it became unnatural. "I was always drawn to death. I have never thought there was any particular need to stay alive. But a man on the street tried to steal my purse the other day, and I was frightened and outraged. Never before have I ever been frightened."

This dream reflected marriage as death, one theme in the Eleusinian mysteries that was memorialized in friezes of the Funeral Banquet of Hades and Persephone.[11] The hidden reality in this ancient motif was the threat to a girl of dying in childbirth. On the archetypal level, it commemorated Persephone's descent to the realm of the dead, her encounter with the dark "other" in Hades, and her destiny of becoming queen of the underworld. Beatrice's willingness to endure her descent and face the horrors of her own unconscious paralleled Persephone's experience. In the marble frieze, the royal wedding is depicted, with Persephone holding the double torches that lighted her way. Demeter is seated on her great mystery basket, which symbolizes the ineffable core of the mystery. Hades is raising an animal-headed vessel full of wine in a gesture of celebration.

Now that she was pregnant, Beatrice was experiencing a new feeling for her, fear. This dream not only affirmed the death of the maiden as she entered into marriage but also evoked her initiation into motherhood. A sense of self-preservation continued to grow on behalf of her unborn child. The hormones of pregnancy were helping to stimulate emotional attitudes of nourishing and protecting a vulnerable newborn. These attitudes contradicted and subtly began to change her intrinsic sense of worthlessness, which she had traced to her mother's attempt to abort her.

Around the same time, now in my fourth month of pregnancy, I had the following dream, which showed my role as model and midwife for Beatrice's pregnancy and her therapy:

> My labor begins. I go to the hospital, but hours later I am still not dilated. One or two people examine me and can't even get a finger inside my cervix. I realize that the contractions have stopped. I try to push the baby out with sheer will, but it doesn't work. Finally I have to leave and go home. I wonder if this is false labor. Beatrice is also in the hospital with her husband. It is as if she is learning about the process even though it is not her time yet. I feel it is all fruitless work.

Psychologically, Beatrice accompanied me, followed me wherever I went, two months behind in the gestation process. This was her first child, my second. I was showing her the way, which included the possibility that there could be false contractions and a false start. I too was apprehensive about how my delivery would go; I had already experienced Hecate's dark power.

Beatrice's dream in the same week also was preoccupied with labor and attempted to incorporate her past with her present in the birth-giving process.

> My husband and I are in Russia. It is time to have the baby. We are in the operating room. The doctors are masked. They are debating

about how they are going to proceed with us. Someone comes in with
a book and shows us a Chinese woman doctor's picture, Dr. Liung.
This is the definitive book on obstetrics. Everyone is very happy.

Now that she had reached the three-month stage of gestation, Beatrice
felt more confident, and the dream incarnated her Chinese maternal heritage in a woman obstetrician who had the authority and skill to help her
birth her baby. Russia was her father's birthplace. Such imagery is part of
the dissolution of a pregnant woman's usual psychological patterns, creating
new structures to prepare her for labor, delivery, and mothering a newborn.
The ego's temporary disintegration may feel confusing or threatening, but
the new thoughts and emotions that emerge help make a woman more
adaptable with her baby.[12] The breaking down of old patterns engendered
by the state of pregnancy, therefore, enhances the therapeutic process of
change.

A week later, Beatrice saw her baby through a sonogram. She said she
could count the baby's fingers, watch it suck its thumb and explore its own
face. She was ecstatic. As she felt the baby moving within her more and
more, Beatrice continued to plan her marriage to the baby's father. Their
union promised to provide a much-needed container of security for Beatrice as well as for their forthcoming child. In ancient Greece the abduction
and marriage of Kore guaranteed the return of the Goddess and with her,
fertility of the fields. It became the prototype of all marriages, with its
promise of reproduction.

Beatrice's dream about me being "a calming mother figure soothing my
nerves" occurred the night before her wedding, almost one year after Beatrice began therapy. Her stepmother's abusive telephone call from England
provoked a healing response in the unconscious. We did not talk much
about this dream, but it supported my feeling that the reunion of daughter
and mother had taken place between us in the unconscious. This relational
reality was carrying the healing value in our work. Beatrice's ability to feel
had been drastically blunted in her childhood trauma. In the dream I infused her with calmness and comfort that stabilized her emotions for the
imminent wedding. She had never been able to depend on anyone; this
dream was the beginning of her being able to depend on me. My function
here was magical, as if I were the good witch whose power could counteract
the bad witch. The moon goddess was subliminally present in our interaction. My therapeutic role with Beatrice included all three aspects of Hecate
Triformis: I had been blessed by Selene's power of fertility. I had been
through the initiatory ordeal of birth and had become a mother; Artemis,
the midwife, had opened my womb. But I had also encountered dark

Hecate—I had lost two children, one by abortion, one by miscarriage. Now I was midwifing not only Beatrice's biological pregnancy but also the progress of her therapeutic development, the progress of her soul.

When I told SARAH about my new pregnancy and forthcoming amniocentesis, she wished me well and subsequently asked with concern about how the procedure had gone. Sarah's new initiatory effort against her father-identified complex was proving a difficult task. But fantasies about having a daughter continued to arise, along with feelings that she barely had time and energy for her son. The discrepancy between the reality and the fantasy led to our talking about how the wish for a baby girl might be symbolic of the embryonic femininity that she was trying to birth in herself. During this month she told me, "It has taken me such a long time to accept you as a role model. The way you dress is so feminine." Sarah had difficulty allying herself with women. Her power struggle with her mother came up with me and other women in her life. Alliance with the feminine, with me, was necessary for her to submit to her own initiation. Respecting a feminine mode of dress symbolized Sarah's accepting me as her sponsor or midwife for the deliverance of her own new identity. Sarah said to me shortly after my miscarriage, "I keep asking myself, what is it going to take for me to change?" Sarah recognized Changing Woman in our work but was as yet unable to embrace her.

A few weeks later, I had a dream about Sarah in which my whole family was involved in Sarah's changing:

> My mother is trying to help me with Sarah. Mother has spent
> some time with her. I'm explaining to my mother how difficult Sarah's
> husband's job demands are on her. I have the feeling my mother thinks
> that it's Sarah's place to go where her husband goes. Then my husband
> enters the discussion. He's trying to help me with Sarah too. He says
> the problem in her home life is the conflict between her son and his
> little sister. My husband is helping with her son because Sarah is being
> abrupt and impatient with him and not giving him time for transitions.
> My husband is trying to mitigate this somehow.

Shortly after I had this dream, Sarah told me she had been trying to get pregnant since I had told her about my pregnancy. She hadn't wanted to discuss it, because she felt she needed to try to separate herself from me and sort out how much of her wish was connected to my being pregnant. Her son was now four years old, and she had wanted another child for some time. My pregnancy confused her, because she didn't feel secure about knowing what she wanted. Sarah also had a dream at this time about a woman wanting to steal her pregnancy. Was this shadowy dream expressing

Sarah's fear that I had stolen her pregnancy or that she wanted to steal mine? Was it also Hecate lying in wait? The dark Goddess is the shadow of the birth-giving Goddess; they are always side by side.

My dream, as with my dreams about Beatrice, showed the permeability between the psyches of two women working in depth together. I was pregnant with a baby girl and had an older son, then two and a half years old. I was going to have to deal with the sibling jealousy that inevitably arises with the birth of a second child. For years my unconscious had also been concerned with the well-being of Sarah's son. My dream included my mother and my husband both engaged with helping Sarah (my shadow) deal with all the changes. Sarah asked me many times if I had chosen a name for my baby girl, showing how commingled her own fantasy wish for a girl was with our therapy and my pregnancy.

In the midst of wanting a girl child, the threat to Sarah's newly emerging inner femininity was dramatically illustrated in a dream about her younger sister:

> My sister is eight years old. We are in Mexico together. There are many stairs, rocks, and swimming pools. My brothers and she come down into the water, waist deep, playing around. I am not paying attention, but suddenly she isn't there. I start looking for her and tell the boys she has drowned. I get up on a ledge and see the body in the water. I get her out. I am frantic; I can't remember the details of CPR. She does have a heartbeat. The lifeguard comes and won't help. He just asks questions like, "How many minutes was she under water?" I am furious and think he doesn't want to resuscitate her because he has made some clinical/rational decision that she has been under too long. When I wake up, I have the sense that she is alive, but I feel terrible and responsible.

Sarah said, "I don't know how to take care of myself. It doesn't come naturally or spontaneously to identify with being female. The dream shows how drastic it has to get, how dangerous, before I pay attention." Sarah's real sister did embody the feminine. Her eight-year-old sister in the dream symbolized Sarah's therapeutic shadow or twin. Sarah could still lose her by falling into the unconscious, drowning again in pleasing the father. The male lifeguard in the dream, as well as her brothers, are ineffectual in helping her revive her sister (shadow). Only Sarah's passionate feeling for her own submerged feminine voice could bring her femininity to life. The positive prospective energy in this dream was that she *cared* about what was happening to her, that she was frantic and furious and felt terrible. She usually tolerated work (male) expectations with an attitude of resignation and sacrificed self-nurturing to the "higher ideal."

Change was finally forced upon Sarah by her own body. Hecate the witch—the dark, the shadow—was unconscious in Sarah, so She manifested in bodily ways. The dream Sarah had in the early weeks of therapy, in which she had borne a retarded child without knowing she was pregnant, proved to be prophetic. Sarah abruptly had to confront the "dread goddess." One night she awoke with severe cramps and found herself discharging a three-month-old fetus and placenta, even though she had had no inkling she was pregnant. In retrospect, she realized the miscarried pregnancy explained her fatigue and her sense of things not being right over the past few months. Sarah was devastated by her own unconsciousness, and by the loss of the baby. She was appalled that she could ignore her body and function like an automaton, driven by achievement values. Ironically, as a doctor with a subspecialty in endocrinological aspects of fertility, she worked on a daily basis with women and their relationship to their bodies.

Subsequently, Sarah had a dream that underlined the severity of her patriarchal wound:

> It is nighttime. I am walking along with my husband and his parents in a resort area carrying old-fashioned woven wood baskets. They go inside to eat. I want to go look at the beach in the moonlight. The waves are getting higher. A storm is coming up. I'm at the top of the beach trying to climb to the top where it is flat. I can't make it alone. A polite man from the restaurant helps me up. He also helps the other three people who have been on the lower beach. As we walk back to the resort, the waves are immense and crashing. We're safe, but the man remembers a young woman in a body cast who is fishing on the beach and realizes that he forgot her. Then we hear the loud, screaming call of a bird and a woman's screams. We look into the moonlit sky and see a huge, white bird with a woman all in white on its back, flying away.

In the dream Sarah identified with the woman in the body cast. She said, "The woman was totally immobile; the cast included her neck. It was obvious that she had spinal injuries." For Sarah, this brought to mind her own physical lack of sensation. It was as if she were encased and couldn't differentiate her bodily responses or limitations. Her immobility in terms of psychological change was also reflected here. But at least Sarah was a woman in this dream, a wounded woman, not a pseudo-man. The bird is an ambiguous symbol. It comes from the sky and could be the beady eye of the death goddess, or it could be Sarah's deliverer. The unconscious brings together opposites, negative and positive. It was up to Sarah to act in a way that would creatively resolve the opposition.

The constructive energy in the dream came in the image of the woven baskets, which Sarah said were gifts from her beloved Aunt Maisie, who had died recently. Maisie had been a positive role model for Sarah. Baskets are traditionally feminine products of creativity. The making of such objects requires introverted energy and quiet concentration. This mode was the opposite of Sarah's extroverted, professional attitude. Sarah realized that she needed to spend more time on the activities that nurtured her, sewing and gardening.

The unconscious mother-daughter mirroring relationship became apparent during this time through bodily synchronicities between Sarah and her mother. Sarah's mother, whose immune system was compromised after treatment for breast cancer, contracted infectious hepatitis. Her mother was completely demoralized; she couldn't see her grandchild for months, and her condition, understandably, brought her to a nadir in her life. Sarah felt ambivalent about coming to therapy. She said it reminded her of the sacrament of confession in the Catholic church because she had to talk about things that made her feel guilty. "I can't trust my body," she said. "What if I become pregnant again without knowing it?" Indoctrinated with Catholic dogma as a child, she felt her spirit and soul to be at odds with her body. Her martyr mother had been her model. For a martyr, the body is sacrificed in the alleged interest of the soul. Possibly the white bird's abduction was the psyche's attempt to bring about a union between the two.

In the midst of her struggle to bring body and soul together, Sarah discovered a lump under her right breast, on the wall of her chest. With trepidation, she scheduled a mammogram and biopsy. The results of the tests proved negative for cancer, but the experience had an important psychological consequence. This second brush with the dark side of the Goddess strengthened Sarah's resolve to move into more depth in her work with me. She was able to see the ways in which she avoided taking herself seriously. She felt safer if she stayed on the surface in therapy and kept moving from one task to another in her external life. One of the most telling things she realized—through tears—in the next few months was, "If I really let myself look at how much I'm away from home, I would quit work."

Finally, her body made the decision for her. Five months later, Sarah began to experience Crohn's disease symptoms again after a ten-year remission. A month later, she was forced to take a leave of absence for illness. Frightened for herself and her family, she said, "There are only two things I want now: my inner life and my health." Body and soul had converged to help Sarah ally herself with new values. Her body refused to be ignored; that old pattern, laid down at menarche, was broken. Her psyche persisted in showing her the consequences of death and loss if she continued on her path of martyrdom and achievement. She was able to stop, stay home, and reexamine her life. I admired Sarah's willingness to persevere in therapy until she could come to a meaningful experience of transformation. Despite her resistance and fear, she remained dedicated to realizing her own changing nature.

CARMINA's struggle with Hecate, the dark side of the Goddess, appeared in the form of a deadly witch late in her analytic process after she took up the challenge of intimacy with men. A few months after my miscarriage, Carmina left therapy. This was the point at which she had announced to her parents that she was a lesbian and had satisfactorily worked through their reactions with me and with them. Involved with a woman in a difficult but stable relationship and working productively at the bank, she felt she did not need to delve deeper into her psyche. I knew she had reached a plateau in her work, but I also felt that her journey was not over.

After a nearly two-year interval, Carmina called me and returned to analysis to complete her initiation process. When I first talked with her on the phone, I suggested that she might want to see a lesbian or gay therapist instead of me. But she rejected this idea and told me about the dramatic change that had occurred in her in the interim: "I feel relief at calling you. I've had another terrible relationship with a woman. I want to have a relationship with a man." Carmina said that she had been having bad dreams about distressed babies and children that she was powerless to help. "One baby I was holding kept falling apart." In addition to relationship issues, Carmina was feeling the loss of her art. She had been frozen artistically for years, unable to put pencil or paint to paper. She was adamant about her change; her identity had come into focus. In her absence from therapy, she had lived her lesbian life to what was, for Carmina, its natural end. The pendulum had swung back inside, to taking up the father-brother problem as a psychological demon. This return to therapy and to her own unconscious journey signaled the beginning of the dark descent that was to last four years. Only Carmina's courage and determination allowed her to achieve her initiation into womanhood.

At the outset of this phase of our work, Carmina had a dream that echoed her initial dream in therapy seven years previously:

> I haven't seen you in a long time. Then I see a woman from the back and think I recognize you. I'm so glad it's you. Then she turns around; it's not you, and she's covered with a horrible disease like poison oak, creeping, crawling, horribly infected, repulsive.

Carmina's fear of her own woundedness, which she often experienced as repulsion, was dramatized here again in relation to me. In the dream seven years earlier, it was simply our contact that frightened her and stirred up her intimacy issues. But here she was faced with a deeper level of what she had to confront in the unconscious, her fear that the therapeutic descent would confirm her own diseased view of herself, that she was an outcast, doomed to remain separated from the creative life she longed for in art, marriage, and children. The dream image is that of the terrifying witch, the dread aspect of Hecate's magic. The horrible aspect of the witch had to be encountered in Carmina's journey.

The witch first appeared in the following dream:

> I am at a summer camp for young women. It's not clear if I am a worker or a child participant. The camp director is a tiny society fund-raiser, a matron who has blue cloisonné teeth and expensive shoes. She is very intimidating. People are afraid to approach her. I am supposed to teach a class, but I have poison oak and a sprained ankle. I'm intimidated by the woman with the teeth.

Carmina saw the woman with blue cloisonné teeth as the control element in her psyche in conflict with the chaos element embodied by the ugly adolescent girl in the raincoat that had come up in previous dreams. The woman's voice in Carmina's head said, "Your body cannot be trusted; it doesn't have a law of its own." The girl's voice, contaminated by the demon's voice, said, "You will never be able to live up to your own aesthetic standard." Carmina's natural talent as an artist did include a high aesthetic standard, but it had been years since she had been able to express herself as a painter. Abandoning her own talent as she had, she found that the aesthetic impulse had been frustrated and her creativity dammed up. Together with her skewed body image from childhood, this frustration was being vented on her body. The woman with the blue cloisonné teeth was a perfect image of her frustrated unconscious attempt to make a work of art out of her body. This image proved to be helpful to Carmina in identifying her enemy. When Carmina could make art again, the positive shadow, the initiating motif of the blue cloisonné woman, could be revealed as Turquoise Woman.

The blue cloisonné teeth woman was Carmina's personal witch shadow. But in the course of her descent, she encountered several archetypal aspects of the witch known to us from Greek Olympian mythology. In the following dream, the witch was Medea, who murdered her children when Jason betrayed her.[13]

> I am the daughter of a hero, a Harrison Ford character. I'm young and dependent on him. We are trying to escape from an evil, meddling witch. He protects me from her. During our struggle, I see the inside of her vehicle full of nasty, slimy water. She has tricks to snare us; I jump back from an electrical shock. She's most powerful when she's

asleep. I recognize her Medea crown. She has chains and an ornament woven into her hair. The hero and I escape on bicycles.

I'm separated from the hero, riding my own bike, holding my favorite jacket. I see a jacket like it and realize it's a witch's trick, so I don't touch it. But the bicycle is drawn to her magnetically. She has captured my hero. In a crystal ball, she shows me how she's torturing him, physically ripping him in half. I see his tortured face in agony. I can't do anything about it, because he is separated from me, and I'd rather not have the vision.

I am standing at the edge of a deep pool. Medea is asleep beside it, and I can see the hero at the bottom of the pool. I realize he must be suffocating. I want to show him that all he has to do is come up and break the surface of the water, and he'll be free. Standing at the edge, I will him to come up. He does it, and he breaks the surface with a gasp.

I'm going into a house where my maternal grandfather is welcoming me, opening the door. I see that my old bed, a futon, is covered with wet towels, and I realize that my brother has been sitting there after a bath. I'm angry and tell my mother. She says, "You're absolutely right. I shouldn't have done it."

Medea was seduced from her own land, then betrayed by her lover, and murdered their children in despair and revenge. Carmina was betrayed by her father and had murdered her creativity, her own symbolic children, for some years. The striking element of this dream is that Carmina feels compassion and sympathy for the hero. She feels for their shared wound. Previously, she had often been identified with the witch in her murderous feelings toward men. Carmina thought that her mother's unconscious witch lay both in her mother's negative relationship to her own mother as well as in her ineffectiveness in dealing with her husband. Patriarchal power had dominated. This absence of power or ability to affect Carmina's development in relation to her brother created an unconscious witch complex that Carmina had internalized. In this dream, for the first time, Carmina's father figure and a potential hero figure are fused. In rescuing her inner father, she redeemed her healthy relationship to the masculine.

Whenever Carmina allowed herself to think about going toward a career goal in the field of art, the witch came up to block her. Typically, a witch attack descended when she was playing with drawing or making a piece of art. "The spontaneous image of pursuing my art arises, and then immediately the feeling gets rigidified, then hazy and unobtainable. I think, 'I can't do it,' and am paralyzed. I start to obsess about food and feel the old conflict between control and chaos, and I have to take a break."

Carmina saw the woman with blue cloisonné teeth as devouring. This witch represented formal, frozen, organized control without any life. She was creativity rigidified. Fighting the witch was empowering, but the fear of her body or instinct lay on the other side of the conflict. "If I get fat, my mother won. If I'm thin, I won. My mother always said I was 'healthy,' as a child, meaning I was fat. By the age of ten, I had a terrible body image." The next dream in this series showed how the witch was interfering with Carmina's attempt at intimate relationships with men:

> I go running across a wide open field. It feels really good to be running.
>
> I am with an Asian man, and I want to make love with him. We both want to. Something structural like time is preventing us. I have to be surreptitious because the woman with the blue cloisonné teeth has to be put off and avoided. We do get rid of her.
>
> I am lying on a couch in the living room in front of a big window. I think, "I will see someone come to the window, and he will hurt me." I look up, and he bursts through the glass. I'm terrified.

The initial image in the dream evoked, once again, the Navajo Kinaaldá image of the initiatory race. In reality, Carmina effectively used long walks to counteract the negativity of her witch complex. While walking or running, her psyche and body fell into harmony. In the second part of the dream, her instinct toward a man is flowing freely but only with careful strategy against the blue cloisonné teeth woman, who could undermine her trust in her own bodily instinct. Being grounded in her body was essential for Carmina's initiation into relationships with men. The third image in the dream reverted to fear of the masculine again. This was the week that her grandmother was raped and robbed. In the midst of her personal struggle with this complex, the cultural violence of men against women in our society had struck Carmina's family again. Curiously, in the wake of that assault, Carmina and her mother were having an unexpectedly enjoyable visit together at Carmina's flat.

During these months Carmina was in hell. Although she continued to function adequately in the world, internally she felt as if everything were lost. Her premenstrual distress with short cycles intensified, and she stopped smoking. She felt simultaneously agitated and depressed. The presence of the witch was felt even in our meetings. Carmina needed me to understand and reflect her despair, even as I carried the hope for her that eventually she would come up out of the underworld again. Hecate helped me to ride the fine edge between life and death. But the cloisonné witch tried to sabotage her and my efforts at every juncture. And whenever Carmina felt disconnected from me, she despaired even more. She needed to know she could contact me between sessions if she lost hope. "I fear that I am a casualty, a lost cause. I fear that I'm going to tell you a dream so bad

that you are not going to be able to do anything except give up on me."
Carmina had no compassion for herself during these months. The blue
cloisonné witch had the upper hand. I was the compassionate one.
Carmina dreamed:

> A friend is suffering, near death, because I have not called or vis-
> ited her. I have been repeatedly contacted by friends who tell me that I
> am being cruel by refusing to see her. Finally her mother comes to me
> and begs me to see her. I refuse again. I feel I am being cruel, and yet I
> cannot bring myself to go see her. It would be like sinking into quick-
> sand. The mother changes into a witchy, harpy creature who screeches
> at me and tells me what a monster I am. We begin to struggle physi-
> cally, and I am relieved to find that I am easily strong enough to throw
> this creature down. It feels good.
> After I leave the harpy creature behind, I go up a hill to a wooden
> house. The air and light are extraordinarily beautiful, electric blue like
> desert light. There is a strange, animal-shaped piece of wood on the
> lawn. I have forgotten my keys, and when I knock my father lets me
> in. I am welcome. I am happy to be there.

Carmina had had a terrible fight with her mother that she felt validated
everything she suspected about her brothers' priority over her in the family.
After the argument, she felt she hated her mother. The quicksand in the
dream reminded her of the bodily weight she sometimes felt when the
witch was attacking her. She could fend off the witch mother but only by
giving up her identification with the suffering girl she had once been. Her
refusal is a triumph. It seemed the argument with her mother had released
Carmina's energy for this next step. But she still needed to learn to feel ten-
derness toward herself. In this dream her father is her savior, her refuge.

The final dreams of this witch series extended the powerless image of
quicksand to that of falling asleep. In this, Carmina saw the Medusan
image of paralysis, being turned to stone.

> I am in a class. I am having difficulty maintaining my concentra-
> tion. We are told to turn to a certain page to read a poem. I can barely
> find the page. I feel dazed or sleepy and weak. I am vaguely aware that
> the poem is an invocation to the Goddess. The prayer is moving, sim-
> ple, and beautiful, but can I trust it? Is it just another witch's trick? As
> we read, I am looking at a beautiful alabaster sculpture, gracefully
> standing in a fountain of water. It looks like *Bird in Flight* by Brancusi.
> But I am dazed. Can I trust the beauty of the sculpture? What if it is
> only a copy? Another witch's trick?
> I am in my room sorting through a mess of clothes and junk on the
> floor of my closet. I am very tired, very afraid. I feel ill, but I know that

> I must concentrate to keep the witch out of me. My job is to clean up this junk, but the job belongs to the witch. It is an enormous task to sort out shoes, bobby pins, hats, and clothing and bring order to the chaos. The things have the same debilitating, hypnotic effect that the witch does. It is as if I am touching *her* things. A doll-like puppet leans against the wall. As I watch it, it becomes the chattering, terrifying, horrible head of the very witch I fear. I scream "No, no, no, you wait . . ." The witch becomes a woman—a lesbian?—who takes my hands and says, "I am Judy, I am Judy." She is no longer threatening, but how can I trust her? She is the witch.

Carmina felt that her desire was poisonous. She said, "If I want something, I can't have it. The witch hates joy." She felt she had been denied joy as a child because of the seriousness of her brother's condition and her subsequent identification with his distorted body. She also associated the sleeping image with her mother, who she recalled sleeping a lot in her childhood. "I was always waiting for her to wake up." The passivity or ineffectiveness of her mother complex was reflected here. But with great effort Carmina was maintaining her concentration on an inner awakening. A new feminine principle was defined in both the poem/prayer and the beauty of the bird sculpture, which alluded to the Goddess in her death aspect, but now in aesthetic form. Hecate's magic was beginning to transform. Carmina was seeing inner, joyful beauty, even if she did not trust her perception yet.

The second dream sets her a task that brings her into direct confrontation with the witch. By taking action, daring to effect something, she directly confronts her nemesis. Because she had been paralyzed for so long, her own deepest motivations and her belongings had fallen into the witch's domain. She had to reclaim them. The task of sorting is one of Psyche's tasks in the tale of Eros and Psyche. In the myth she is given a pile of seeds to sort, and ants come in the night to help her.[14] In this dream, once Carmina begins to sort, the witch is reduced to a manageable human shadow figure, Carmina's lesbian shadow. The shadow took this witchlike form because Carmina unconsciously used her lesbian identity to avoid her father-brother issues. Carmina painted a picture after this dream that further diminished the witch's destructiveness.

After her dream about wanting to make love to the Asian man, Carmina told me that as a child she had wanted to be Asian. Then she had another dream in which Asian babies appeared:

> I am playing with Asian twin babies. One of the babies is sick, deformed. It feels like a cat in my arms. It is heavy, but small, with almost no arms or legs. I am taking care of this baby while the mother

takes care of the healthy twin. Gradually the sick baby begins to move and breathe and heal. I am holding it, and it begins to take steps. I quickly call the mother. She comes with many women to see this miraculous change. I am deeply moved, and yet it is hard for me to feel. I am once again embarrassed by the stoniness of my heart.

Carmina desperately needed to feel compassion for herself. Although she relied on my compassion for her, she had trouble accepting it, because she felt so much self-denigration. As she described her fascination with Asian culture, I was moved to tell her about Kuan Yin, the Chinese goddess of compassion and mercy. I suggested she look at John Blofeld's book on Kuan Yin, in which he beautifully describes his devotional journey in Asia searching out this goddess and her lore. I had an intuition that the Eastern concept of devotion to the deity as the way to grace, rather than the Christian idea of behaving in certain ways in order to earn grace, could have an impact on Carmina's sense of unworthiness. Carmina's analysis with me, her commitment to the work, had become her devotion. Her sheer courage in withstanding the onslaught from the unconscious and penetrating the meaning of her fate as it was revealed to her day by day was commendable. She deserved to feel proud of herself.

Suffering the loss of my miscarriage, then pregnant with my second child, my daughter—embodying the mother-daughter relationship both within and without—I was the initiating sponsor and Great Mother's midwife, the guardian of the container for the inner and outer transformations that Beatrice, Sarah, and Carmina were undergoing. I carried the hope and the trust for the eventual emergence of *all* the new life that was gestating.

CARMINA's relationship to the Great Goddess of birth, death, and regeneration was lived in the inner realm of dream and fantasy. Her psyche reached back to prehistoric symbols to liberate her emerging feminine power. Her feminine rebirth and her fear of death or genetic alteration were revealed in dreams of pregnancy, miscarriage, and ailing newborn babies. Birth imagery revitalized Carmina's creativity and asserted her artistic vocation. As with her menarche, spirituality, sexuality, and psychological awareness were always intertwined as Carmina transformed. My first pregnancy allowed Carmina to participate in a woman's healthy gestation and birth through our relationship. At some deep level, this helped her to trust her own body and instinct more. From the beginning of our work together, I had always sympathized with Carmina's deep resistance to the patriarchy and to her childhood wound that involved her relationship to her genetically affected brother. But after the birth of my son, delighting in the specialness of that early infant-mother relationship, I found my feeling also going out to Carmina's mother, overwhelmed by a newborn who required so much care when her first child, her baby daughter, was two years old. I felt sad for both of them at their premature loss of each other. I could also feel more immediately how the birth of the third child, when Carmina was four and her brother two, must have further burdened her mother and made Carmina feel more abandoned. Given the challenge of their family fate, I thought both mother and daughter had done well by building a relationship that included much love as well as animosity.

SARAH's experience of the Great Goddess in her birth-giving and her death-receiving aspects encompassed both inner and outer life. Birth imagery often came up in her work, reflecting both her struggle with changing and her feelings about having a child. Transformation for Sarah involved recognizing that she could no longer ignore her body as her menarche had been ignored by her culture and her family. Her arduous labor with the birth of her son exposed her to the realm of the dark Goddess. Her mother's breast cancer, finding a lump in her own breast, and the exacerbation of her symptoms of Crohn's disease reinforced her psychological descent. During her pregnancy she felt closer to her mother, less competitive, more supported. Similarly, my first pregnancy and the birth of my son allowed our therapeutic relationship to develop. A few years later, we became more intimate because we shared an experience of the dark Goddess, when, within a year, first I, then she, miscarried a baby. My subsequent pregnancy and her desire for a daughter intensified the therapeutic process of change around the mother-daughter relationship.

With BEATRICE, the synchronicities of our pregnancies created a powerful constellation of the Great Goddess between us. As the receiver of the dead, the Goddess took back the souls of our aborted babies. As birth-giver, full moon, giver of fertility, Selene, She blessed us both with new pregnancies in which we rejoiced and feared, waiting for safe deliveries. Beatrice's initiation into womanhood was encumbered by the cumulative forces of death and evil she had experienced in her life. Any new challenge or change was fraught with the fear of death that she had experienced at menarche and earlier at the loss of her mother. But the new life incubating within her lent her power to change.

PART III

Emergence

Figure 10.
Kuan Yin.

7

Healing With Compassion

A woman in psychotherapy experiences her transformation as an open-ended, multilayered self-examination in which the time of her sessions and her relationship with the therapist are her only guidelines. Without a defined order or set time for her ritual initiation, she has to trust her psyche—her ego and unconscious work—to evolve structure, form, and an end or completion to her initiation. Emergence from our ritual enclosure takes many forms. Along the way she experiences many small openings or illuminations that herald her psychological arrival. She may emerge from a dark tunnel of depression, from a particular inner conflict, from a deadlock with an external problem, or from a state of chronic anxiety. Or she may feel the release that new insights, feelings, and attitudes bring. These are precursors of the larger emergence from the container of our woman-to-woman relationship that lies somewhere in the future.

As a woman's own inner guides emerge from her unconscious, they spontaneously enact rituals through her dreams and fantasies. These rituals fall into an order or pattern leading to the goal of realizing her individuality. The inner feminine archetypes or authorities help a woman form a conscious life that mirrors the biological rite of menstruation already within her. The figures weave the woman's destiny, forming her unique story or myth. The archetypal guides support the power of a woman's own voice, which initiates her separation from the therapy and from me. By leading her deeper into her own feminine mystery, they lead her to the natural termination of her therapeutic work.

Several years before I met Beatrice, the symbol of the lighted lamp magically brought Kuan Yin, the Lady of Compassion, into my work with SARAH. When, after eighteen months of therapy, Sarah had to move, the next to the last time we met she cried about the loss of her therapy and her relationship to me. At the time, she and her husband saw the move as a permanent one. She said, "I want to give you a gift, but I don't know if it's appropriate; I'm worried about boundaries." Sarah had not demonstrated any boundary problem in relation to me, and her feeling awakened in me the wish to give her a token of our work when we parted. We had planned to continue having therapy hours by telephone for a time, so my gift would represent both our past therapeutic work and its transformation into another form. Browsing in an odd little antique store, I was drawn to a tiny silver charm, resembling both a vessel and a lamp. I associated it to Psyche's lamp and to Aphrodite's casket of beauty ointment that Psyche could not resist opening,[1] as well as to the alchemical container in which transformation takes place. A small card that accompanied the charm said the lantern was an attribute of the Chinese bodhisattva Kuan Yin. I did not know of Kuan Yin, but I gave the card and charm, together with my sense of its meaning, to Sarah in our last meeting before her departure. She was touched by the gift and curious about the enigmatic Kuan Yin. Neither of us could have anticipated that Kuan Yin would become a motivating archetypal and spiritual force in Sarah's therapeutic work.

A week later, in our first telephone hour, Sarah told me that after our session the previous week, she had been driving home when her eye was caught by a jewelry store. She stopped and entered the shop, where to her amazement she found Kuan Yin in the form of a small, carved mother-of-pearl pendant, a woman with flowing robes set in gold. "I also found a single rough pearl for you," Sarah told me. She did not buy the Kuan Yin, because the piece was expensive, and she wasn't accustomed to spending money on herself. But she did buy the pearl and sent it to me with a note:

Dear Virginia,

You are the touchstone of my analysis and the bridge to the wisdom of the treasure. I hold our therapeutic relationship to be sacred. The opportunity to continue our sessions by telephone has provided me with a sense of inner stability and joy during what is externally a very difficult time.

The beautiful lantern you gave me is a symbol of this chance to continue to look with my eyes open as the lantern casts a pattern of light and shadow on the unconscious. Thank you for the light, Virginia.

Fondly,
Sarah

Accepting the pearl meant that I had to hold the value of the feminine for Sarah until she could acknowledge her own worth and validate it for herself. Our exchange of gifts at this juncture brought us to a new level of meaning in the work. We both remembered her early dream of the archetypal Queen/Princess, mother/daughter guides in which the pearl ring had appeared. The inner relationship symbolized by Sarah's pearl ring in the dream had found outer form in both our relationship and her potential relationship to Kuan Yin. Entranced by the synchronicity of finding the pendant, Sarah continued to pursue her inner development in conjunction with our work on the phone.

The deity Kuan Yin is said to be "She-Who-Hearkens-to-the-Cries-of-the-World."[2] According to myth she was so concerned for humanity that, upon receiving enlightenment as a man, she chose to return to human form as a woman.[3] On earth, she sits on her island in the sea answering every prayer addressed to her. She is said to save her devotees from physical and spiritual harm. Peace and mercy are her blessings. Her most effective meditation is the constant repetition of Her name. Over the years I have found Kuan Yin's compassion to be redeeming for many women. She has become one of the central feminine images in my office (figure 10).

Compassion for oneself and others opens the door to grace, to a spiritual dimension of existence that includes and transcends everyday routine. The problem for a woman is that she has been taught to feel compassion for someone else: a child, a friend, a lover, a husband, a parent, or for suffering humanity. A woman rarely feels compassion for herself; if she does, she risks being told by those close to her that she is weak and selfish. In the process of deep psychotherapy, a woman comes to feel compassion, love, and care for herself. Once she begins to soften in this way, she can see how strong she has been to survive her personal and cultural wounds and to engage in a descent that eventually frees her from her role as victim of fate. By doing her individual work in psychotherapy she liberates herself from the constraints of our patriarchal society and influences those around her in an ever-rising tide of feminine consciousness.

Inspired by Kuan Yin and the reappearance of the pearl, Sarah chanced on the myth of Atalanta and felt the story of this mythic heroine best fit her early development.[4] This ancient Greek heroine was left on a mountainside to die as an infant because her father had wanted a boy. A wild bear nurtured the child, and then hunters took her in. Atalanta grew up hunting, shooting, wrestling, and competing with men. Her father reclaimed her after he found she was an athlete. When he wanted her to marry, she declared that she would marry whoever could beat her in a foot race, knowing well that there was no such man alive. She defeated all her would-be suitors until Hippomenes asked Aphrodite to help him to win.

Aphrodite helped Hippomenes seduce Atalanta from the race by giving him three irresistible golden apples to roll on the ground as she ran. Delayed by a few seconds each time she swerved to pick up an apple, Atalanta lost the race to Hippomenes and became his bride. Sarah felt her identification with her father, her competitiveness with men, originating in her relationship with her older brother, and her unwillingness to value the feminine were mirrored in this myth. Putting her experience in this archetypal context enabled her to be more conscious of her competitiveness with her husband and to change her automatic patterns of response to him.

Sarah attended a lecture on synchronicity and heard the story Jung told about an Egyptian scarab appearing on his office window in Küsnacht, Switzerland, at the moment that a patient was describing to him a dream of a golden scarab.[5] Moved by her own experience of synchronicity in relation to Kuan Yin and our work, the lecturer's statement "When the student is ready, the teacher appears" had struck Sarah as apt to our meeting. Although I was her psychological teacher, Kuan Yin's synchronistic appearance had also been a spiritual lesson for me. I knew intuitively that Kuan Yin would be meaningful in Sarah's development. I did not envision that she would also appear in my work with other women.

As Sarah tended her infant son, her dreams took up the issue of her father problem and the archetypal feminine.

> I am with my family, dressed up, attending a gathering. Afterward Mom and the rest of the children get in a cab to go to the cemetery to visit three male relatives' graves. The first is my uncle's, the second my grandfather's, and, I am shocked to find, the third grave is my father's. I don't know how or when he died. It is Eastertime.

> A beautiful woman and I are going places together. She is like the Queen. She is in real estate, very wealthy. She takes me in her sports car to a house she owns that overlooks the ocean. It is a contemporary house, all wood and decks.

The first dream reflected the death of the ideal patriarchal figures in her unconscious. Sarah's father's death suggested that she had been subtly freed from her dependency on him by the manifestation of Kuan Yin. Easter implies the possibility of resurrection, which pointed both to the tenacity of the complex and to the hope that a new attitude would be reborn in her. The archetypal figure of the Queen, the primary ordering principle of Sarah's psyche, which was previously relegated to a remote castle, has become a more immediate guide who operates in the modern world. In this dream Sarah has an internal feminine guide, wealthy in feminine riches, intelligently and lucratively connected to the land. Kuan Yin's appearance had caused a change in the Queen. The Queen archetype seemed to belong to both the spiritual and the psychological realm. Now that Kuan Yin was providing the spiritual container for the analysis, the Queen was more accessible to Sarah. This was particularly important, because Sarah's soul energy needed to be embodied, not projected out onto the spirit.

In the midst of grappling with uniting body and soul elements, Sarah continued to fear the descent that her psychotherapeutic work entailed:

I take my four-month-old son to visit Aunt Maisie at her house. There are more stairs than there used to be. She is in a little room in a bed like the one in the rest home where she now lives. I leave my son there to be taken care of. I am living at my parent's home along with my brother and his friends. I'm worried I won't be able to protect my son. I go to a garage sale and buy a huge machine gun. I bring it home. Joe and his friends say it is too big. Maybe I would want to stop someone but not kill them. The five of us drive to my Aunt's to see my son. I change him and take him to my parents.

Then I am driving a large car with my son and a woman friend through a kind of obstacle course. I have to get past a fruit stand and a huge hole in the street. As I am maneuvering around a deep ravine, both wheels go off the edge. The car is tilted. I calmly ask the woman to get out and take my child with her. She says the car will fall over. I tell her not to worry. I do fall down into a construction site, but by some miracle I land upright and I can drive away.

Aunt Maisie was Sarah's great-aunt on her father's side and lived in the same neighborhood when Sarah was growing up. Sarah visited her constantly. "I found a separateness from my family there. She is an honest, wise, very intelligent woman." This great-aunt epitomized the positive feminine for Sarah against all the masculine forces in the family. Sarah's fear of the unknown was projected into her child in the dream. She feared she had to resort to male weaponry to protect him. The guns symbolized her patriarchal complex. Her preschool son needed her nurturing presence as a mother, not her achiever identity as a doctor. In the second dream she descended alone, albeit awkwardly, without her child and survived to drive away, to pursue her therapy. In spite of her deep fears, Sarah remained dedicated to her work. She said her love for Kuan Yin was growing. And she cherished the lamp charm; the lamp-lighting image gave her hope. She felt that doing endocrinological training and going into analysis were both lamp-lighting experiences.

A year later, after Sarah had moved back to San Francisco with her family, her Aunt Maisie died. At her funeral Sarah read excerpts from Thomas Mann's *The Black Swan*. The action in this book revolves around a mother and daughter's intimate relationship during the mother's mid-life transition to menopause. The mother, Rosalie, is completely identified with nature:

> Words cannot express how she loved the spring, *her* season, in which she had been born, and which, she insisted, had always brought her, in a quite personal way, mysterious currents of health, of joy in life. When birds called in the new mild air, her face became radiant. In the garden, the first crocus and daffodil, the hyacinths and tulips sprouting and flaunting in the beds around the house, rejoiced the good soul to tears . . . her daughter had to admire it all with her and share her ecstasy.
>
> The rose season was utter bliss to her. She raised the Queen of Flowers on standards in her garden, solicitously protected it, by the indicated means, from devouring insects; and always, as long as the glory endured, bunches of duly refreshed roses stood on the whatnots and little tables in her boudoir—budding, half-blown, full-blown—especially red roses (she did not favour the white), of her own raising or attentive gifts from visitors of her own sex who were aware of her passion. She could bury her face, eyes closed, in such a bunch of roses and, when after a long time she raised it again, she would swear that it was the perfume of the gods; when Psyche bent, lamp in hand, over sleeping Cupid, surely his breath, his curls and cheeks, had filled her sweet little nose with this scent; it was the aroma of heaven, and she had no doubt that, as blessed spirits there above, we should breathe the odour of roses for all eternity.[6]

Sarah too had been born in the spring and felt it was her season. She had shared this preference for spring with her aunt. In the face of her family's denial of negative feelings, it comforted Sarah to place her aunt's death in the context of the natural cycles of the earth and of the feminine. She and her aunt had shared their love of gardening and had taken long walks in the woods together. Sarah's interest in observing and classifying things in nature had led to her becoming a doctor. As a child she had liked categorizing rocks and trees, animals, and fish. As a teenager she had spent summers at her Aunt Maisie's country farm, tending goats.

Losing her aunt, who modeled a femininity that Sarah was trying to amplify in herself, left Sarah feeling adrift. In the wake of her aunt's death, she was sick with a feeling of failure in regard to the tenacity of her father complex. She missed one therapy appointment because she was afraid of facing her feelings. Her vitality visibly diminished during this period. Then suddenly, with the advent of spring, she found herself furious with all the men she was trying so hard to please, and her zest for life began to return. One day, bereft at her aunt's death, Sarah returned to the jewelry store to buy the pearl-and-gold Kuan Yin. She cried in gratitude when she found the pendant there, as if waiting for her. As the spring season blossomed, she turned to nature, to plants and flowers; Earth received her mourning and healed her loss.

Sarah came in one session and said, "I feel wonderful about my Kuan Yin; to think I might not have bought her!" Acquiring this jewel was an outer manifestation of the inner initiation that she was accomplishing. She valued herself enough to feel worthy of it. Although she was still working hard at the clinic at this time, having the pendant and wearing it like a talisman in a velvet pouch subtly influenced her. She became aware of her developing feminine spiritual life. The Chinese say that if a devotee continually reminds herself of Kuan Yin's peace and generosity, she brings those qualities into her own life.[7] Sarah realized that Kuan Yin's compassion for the world resonated with her own ideal of saving humanity, which compensated for the guilt-ridden child in her psyche. The physical presence of Kuan Yin in her life reminded her to be compassionate toward herself.

Sarah's discomfort with turning toward her inner world and voice was reflected in a brief meditation she did in one therapy hour. With eyes closed, she looked within and said:

> Kuan Yin's spirit begins to break through the layers of masculine negativity. I'm never alone in the world. All my energy goes out. I avoid going in. Inside it is dark, a cave; it doesn't draw me in; it's cold, not lived in. I hear the voices of all I haven't done and should be doing. If I let the voices go, what comes to me is light, votive candlelight all over the cave like stars. It feels better, but it's still empty. The inside needs more time. The outside is all chaos and clutter; sparkling glass shelves, cut glass and cut stone, with light bouncing off all the surfaces. The skylight brings light in. Outside is a warmer, more positive, inviting place to be.

The Kuan Yin piece was the touchstone of Sarah's nascent inner life. As the Kinaaldá girl derives energy from the jewelry and clothing she is adorned with in the ceremony, so Sarah derived comfort and contact with the divine by wearing the Kuan Yin image. To access her Self, she needed more time. It was a slow, gradual process to let go of the compulsion to do more, to adopt a heroic attitude even when it was not called for. The theme of the garden continued to recur in her dreams and experience:

> We are living in an apartment house. Outside the windows of our apartment are two eight-by-ten-foot square plots, one my vegetable garden, the other my flower garden. The landlord rents another apartment to a family with a toddler. Without saying anything to us, the family builds a deck that covers my whole garden. I think it is good for the toddler, but I am devastated.

Sarah felt on a literal level that she planted gardens and lost them, because they had moved so often in the past years. But on a symbolic level the dream referred to the way she mercilessly sacrificed her own feminine nature to the needs of others. Her feeling of being devastated showed promise for change. Once again, she cared about tending her own garden.

Three years later in the springtime, after buying a house in the Bay Area, Sarah was able to express her special relationship to "her season" in her home. She stenciled a design of flowers—crocus, tulips, and anemones—on the walls of her bedroom and bathroom. Outside the windows, she planted a garden of these same flowers. She said, "With the murals, it doesn't have to *be* spring for me to feel that energy." She felt she was amplifying her inner home in the outer one. Meditating on Kuan Yin, she felt calmer at work. The book *The Black Swan* continued to be a source of Sarah's relating to nature as her feminine nature and feeling grounded there.

As Sarah developed a conscious relationship to Kuan Yin through the pearl image of the bodhisattva, she recognized the folly of her inability to set limits. Just before her illness called her back to herself, she talked about the exhausting possession with her work that she felt:

> I'm looking each day at the discrepancy between my stated values
> and what I do. It is painful for me to see myself making choices at
> every point about "time" and not feeling good about any of it. I feel
> like Psyche in the two tasks of sorting seeds and having to say no to the
> souls in the underworld who beg her for help. The only place I feel
> support for this work, for feminine values, is from you.

Sarah was feeling the loneliness and isolation that each woman feels who is in a deep analytic process toward becoming a woman-identified woman. Her work environment and colleagues supported patriarchal values of achievement and power over nurturing of self and family. Even her husband's pride in her accomplishments as a physician covertly undermined her attempts to free herself from her career obsession.

But Sarah was working on sorting out her priorities as Psyche had sorted the seeds. Psyche's final task is to go down to the underworld and receive a cask of beauty ointment from Persephone. Psyche is told that she has to ignore the dead souls who plead for pity along the way.[8] In this motif Sarah found her own instruction: for the sake of her development, she had to focus on her own inner path and not be lured into overextending herself on behalf of patients and friends.

As a participant in Sarah's meeting with Kuan Yin, who became her guiding spiritual light, I knew this goddess before BEATRICE came into my life. Thus when she appeared in Beatrice's early dream adorning the pin for her hair, I felt attuned to her. While Beatrice and I were pregnant together for the second time, she spoke of praying to Kuan Yin as her sole means of comforting herself. Beatrice's devotion to Kuan Yin provided an emotional tie to her lost mother. The feeling of compassion that had arisen in me from the moment we met dominated our relationship. Out of my own positive mother complex and affinity for the Virgin Mary, I resonated with her mother-daughter wound. The progress of our work seemed determined or fated by this deep spiritual constellation.

In a session when Beatrice complained that she was bothered by becoming more and more vague as she became more pregnant, I commiserated and shared with her my own increasing inattention to time as my pregnancy progressed. This was one of the rare occasions that we compared our experiences of pregnancy. The conscious focus in therapy continued to be on Beatrice; in the unconscious, the psychological reunion of mother and daughter quietly did its work.

A month after her wedding, Beatrice dreamed:

> I see the back of a woman, a gypsy woman. But I can see my own face. She says, "The baby is a girl."

A gypsy woman—Beatrice's own mediumistic shadow—tells Beatrice that the baby is a girl. At this point in the therapy we had activated several symbolic forms in the unconscious: the myth of Demeter and Persephone, that is, the reunion of mother and daughter; three other archetypal or spiritual female figures, Kuan Yin, the Virgin Mary, and Hecate; and two women with their baby girls *in utero*. It was a powerful feminine constellation including varying manifestations of body, ritual, time, instinct, archetype, and spirituality.

As if in response to the compelling combination of forces working between us, I had the following dream:

> Beatrice's baby is stillborn. She is in an hour with me, shocked, grieving, and angry, roaming around my office. I ask if she saw the baby. She says, "No," furiously. We end up physically wrestling as I try to talk to her about her grief and she responds with anger. I mention the miscarriage that I had last fall; she listens and calms down.
>
> Then we are in a hospital in the maternity ward with many babies. Some of them are ill. Two nurses each bring a baby to me where I am sitting on a long, low bench. I want to change the babies' diapers. I'm semi-bare at my midriff between trousers and shirt. One baby who has a disease puts its head against my bare back. Another baby also rolls over and touches me. I begin to worry about infection and my own baby. I go to ask one of the nurses about contagion. I am left with a vague state of anxiety.

The dream brought up the shadow of the process between Beatrice and me. In the dream, Beatrice's stillborn baby symbolized the psychic child poised for rebirth that Beatrice and I had been gestating between us. This dream occurred in May; my baby was due in July. Beatrice knew that I would be taking a six-month leave of absence from my work at the beginning of July. My dream reflected my concern about abandoning her; it dramatized the anger and fear she could never express about my leaving. Inherent in her fear was the threat to her psychic development and the loss of the nurturing mother she had regained. Beatrice had never truly mourned the loss of her mother. Instead she had maintained a fantasy that her mother would one day return to her. Here, the only way I had to speak to her pain was to remind her of my own loss the previous fall; invoking the dark Goddess had a soothing effect on Beatrice.

The dream also alluded to the permeability of the whole psyche in the mother-daughter relationship. Each of us was carrying an unborn daughter within us. In my dream, her stillborn daughter is now herself, and I have become her mother. This shifted us into a collective realm, the maternity ward, where I became afraid that my own caring for others' children would put my daughter at risk. My daughter is also myself. As a pregnant woman, in the intensity of carrying the weight of a deep healing process, I was concerned for my own psychic and physical contamination. I had to protect the incubating life from harm.

Psychically, Beatrice and I moved in and out of being and experiencing ourselves and each other as sometimes mother, sometimes daughter. With imperceptible shifts in identity and relationship, we merged, separated, and overlapped all at the same time. Our personal histories, our cultural adaptations, our ancestral predispositions, our present biological and spiritual realities intertwined and interacted, separated and reunited in a reenactment of the ritual experience of the matriarchal mystery. The reenactment was unique—a result of the unique combination of our individual personalities with the participation of our daughters *in utero*. Her despair at her mother's abandonment, my absolute knowledge of a mother's constancy; her wandering, my rootedness; her relationship to Kuan Yin, mine to the Virgin Mary; our shared experience of Hecate: all this wove back and forth into the complicated pattern of a ritual that induced healing.

The period of time following this dream was a pivotal point in our relationship. Nothing was interpreted; I did not tell her my dream. But I took the meaning to heart. I already felt a deep commitment to her and to our work, which included her pregnancy and the forthcoming birth of her baby in September. I told her that I would call her after my daughter was born and before her baby was due.

Three weeks later Beatrice had a dream that echoed the theme of the dual pregnancy, the psychic child and the actual child within her.

> I am in the hospital. I have been asleep. My husband and the medical team tell me I have had the baby. I can't recognize it. The baby is crying, wanting its mother. I know it is too early for my birth, and I can feel my baby kicking inside me. I am frightened to tell them. I don't want to reject the baby, but I know I am still pregnant.

Beatrice was in tears when she told me this dream. Her husband's band had had no engagements that month. They had not been able to pay the rent and other bills that were due. She said, "I can't take care of my own survival." There were multiple meanings to the dream. The psychic child was being born prematurely by my taking a leave of absence from our work. Beatrice was not ready to recognize or take care of her nascent Self; it still needed to develop in the womb of our relationship. She doubted her capacity to mother herself and/or her child. The next set of tests for the baby due to Beatrice's Rh-negative blood factor were also coming up. Without my support she was afraid of being at the mercy of an indifferent, impersonal institutional system.

The last dream Beatrice told me before my leave of absence also dramatized her fear about my not being there to support her through the birth:

> I am in labor in the hospital. My husband and a nurse are there. I decide to go visit someone I know in another room. She has already left. I am alone and realize the baby is coming. The baby comes. I need someone to cut the umbilical cord. I call for help; no one comes. I hobble back to my room. My husband is in bed, as if he is the patient. The nurse is having a cigarette.

In Beatrice's dream I have left the hospital before her, so she has to deliver her baby alone. In reality her husband was completely involved with her pregnancy and with the birth of their child. But given her history with unreliable men, she feared the worst. In a sense I was, like her mother, abandoning her to a man while she was in a vulnerable condition. Beatrice had no close friends to attend her during this time. With the exception of her husband, she had to face her initiation into motherhood alone. Before we ended that hour, I confirmed that I would call her a few weeks before her baby was due. I anticipated my daughter would then be around a month old. And I also told her that she was welcome to call in the interim.

I did not speak to Beatrice for six weeks. In the meantime, two weeks before my daughter was born, Hecate returned to visit me in an elaborated form:

> I am in the strangest den of enigma. It is the bottom floor of a house, but the windows are at ground level instead of in the wall or near the ceiling. It is a cellar or cave. I am there with my son. A witch-like woman is in charge of many little children and many animals.

Lions, tigers, and their cubs are all intermingled with the children. Both animals and children are eating from bowls on the floor. The witch is talking about having developed a new vegetable crop and shows me a closet or tiny cave in which she is growing mushrooms. I taste them, and they are surprisingly sweet, with a faint hint of mold. For some reason, the whole situation, though there is nothing overtly frightening about it, disgusts and terrifies me. It feels as though the space is a prison, stunting normal growth. My son is looking out the window saying, "Look, Mommy, streets!" He is completely unaffected, related to normal life. I wake with a terrible, stifling fear.

Hecate is there in a subterranean room amid the organic, undifferentiated nature of life. Animals, children, and mushrooms are all mixed together. The mushroom, fruit of darkness, is the nurturing food for childbirth. It may refer to a sacred mushroom, varieties of which are known to have been used in Dionysian and Orphic mysteries to induce an altered state of consciousness.[9] Hecate, the midwife, has produced her own variety of mushroom to expedite my delivery. Two weeks before labor began, I was psychically experiencing moving down and away, losing my hold on external reality. My three-year-old son remains the delightful link with the outside world. In the dream he keeps trying to draw my attention to the streets. My capacity for functioning was diminishing, even as I continued with the rituals of preparing the baby's room and closing up my office for my leave. Internally, I was withdrawing to Hecate's realm, feeding on her food with the animals and the children. Amplifying my inner withdrawal were my meditations on relaxing and riding the contractions. Every preparation was in the service of the archetypal and spiritual ordeal I expected the birth to be.

One week before I gave birth to my daughter, I dreamed about Carmina, who had suspended her therapy with me indefinitely about ten months previously:

> I am visiting Carmina at her home, observing her in her current situation, evaluating how she is doing since the last time I saw her.

This unexpected dream once again reminded me that a deep therapeutic relationship has a life of its own that goes on independent of face-to-face contact. In this way it is like all important relationships. My connection to Carmina and hers to me had always included the archetypal depths. On reflection, I knew that she would be happy for my forthcoming birth of a baby girl, and that the Demeter and Persephone myth that had been active in our analytic work together was being lived out in my life in a new form. Intuitively, I knew this would someday be important for Carmina, although I had no idea if or when I would ever see her again.

My daughter's birth proved to be different from my son's. My daughter was in the optimal position for delivery. When my labor began at home, I breathed through my contractions so well that I barely arrived at the hospital in time to deliver her there. Four or five pushes and she was out. Although the archetypal aspect was certainly there, earthquakelike, the brevity and abruptness were more like the animal instinct in my dream. There was no long, slow, gradual process of deepening relationship with my husband, the midwife, and the doctor that I had experienced during labor with my son. And there was no transcendent spiritual vision as I had experienced with him. It was something of a shock after the trauma of the birth to find that I had not left ordinary life at all for this event. The true initiation into motherhood had come with my first child. My relationship to Hecate was more developed than it had been with my first pregnancy. She had helped me to prepare and go into the descent in advance and nurtured me with her food.

The miracle of welcoming a daughter into my arms was no less enthralling for the brevity of the labor. I saw my petite girl baby with her perfect flower face emerge from my womb with great joy. When my daughter was three weeks old, I called BEATRICE. She was delighted to hear from me, wanted to hear about the birth and how my daughter was faring. She also told me the following dream:

> Kuan Yin presents me with a biblike affair, which she hangs around my neck. It is heavy, and I am rather frightened of it, but I don't think of taking it off. The fabric is dark green silk, and many buttons are sewn on it, with one continuous red thread in quite neat rows. At the outer edges the rows become untidy, as though waiting to be pulled into place. Even farther out, the buttons are just floating, as though their time has not yet come. I am fascinated by the bib, but every time I make a conscious effort to "read" it, it seems out of focus.

Here again the bodhisattva embodying wisdom and compassion emerged from the unconscious with intense purpose. Beatrice said, "It seemed like a life history, past, present, and future." The bib was reminiscent of the bib sewn in the Buddhist ceremonies to commemorate an aborted baby. The bib also looked like the cloth slings mothers use for carrying a new baby. Beatrice and her husband had been preparing for the baby's birth by acquiring such items. The responsibility of bearing a child and of having committed herself to life by becoming a mother felt heavy and somewhat frightening to Beatrice. The goddess Kuan Yin adorned Beatrice with this garment of honor and bestowed her with the psychological gift of life because her natural mother and stepmother had both neglected to do so. The threads of the future were "waiting to be pulled into place"; she could not read her fate. But the present was viable and blessed by a sacred feminine spirit. Kuan Yin had appeared in my absence to prepare Beatrice for her initiation into motherhood.

At the end of our telephone conversation, I told Beatrice that I would call each week to check on her until her baby came, and that I would be glad to come to the hospital to visit her. Two weeks before her baby was born, I had the following dream:

> I am visiting Beatrice and her husband prior to the birth of their baby. They live in a communal situation. They have another baby whom Beatrice is still nursing. I'm concerned about how they are going to handle the new one in relation to the older one of indeterminate age. I say to her husband, who is showing me their layette and buggy, "Poor thing, she never was the only one until she found you two. It is too bad it is going to be so short-lived." He doesn't understand. I tell him he is not taking the problem of sibling jealousy seriously. Later I advise Beatrice to continue nursing the older one as well as the new baby for the time being. She is relieved because her instinct had told her as much in spite of her husband's arguments against it.

This dream continued the theme of Beatrice's inner child's being under my protection. But her fear of a stillbirth, of death at my departure, proved unfounded. Here the baby is of indeterminate age but still nursing. Beatrice's husband could not know her inner struggle. But in the dream I enter their world in order to help him understand her. My calling Beatrice and affirming my relationship to her at this crucial time when her baby was imminent bolstered her sense of self-worth. It also encouraged her to tend to her inner development instead of completely sacrificing it to the external child.

The dream introduced a new theme, that of my relationship to her husband. I became the mediator with the masculine. A woman often needs to invoke her woman therapist as her double to empower her to stand up to patriarchal responses that could prove destructive to her budding development. In analytic work I at times have to be the psychological liaison between a woman and her mate, both affirming the woman's need to individuate and validating her partner's difficulties with her changing.

Two weeks later Beatrice's baby girl was born. Her husband left me a message, and I arranged a visit the following day. He said, gratefully, "You were the only person she really wanted to be here for this." This was one of the moments in which I realized how much I meant to Beatrice, not only for her inner life, but also as the sole intimate relationship in her life apart from that with her husband. The single other person she could claim any connection to was her stepmother in England, with whom she had such an ambivalent relationship.

I brought my two-month-old daughter to the maternity ward to visit Beatrice. She and I were together with our babies. We talked about her birth experience and about nursing. Her husband had valiantly seen her through the delivery, so her fears of being abandoned in need were not substantiated.

Subsequently I discovered that Beatrice's baby was born during one of the three main annual festivals of Kuan Yin, Hearer-of-Cries, which culminates on the nineteenth day of the ninth lunar month, September. The baby was born on September seventeenth. These festivals are celebrated by week-long gatherings during which rites and meditation center on Kuan Yin.[10] This synchronicity reinforced my sense of Kuan Yin's special secret relationship to this child.

In October I arranged to visit Beatrice at her home, again bringing my daughter with me. Beatrice served tea and biscuits, and we talked more about the early weeks of life: nursing and changing diapers and soothing and rocking and being on call at every moment. Beatrice was disoriented and felt a little lost, yet she was coping with the necessities and was concerned about what to do for the baby. She was experiencing the fuzziness of mind that ensues for a mother with a newborn. At the end of this visit I told Beatrice I would call her when I resumed work in January, but that she could call me in the interim if necessary.

My visits to the hospital and subsequently to Beatrice's home were the ritual culmination of our abortion, miscarriage, and birth synchronicities. It was part of our mother-daughter reunion in the unconscious, a celebration of life and of our being the vessels of life, a tribute to the Great Mother. Beatrice had told me during the course of her pregnancy that in England the National Health Service provided a trained nurse to visit new mothers weekly in their homes for a certain period of time after delivery. The nurse's function was to help the mother emotionally and practically with her new role. As her therapist I functioned as a symbolic visiting nurse in this capacity for one visit. The role of visiting nurse resonated with a childhood fantasy I had as a young girl of becoming a rural nurse and visiting people in their homes as doctors then did.

The extension of the therapeutic container to hospital and home, then, mirrored the internal process already active between us. The visits suited the need for a compassionate, present spirit of mothering and caring that is Kuan Yin. The mother-daughter axis and the Kuan Yin–Virgin Mary dyad in the unconscious provided a symbolic ordering of the boundaries between us. The archetype of birth flowed into that of mother-child relationship. Beatrice and I talked, nursed our babies, and experienced our rapport with our daughters and with each other during this critical phase of their new lives. The visits amplified the ritual that our once-weekly sessions had been and allowed us to resume work that January without a breach.

In the early weeks of my daughter's life, I immersed myself in the blessing of our milk bond. The day we came home from the hospital after the birth, my husband brought me a gift from the bookstore where he and our son had been browsing, the newly published *The Mists of Avalon,* by Marion Zimmer Bradley, which tells the legend of King Arthur through the lives, visions, and perceptions of the women in the story. Morgaine, priestess to the Great Goddess, has the strongest voice in the narrative. I read the book while nursing my newborn daughter. Existing in a state between waking and dreaming, day and night, the atmosphere of the isle of Avalon permeated me as my milk flowed. I saw my mother's face in my daughter's as she suckled and felt myself returned to my mother's arms as a baby at the breast. The gift of a second healthy child moved me to prayers of thanksgiving. Daily chores were once again infused with a devotional quality. And seeing my daughter's body each time I changed her clothes and diapers, I was struck with wonder, knowing that one day life could also be born from her. She was a manifestation of the unbroken, ongoing generational line between mother and daughter. My mother was present too, the grandmother in the line, tending our son and her granddaughter and me.

I loved the feeling of life moving through me, nursing my daughter, caring for my son. I was slow-moving, involved in day-to-day affairs in outer life; inwardly, I traveled to other worlds. I was pulled back and forth from moon realm to earth realm. I felt that once I had given myself to the gift of motherhood I would be able to go on to other transcendent realms with the inner certainty and satisfaction that I had served life in the fullest possible way. It was difficult for me to imagine ever being that fundamentally happy again. The primary beatific relationship with my mother was reborn in relation to my own children. My son took me out of myself into the world; my daughter brought me deeper into the inner reaches of myself.

The coincidence of my early nursing relationship with my daughter and my reading of *The Mists of Avalon* intensified both experiences. The book validated and confirmed many half-formed thoughts, impressions, and feelings I had been gestating for years. All the manifestations of the divine feminine that I had had in my own analysis, my life, and my work coalesced into a revelation of the Goddess's living mystery in women. I had always yearned for a devotional life. I had found a devotional place in my work, then in my marriage, and then in relation to my children. I felt knowledge and power grow in me as I meditated on the female mystery. The priestess training on Avalon resonated with the analytic training I was undergoing, but in a pure feminine way. The isle of Avalon reminded me of the Greek islands, where I found the power of the Goddess time and again after my travels initially took me there. There, where the Eleusinian mysteries were born, home of the myth of Demeter and Persephone, was my soul's home.

In the months during and after reading Bradley's book, one synchronicity after the other led me deeper and deeper into the mysteries of the Goddess and the practice of feminine spirituality. A woman analyst friend of mine who is a Buddhist priest came to visit and shared her perceptions with me. I felt a longing and determination to find a feminine collective with whom I could crystallize the experience of being a woman in a patriarchal society while working with the depths of people's psyches. I had several dreams in which I tried to no avail to connect with Marion Zimmer Bradley as a teacher.

When I emerged from my six-month leave of absence, I returned to my therapeutic practice with a richer sense of the mother-daughter mystery. The first week back at work I dreamed:

> I am in a small wooded park near my home. I see a briefcase lying open on a tree stump. The briefcase is leather, zippered, but has a feminine style about it. I look in and see a black pen with the name *Marion Zimmer Bradley* stenciled in white on the shaft and other papers of hers. I think "Aha! I didn't have to go to her. She came to me. I'll meet her when I return the briefcase." I think it must be her work from teaching at a school. But when I do meet her, nothing comes of it. It's not that interesting.

I recognized the pen in the dream as my black fountain pen. And I realized that I did not need Bradley as a teacher in the outer world; I had projected my own creativity into her. Reading *The Mists of Avalon* and knowing that other women were also finding themselves in God the Mother, amplified my personal spiritual source in the divine feminine. After this dream, I redirected my energy to the immediate reality of the Goddess in my life and my work and followed every vein of gold that glimmered in her direction.

Resuming therapy with my patients, I was struck by how in the course of our work many of them had found some aspect of the Goddess. Both Sarah and Beatrice had their deeply personal relationships with Kuan Yin. But each of them had found other feminine guides spontaneously arising to help them in their dreams. Sarah had, for example, the Queen, Atalanta, and Mother Nature; Beatrice, the gypsy woman and the Chinese obstetrician. And as the analyst and symbolic priestess, I was aware of other aspects of the archetypal feminine that were moving in their therapies: Changing Woman, Demeter/Persephone, the triad of Virgin Mary, Mary Magdalene, and Mary the Gypsy, and Hecate. I felt affirmed and sustained in my work with these and other women by seeing the Goddess's power in our culture reviving in their psyches.

Figure 11.
Demeter and Persephone at Eleusis.

8

Celebrating the Mother-Daughter Mystery

*T*he mother-daughter mystery is activated within each woman in the psychotherapeutic container as each relates to the other in ever-changing patterns of mother and daughter. These patterns may include any feminine dyadic relationship: sister-sister, granddaughter-grandmother, niece-aunt, friend-friend, student-mentor. Multiple variations on these interactions result in a dance of merging and separating that has a twofold goal of reconnecting the woman with her matrilineal strength and wisdom and facilitating her emergence as an individual. A woman experiences the initiatory mystery element through her own blood mysteries. In her therapy she becomes increasingly conscious of the meaning that these mysteries hold for her emotional and psychic life and, therefore, for her life in the world.

The archetypal mother-daughter pair in our cultural heritage is Demeter-Persephone (figure 11). The Eleusinian mystery ceremony that celebrates Persephone's descent and return reflects the deepest elements of a woman's psychotherapeutic descent, transformation, and emergence. The Greek word *myo*, from which our word *mystery* is derived, means "to be closed or shut,"[1] or "to close oneself after seeing the secret."[2] *Mysterion* means "a secret rite." A *mystes* was one initiated in mysteries or close-mouthed.[3] The Latin translation of *mysteria, initiatio,* brought the word *initiation* into our language.[4] In ancient Greece the Lesser Mystery, the *myesis*, took place in the spring at Agrai. The Greater Mystery, the *epopteia*, where the state of "having seen" was attained, was performed once a year in the fall at Eleusis.[5]

In the Homeric Hymn, veiled Demeter wanders, distraught and mourning for her daughter, until she reaches Metanira's house in Eleusis, where she sits grieving and silent.[6] All those seeking initiation had to imitate the goddess in her grief.[7] Veiling is introductory to the mystery ordeal. In an ancient Greek frieze, the initiate is depicted at the spring purification rite seated with head and face covered by a veil.[8] Shrouding of ordinary sight is a condition of any initiatory process that leads to personal transformation through contact with a divine source of life. In the dream incubation at Epidaurus, the supplicant closed her eyes in sleep, seeking a healing dream. A woman's inward-turning enactment in psychotherapy parallels the veiling and the dream invocation.

Confidentiality is a condition of the psychotherapeutic container, and secrecy was stipulated in the Eleusinian mysteries, symbolized by the *cista mystica*, a wooden basket closed by a lid.[9] Two Greek words differentiate secrecy: *aporrheton*, "that which was kept secret under a law of silence," and *arrheton*, "the ineffable secret."[10] The ineffable secret was the unknown and unknowable core of the mystery. Mysteries were not obligatory. Each person made his or her own decision to undergo initiation.[11] The terms *adelphos*, "brother," and *adelphi*, "sister," were used at Eleusis for those who received initiation together. Close ties of friendship developed through common participation in the mysteries. *Mystai* were encouraged to seek one another out.[12]

In long-term psychotherapy and analysis, a woman makes a voluntary decision and commitment to enter therapy. She must be "close-mouthed" about her process at certain times in order to protect the work simmering in the container. She must honor the secrecy of both what she chooses to protect and what is ineffable, or impossible to describe. In performing the ritual of psychotherapy, she undergoes a psychological initiation. By withdrawing behind the "veil" for a time, she dedicates herself to a new state of consciousness. At the end of the ordeal, she has enfolded her experience within, and the veil is lifted. And finally she develops an affinity with other people who have been analyzed or initiated, an affinity based on a shared experience of depth or meaning that leads to a more conscious worldview.

In the Greater Mysteries practiced in the city of Eleusis, the myth of Demeter's search for her abducted daughter Persephone was enacted once a year for over two thousand years—from before 480 B.C. to after A.D. 364.[13] Originally, only women were admitted to the Mysteries, but after the seventh century B.C., both men and women participated. The rites took place after the last harvest, on the nineteenth of Boëdromion, corresponding roughly to our twenty-seventh or twenty-eighth of September.[14] The initiates, who sometimes numbered in the thousands, relived Demeter's mourning, her search for her beloved daughter, and Persephone's return.

My fascination with the mother-daughter mysteries and ancient Greece arose out of my intimate relationship with my mother and the Mediterranean heritage she handed down to me. Through the rituals of the Roman Catholic church, especially the transformation mystery of the Mass and devotional rites to the Virgin Mary, I awakened to a sense of mystery as a child. One of my earliest memories is of being in a darkened church enveloped by the scent of pungent incense, the ringing of bells, candlelight, and the Latin liturgy of the Mass. Another is the feeling of being at the center of a secret as a six-year-old when playing in the nun's enclosed flower garden at recess. In high school, I fell in love with Greek mythology, and in college I studied art history. Then, in my early twenties, I found myself on an odyssey to Greece, where the ancient mysteries still live in the land, the sea, the language, the people, the temples. There, my past, my present, and my unknown future fused into an awesome experience of feminine wholeness. Every return to Greece for me is a ritual Self-renewal.

In woman-to-woman psychotherapy, the personal mother-daughter relationship is amplified by the archetypal dynamic of the Demeter-Persephone myth so a woman may experience the inherent mystery rite in her own psychology. In ancient Greece, the Lesser Mysteries at Agrai were required as preliminaries to the *epopteia* in the fall. The hero Heracles was the prototypical initiate for the ancient Greeks. He sought initiation before he attempted the final and most perilous of his twelve labors—to bring up Cerberus, the three-headed guardian dog of Hades. Heracles had to undergo formal cleansing of his blood crimes in order to be worthy of initiation at Eleusis.[15]

In the frieze portraying his purification, Heracles is barefoot, signifying his status as initiate.[16] He offers a pig to Demeter. The animal died in the initiate's place, symbolizing the death that the initiate would undergo in the rite.[17] In the Thesmophoria, one of the antecedents to the Eleusinian mysteries, women sacrificed little piglets to the Great Snake who lived underground, honoring the unrelated aspect of woman's nature so that they could return to their demanding lives of relationship with renewed energy.[18]

After the sacrifice, Heracles is shown seated and veiled as he is consecrated to the ceremony. A priestess waves a winnowing basket, *liknon*, above his head. The basket was an instrument in which grain was cleansed or sieved, to separate the wheat from the chaff. For some ceremonial purposes, the basket held symbols of fertility—bread in the shape of a phallus or pudenda or an infant, seeds or fruit. In this Mystery rite, the empty basket was waved over the initiate's head in order to purify him.[19]

Some years ago, when I was on the verge of entering a new stage of my analytic training, I had a dream in which my analyst was insisting that I buy a sieve to put in my office. I could not understand why he thought this was important. All he said was that he had had one in his office for years. He pointed to his sieve, from which emanated a golden light that flooded the room. I have come to understand that the sieve, or *liknon,* is a perfect image of the winnowing of psychic contents that goes on in analysis. A woman in psychotherapy unburdens her soul, which cleanses her in preparation for new patterns of consciousness. She and I continually sort and select out what is valuable to her, what will nurture her feminine individuality, and what will not. Purification alone has the power to make sacred.

At the end of the purification ceremony, Heracles is shown standing before Demeter, who is enthroned on the basket, *cista mystica,* holding a torch. A snake is coiled around her torch, another around the basket that contains the "secret things." A third lies in her lap. Heracles may now commune with the Goddess, signified by his caressing the snake on her lap. Kore is standing behind her mother, also holding the torch, the fire of purification, with which she lit her path out of the underworld. She and her mother both bear the light of consciousness.

The sacred snake, like the horned bull, belongs to the Goddess but also carries phallic energy. An ambiguous and bisexual symbol, the snake has always been associated both with earth's life-giving energies and with the abyss of the land of the dead. Coiled around the belly of a prehistoric goddess figure, the snake symbolizes pregnancy. Snakes live in the ground, communicate with the underworld. Persephone opened the path to the underworld, the unconscious, for humankind. To return to the snake is to go down, to return to primeval origins in order to be reborn. A powerful deity of rejuvenation, a snake was the guardian of the house in Greece. House snakes were fed offerings of *pelanoi,* honey cakes. The earth-born Kore, the maiden goddesses, were all originally house-guarding snakes.[20] When a Kore took human form, the snake became her attribute, the symbol of wisdom.[21]

In dream incubation the snake's appearance brought healing. Demeter, called *phosphoros,* "light-bringer," was worshiped with her serpents as a healing goddess in some temples.[22] Cold-blooded, invertebrate, the reptile is remote from us. The Goddess can be familiar with the snake, divine its wisdom, because she too is nonhuman, otherworldly. Heracles may touch the sacred snake only after he has been initiated into the mysteries that the snake and the Goddess share.

The meaning of the Eleusinian initiation lay in a ritual experience of the mystery of death and rebirth. In psychotherapeutic initiation, the heroic ego gives up its investment in control and willingly submits to an encounter with the unconscious. I find it fitting that the prototypical initiate for the ancient Greeks was a male hero who sought induction into the

Mysteries only when he realized the limits of his power. Significantly, his last labor involved a descent to the underworld. He had to submit, sacrifice, and turn inward in order to accomplish the descent. A woman's ego is often modeled on the patriarchal heroic values of our society. Her ego's perspective, or conscious attitude, has to be lived out to its end in order for her to see that a different approach is needed. She, like a man, has to experience the limitation of the patriarchal attitude before she seeks a deeper, life-renewing experience that has the potential to heal her wounds, restore her feminine Self, and re-form her feminine ego. Such a submission may take many years.

CARMINA's dream about doing a ritual of purification at the sea was one of many in which she was living the archetype of initiation inherent in the myth of Demeter and Persephone. In that dream, Carmina found her pregnant double at the sea. Her impulse toward ritual cleansing promised to lead her to self-regeneration. Carmina entered therapy at the age of nineteen, which meant she had to live into adulthood on her own for some years before she was ready for psychological initiation. An early dream while she was still in college made a clear statement that she could not yet submit:

> My mother dies.
>
> I decide that I need to go and see a doctor for my back. I am in a more primitive culture. I have to stand in line with many unknown people at the bottom of a hill. A woman appears at the top of the hill and calls a name; it is not always the same woman. She calls me and leads me into the woods. She walks over a black snake in the sand, glistening, coiled perfectly in the path. I say, "I can't go on; it looks lethal; it has a triangular head." She says, "Pick it up, and throw it in the bushes." I can't do it. I walk around it through the bushes. I feel guilty and ridiculous not being able to do it. She doesn't say anything. There is a nice path in the redwood trees. I hear a horrible scream. I know another person has either walked over it or picked it up and been bitten or killed. I ask the woman. She doesn't respond. I never get to the healer.

This dream reminded Carmina of meditating on shamanic paths and seeing rattlesnakes while backpacking in the Southwest. She associated the woman guide, who was wearing jeans and a shirt, with me. Carmina said, "It didn't feel voluntary; I felt helpless. I did a series of black snake drawings after I woke up." The polarity between passivity and active participation in psychotherapy manifested here. She had not yet chosen to undergo the initiation. The dream said that psychologically separating from her mother was related to her seeking that healing. Persephone had to leave Demeter to realize her fate. The reference to Carmina's back was reminiscent of her first threatening dream in therapy, in which I was touching her back: the back is the realm of the shadow; this indicates her healing lay in the shadow.

The theme of Carmina's relationship to her mother surfaced frequently. She talked about their closeness and how her mother's disapproval made her feel "bad." Carmina knew that her mother's intention was to care for her, not hurt her. But she also knew that her maternal grandmother had been cold and destructive toward Carmina's mother, and that the feminine had been devalued in her mother's family. Carmina perceived the generational burden that women carry in our culture; she had experienced similar devaluation in her own family. She said, "My father doesn't like the gut-level spiritual quality of women unless it is dressed up in a play, salt-and-peppered by society." Carmina's description of her father was "pure masculine mind that wants to bottle or contain my spirit, my natural energy, my core place." I wondered if Carmina's mother, burdened by her own lack of self-esteem, felt sad about not having been able to do better by her own daughter. I often found myself feeling sad for Carmina's inability to appreciate her own beauty, intelligence, and capability.

Demeter and Persephone were moving in the unconscious here both between Carmina and her mother and between Carmina and me. Internally, Carmina was experiencing the conflict between her mother-identification and herself as daughter wanting to explore life beyond her mother's realm. Her real mother served as the focus for Carmina's inner conflict. At this point, at the age of twenty-one, Carmina felt that coming out to her parents as a lesbian was less frightening than bringing a man home. Though her problem with her father was obvious, she knew that she would have the most trouble separating from her mother. Remaining in relation to women and avoiding men helped her resist that task of separation. The mystery snake appeared in the dream, but Carmina was not ready to encounter it. She could only objectify the snake in a drawing, knowing that in the future she would have to face the Great Snake.

A year later, another dream brought up directly the theme of the rape of Persephone:

> I am watching a strong black woman walk through some bushes on a hill. She is going to be attacked. I am the woman. I get raped. I am thinking with no feeling, "This is a rape." Then I recognize the hill. There are white buildings and hills with bushes. It is warm like Greece.
>
> Suddenly I'm inside a building. Men are watching women dancing seductively in a room. The men think the women are enjoying them-

selves, but they are actually doing it for money. A young man, a jock, an obnoxious type, is looking at me in an impudent way, staring and leering. I verbally attack him and tell him to leave me alone.

Carmina's fear of men was at its height at this time. She had become more and more separatist as she withdrew into a radical lesbian lifestyle. Her fear grew commensurately. It corresponded to her fear of the snake in the previous dream. The more she retreated into the alleged safety of the maternal or female realm, the more threatening the male world and men became. And curiously, the more intense her fear, the less compassion she felt for herself.

I understood Carmina's fear and knew that these dreams spoke to her fate, because it was at her age that I had found myself drawn into an initiation by the snake of the underworld. Living in the south of France, I had met a fascinating Greek woman, Cybele, twenty years my senior, who asked me to accompany her to her father's village in Greece. Unexpectedly, the fulfillment of my girlhood infatuation with Greece entailed my fall from the innocent paradise of my mother's realm. Like Persephone, I was drawn away from my mother, lured by ancient myths, Cybele's beauty, and my own instinct, into an experience of the underworld and the snake. Beautiful, passionate Cybele had loved dancing, singing, drinking, and the company of men. She had also been emotionally erratic, subject to both effusive demonstrations of love and hateful rages. In her, I had met the dark side of the feminine so thoroughly absent in my calm, constant, capable mother. I lived this experience both adoring and fearing the unpredictable Cybele, who, I learned during our travels, had a deep phobia of snakes. As a child, in Catholic grammar school, I had heard the story of the serpent in the Garden of Eden. Ironically, Eve's snake was the agent of my initiation into darker reaches of the soul.

Years after that first voyage to Greece, I understood that Cybele's fear of snakes was a fear of the unconscious. As Jung wrote:

> Exclusive concentration on the centre, the place of creative change, is necessary if life-mass is to be transformed. During this process one is "bitten" by animals; in other words we have to expose ourselves to the animal impulses of the unconscious without identifying with them and without running away; for flight from the unconscious would defeat the purpose of the whole proceeding.[23]

In fleeing the unconscious, Cybele became susceptible to its dark, cold unpredictability and acted out its primitive forces toward other people. Being involved with her exposed me to the cold, destructive side of the snake as well as to its life-giving, energizing side. Through Cybele, I was "bitten by the snake": I was exposed to a powerful negative feminine shadow and neither identified with it nor ran away. Meeting Cybele, I gained the dark, as Persephone had. I arrived in Greece a girl; I left Greece a woman, my reality changed, my vision altered. I had internalized a more complete sense of the feminine and a deepened, passionate attachment to the country, its people, and its language. Each time I returned to renew myself in the land of my soul, Cybele was always a part of these visits.

The mystery snake continued to be alive in my psyche. In my late twenties, on the verge of leaving for Zurich to begin training in Jungian analysis, I had a dream in which I was traveling with Cybele:

> Cybele and I are in a European town. We arrive at a narrow street that becomes a rope ladder. The ladder is strung across a vast sunny, rocky landscape, a primordial garden. The ropes have a tendency to close in on us as we walk. Inanimate objects follow us when I call to them, as if they were dogs or cats. It is definitely a magical place. Squirming along is unpleasant but exciting at the same time. Proceeding cautiously, I look up and see, far away, on the other side of the garden, a giant golden snake moving slowly, cobralike, toward me. It is almost translucent—at once terrifying and gorgeous. Excitedly, I call to Cybele, "Look at the snake." Then I remember her phobia and fall silent. Quietly, I look around, wondering with a thrill if there are others under our feet. We reach the other side safely.

This dream came at a time when I was feeling a new, differentiated sense of feminine eros. In tantric yoga, the Kundalini—the female serpent coiled in the lowest chakra, the pelvis—rises in the spine, bringing female energy and power to consciousness. Psychologically, the dream pointed to a separation between Cybele and me. Where she had feared the wisdom of the serpent and I had feared her unconsciousness, I was now intuiting a different way, a way that accepted the primordial ambivalent forces of nature within myself. The vision of the golden snake radiated with a light similar to that of the winnowing basket in my analyst's office. At the climax of the Eleusinian mysteries, the ineffable secret is said to have been revealed in a blaze of light. In the dream, I watch the golden snake safely from a distance. This cobra is not accompanied by a goddess; it is wild, free archetypal energy. I had to find a way of mediating its power through my human femininity.

I discovered that in Egyptian hieroglyphics the word *goddess* is expressed by the image of a cobra. The Egyptian goddess Neith appears as a great golden cobra. As the early patroness of the loom, Neith in her snake form is a goddess of life and fate.[24] Neith had been weaving my fate in the fertile garden of the unconscious. That golden presence never left me for long. Now, years later, in the container of my work with Carmina, the golden snake resonated with the black snake in her dream and waited for the time when she would be ripe for transformation.

As Carmina slowly changed, her inner daughter, a little girl who needed to be cared for, appeared frequently in her dreams.

> I am at the zoo, running around barefoot with bruised feet. I have to stop and put on shoes. In another part of the zoo, I'm in a locker room, waiting for girls to come out of the shower. Someone says, "Something is wrong with this little girl." I see a small but sexually developed girl whose beautiful little body is covered in a horrible rash. I wrap her in a towel, which soaks me, and tell her, "You're beautiful inside and out, no matter what they say."

Carmina's inner daughter is here pubescent. As she embraced the child (herself) instead of rejecting her, compassion transformed Carmina's self-image. In the next dream it was *my* daughter who became the focus of Carmina's attention:

> I go into a coffeehouse in Berkeley, order my coffee, and sit down. Suddenly I realize that you are the proprietress. I think, "Oh no, I have to leave; I've invaded your territory." Then I think, "No."
> I go into the back room. And I realize you have your daughter with you. She is a fifteen-month-old baby. I feel out of place again, but I think, "I just walked in off the street." The baby walks up to me. I think that I can't pick her up. Later the place is closing. It's time to leave, and I have to see you. I feign surprise, and you restrain me from speaking, "Shhhh." I walk out; I have lost my two women friends.

Carmina said that this dream felt like her first dream about being in my house, except that here she was of two minds. This was a public place, a place she had a right to be. Her fear of picking up my daughter reflected her old fear of intimacy with me and her deep sense of not being worthy of embracing new life. She continued to fear that she was incurable, hopeless. "I'm so awful. You can't know how awful, because if you did . . . " In the next dream, the relationship between my daughter and her work became clearer:

> I'm in your office. It's gotten very small. There are books all along the walls. You are late, and I think it's because you have to deal with your children. I think that's fine, because I want to look at your books. I am browsing. You come in having a fit, talking to someone. I'm amazed that I haven't seen this attribute in you before. You are much more animated than I'm used to seeing you. It is as if a two-dimensional object becomes three-dimensional. I am listening.
> Then your children are there. I immediately go over and pick up the baby girl. It feels like flexing an atrophied muscle. I know how to

do that; I've done it a thousand times. I am letting myself feel toward the children. I also fear that they are going to reject me.

Carmina told me, "Letting myself feel toward the children is letting myself feel for the work." In the dream, seeing me fleshed-out and vital, a full person, not just a receptor for her psyche and feelings, allows Carmina to engage with her therapy. When she observes me being angry, she recognizes that I have a shadow too; the shadow gives me weight. Only then could she dare to be involved. If the therapist remains detached and shows only partial aspects of herself, a patient cannot realize her own fullness.

Almost exactly five years after her black snake dream, Carmina's snake resurfaced in the context of her personal mother-daughter relationship. At this point she had given up her lesbian identification and willingly entered the mystery of her analytic work. Fifteen months after her return to therapy, the dream of the uncontrollable pet snake, a gift from her mother, occurred. This dream marked the beginning of her renewal.

In the dream the little snake appeared with fire and water, two of the purification elements from the preparatory ritual of the Lesser Mysteries. That the snake was a gift from Carmina's mother suggested that the connection to the Mysteries was alive in the unconscious transmission from mother to daughter. The snake was trivialized as a pet in the dream, yet it displayed an independent energy that betrayed its archetypal power. In the Eleusinian mystery rite, the snake belonged neither in the water nor in the fire, but around the great mystery basket, *cista mystica*, or in Demeter's lap. Carmina could not handle the snake in the dream, because she had not arrived at the final stage of the initiation. Significantly, the snake reappeared only after Carmina had begun to paint again. At this point, her creativity still manifested in unpredictable ways, rather like the snake in the dream. Its small size may have referred to the embryonic quality of her reviving creativity.

A few weeks later, the regenerative energy of the snake erupted:

> I am both a prince and myself watching the action. The prince is undergoing trials. I/we are attacked by pythons, snakes coming out of the floorboards. He has to go through this. Finally it is over. A mermaid appears at the end. She says, "You've gone through it. Here is an omen: Watch out about falling asleep."

Carmina's heroic ego, in the form of the prince, is encountering the snake. She is also a witness to the encounter. The mermaid is the symbol of the feminine shadow emerging at this stage of the process, helpful yet not fully human. Fish, like snakes, are cold-blooded. The mermaid warns Carmina not to slip back into unconsciousness; the initiation has yet to be completed. Carmina was undergoing purification rites of water and fire, feeling tantalizing and frightening impulses of the snake energy that would lead her to the culmination of the mystery.

Carmina's initiatory experience appeared random and tumultuous, reflecting the chaotic opposites of the unconscious. The mermaid guide spoke to an evolution of consciousness that promised emergence. But a woman's initiation in psychotherapy can only be seen in its entirety—structure, form, and meaning—when she is finished. By contrast, the ancient Greek initiate who had purified herself in the spring rites knew the exact form of the ritual she was to undergo in the fall at Eleusis. Accomplishing the initiation depended on her following the prescribed order of the ceremony.[25] She was required to fast for nine days preceding the procession. On the sixteenth day of Boëdromion (around the twenty-fourth of September), she listened for the heralds cry, "Initiates into the Sea," which signaled her to take the sacrificial pig to the sea, to bathe and be purified. On the seventeenth, she went to the temple of Demeter to offer her sow. On the eighteenth, the initiate spent the day at home meditating and making the *kykeon*—the barley drink seasoned with pennyroyal that Demeter had drunk during her mourning. Demeter had refused wine because the grapevine belonged to Dionysus, who was associated with Kore's abductor, Hades.

Early on the morning of the nineteenth of Boëdromion, the initiate joined the procession to walk the fourteen miles from Athens to Eleusis. The priestesses carried the sacred objects in baskets on their heads.[26] The initiates wore myrtle boughs in their hair. They all danced and sang on the Sacred Road. Wearing dark clothes and carrying a pilgrim's staff, the initiate followed in the footsteps of the grieving goddess. She and the other women bore *kykeon* vessels carefully bound to their heads; men carried little pitchers.

At the first bridge, the boundary between Athens and Eleusis, a woman comic played the role of Baubo, telling bawdy jokes. In the myth, her jesting and obscene behavior had moved Demeter to laughter.[27] The origin of her name is "vagina, or mock vagina"; she was always represented as a personification of female genitals.[28]

As stars appeared and night deepened, the initiate broke her fast by drinking the *kykeon* and proceeded with lighted torch.[29] At the second bridge she had to identify herself with a "password," a statement summarizing the acts she had performed to participate. Then, along with the crowd, she passed into the courtyard around the well the goddess had sat beside when she chose Eleusis for her temple site.[30] There the initiates crowded around the Telesterion, the temple center, which contained the Anaktoron, an altar with a pit chamber. In darkness, by torchlight, she waited for the culmination of her journey.

At a certain moment, the skylight, open to the sky in the Telesterion, emitted a great burst of fire and smoke. With this climax of the ceremony, Kore, now Persephone after her sojourn in the underworld, was called up. A gong imitating thunder was beaten, which sounded from the underworld with nerve-shattering effect. Plutarch says that the crowd was noisy pushing toward the drama, "But he who is already within [the Telesterion] and has beheld a great light, as when the Anaktoron opens, changes his behavior and falls silent and wonders." The hierophant (chief priest) declared, "The Mistress has given birth to a Holy Boy." In the profound silence that followed his words, the hierophant displayed a mown ear of grain. Ineffable things were seen. With this vision, birth in death was assured for the initiate. At the moment of dismissal, two huge water jugs at the steps to the Telesterion were overturned, with the injunction *Hye, Kye,* meaning "Flow, Conceive/ Rain, Be fruitful."[31]

Reaching back for renewal into the ancient mystery source, a month after her python and mermaid dream, Carmina's unconscious took her to Greece in the following dream:

> I'm in Greece. I'm trying to return to a place that I've been before. I walk a long way uphill. My beautiful cousin is there and an anonymous man. I feel a little shy. She says, "Oh come with us. We're going over the hill to Daphne's place. We're leaving at midnight." I have a vision of what I know about Daphne. She is a notorious dancer who takes young girls and trains them to be dancers. She lives in a colony on the other side of the hill. The people in the village are suspicious of the colony. It sounds dangerous and exciting. In my reverie, I'm afraid I have missed the time to go, but it turns out they haven't gone without me.

Carmina had studied dance as a young girl and teenager. She associated that activity with a feeling of being carefree and comfortable with her body in a way that she no longer felt. When she had this dream, she was leaving on her extended trip to Barcelona; she also planned to revisit Greece. The unconscious suggested that the journey had the potential to revive her dancing femininity in a ritual context with other women. There was a teacher in the dream, an older woman, sponsor, initiator, me. The beautiful cousin was Carmina's positive shadow beginning to emerge, more differentiated than the blonde or the mermaid. The journey was also the inner journey of analysis, of reclaiming aspects of herself in her pubescent years that would serve the initiation at this stage. The teacher in the dream could further allude to the Greek poet Sappho of Lesbos, who lived as the mistress of a community of women and whose poems rejoice in dancing, singing, flowers, and feminine beauty. Carmina was reawakening to her own beauty.

After Carmina returned from Europe, the mother-daughter mystery was wildly activated. Her seven-month study of Catalan and courses in art, together with other travel in the Mediterranean, had been exciting and fruitful. She also had had a few satisfying affairs with men and had found interesting roommates during her studies. But returning to her analysis she fell into a black depression punctuated by numinous dreams and insights that forced radical changes in her state of mind. First her relationship with her mother came up again:

> I am looking in a mirror. In the reflection, I have no face, it's blurry.
> Then a face is superimposed over the blurry place, a negative female
> image.

The night before Carmina had had a heated argument with her mother, who was devaluing her analysis. Carmina said, "This work means so much to me; I think about it all the time." A few weeks later she dreamed about me:

> You are saying, "You just have to do it; you have to ask." It's hard
> for me to trust you again.

This pair of dreams reflected Carmina's difficulty with separating from her mother. Instead of her own face reflected in the mirror, she saw her mother's negative attitude toward her analysis. Her mother's distrust of me and of Carmina's analytic work contaminated Carmina's trust of me. The shadow side of Kore's closeness to Demeter is the inability of the daughter to feel right when separate or different from the mother. This was a difficult and productive period in our work together. Carmina struggled to stay afloat amid the onslaught of her unconscious. I struggled to carry hope in the face of her anger and despair. I believed that Carmina's core was inviolable. Asserting my faith in the teeth of her distrustful negative mother complex, which was intent on destroying our relationship, felt like a life or death struggle. Some of Carmina's bee and birthing dreams occurred during these months and provided hope from within for her. Her creative muse also attended her; she was able to paint and draw to objectify some of what she was experiencing. Then the mystery snake began to return again and again.

A month after the mirror dream with her mother Carmina dreamed:

> I am in a garden with my family. I am leading the way. There are
> snakes everywhere. I am afraid but not afraid that they are going to
> bite me. My family is afraid. I am waiting for a baby to be born. A
> snake is going to be born at the same time.

Carmina told me, "I have lost my body and self-definition. I think to myself, 'This is so sordid; how can you have any faith in me that things will work out?' I'm afraid to tell you my dreams. I'm afraid that you'll discover something that will make you hate me." Around this time, Carmina's family did seek counseling. Carmina had been the "light-bringer" in motivating a search for consciousness about the family dynamics. In this dream, her feeling begins to separate her from the rest of the family: she is afraid—she recognizes the power of the archetypal world—but she is not afraid of being bitten. She was no longer fleeing the pain; she had submitted to her analysis and was participating in her fate. The birth of a new identity, symbolized by the baby, is anticipated, along with the birth of a baby snake. Carmina was getting back in touch with both her physical self and the natural world. She had psychically returned to the snake, the primordial source, for this renewal. The golden snake in me resonated once again.

A few months later, both snake and baby energy stirred again in Carmina's dreams:

> I am looking down into a rectangular pool. Something is rising, unfurling out of the pool, growing up and out. It is alive. I don't know if it is an animal, a monster, a plant, or a person. I don't know if I should be afraid of it or not. All I know is that it was once one thing, and now it is another.
>
> Then I am watching a creature becoming a snake. I am afraid and fascinated. I am sure this is the creature from the pool in a new form. I watch the snake creature slide under the door.
>
> I am dealing with an unmanageable baby boy, around eighteen months old. I am trying to get him into a special harness, like a safety belt, but he keeps slipping out. Later, I am watching him with his young mother, and he is just as wild, slipping and squirming away from her. I feel as if I am losing my patience. I am aware of a connection between this unmanageable baby and the creature from the pool that changes so fluidly and unpredictably. I don't know what to expect next. It's all a little uncontrolled and frightening.

Living the mystery, Carmina was undergoing a radical transformation that was reflected in the fluid and unpredictable creature changing before her eyes in the dream. The unmanageable baby boy referred to her younger brother, who had been physically and mentally uncontrollable. Both identifying with and feeling an aversion to her brother's affliction of muscular dystrophy, Carmina feared loss of control because she had seen its extreme manifestation in him and felt guilty about her revulsion for him. The snake-child relationship recalls the culmination of the Mysteries, when Persephone is said to have given birth to a boy. The mystery association in the dream had a powerful healing effect on the personal wound between Carmina and her brother in her psyche.

In the dream the snake-child relationship also referred to biological nature. The archetype of birth includes our evolutionary history. Mammals evolved from reptilian life. We carry the memory of our evolution in our bodies, as our psyches carry archetypal memories from civilizations gone by. As the embryo develops in the womb, it recapitulates the stages of our phylogenetic development. Through her brother's condition, Carmina had experienced an alteration in the evolution of a baby *in utero.* So her initiation into womanhood touched the embryonic beginnings of human life within her own body. Carmina was being transformed at every level of her being.

In the next dream, Carmina, as the initiate, drew closer to conquering her fear of the mystery snake. Her sense of trust in me was reestablished as she and the snake became more intimate:

> A woman is showing me her snake in a bag. I know this snake; we have a history in common. I can see the snake watching me through the cloth of the bag. We recognize each other. My friend assures me that I will not be hurt, and somehow I trust her.

Carmina said the snake was "a python with a human gaze." As her own female energy and power came to consciousness, Carmina's relationship to me deepened. Her fear of the snake, her fear of the unconscious, her fear of the unknown, her fear of men, had inhibited her capacity for intimacy. Instead of appearing as an attack by a swarm of pythons, as in the dream fifteen months ago, here the snake was contained. The mystery element is alluded to: the snake belonged to the other woman, possibly me, possibly Demeter. The bag is analogous to the mystical basket that contains the secret. The snake is Demeter's familiar, humanized in our relationship. Carmina saw a larger order of meaning to the snake. Out of that recognition, our intimacy could serve the motivating purpose in her psyche.

Recognizing a higher order of relationship to the snake gave Carmina the courage to separate from her mother. She dreamed:

> I'm telling my mother good-bye, telling her, "Enough. I'm not going to do it anymore."

Powerful feelings came up around this separation. Carmina was intensely angry at me because she felt completely alienated in her life outside analysis. At this point I felt Carmina raging as Demeter had raged, raging at the lost aspect of herself, her innocent daughter self, expressing the inherent feminine cultural wound. At the same time, she treated me as her impossible mother who had yet to rescue her/Kore from her cruel fate. I understood that in addition to her internal mother-daughter split, she was experiencing an as yet unbridgeable gulf between her deep initiation and the role expected of her in the everyday business world of the bank. She could not express this mystery to anyone but me. The discrepancy between her inner work and her outer life isolated and angered her.

But the unconscious continued to insist that she was where she needed to be. Just a few days later she dreamed:

> I am doing a science project about a snake, but I can't see the snake.
> I am watching my friend cure buffalo meat for her science project.

Carmina's association to this dream was that in the seventh grade she had done an interesting project on venomous snakes. She had wanted to be a scientist at that age. Here again, the snake is under control, safe. This reassurance helped Carmina feel more confident about acknowledging her sexual feelings toward men. She told me, "I have a lot of attraction to men these days, which feels like snake energy." One of the secrets in the Eleusinian basket may have been a phallus or a snake.[32] The unconscious was bringing together her fear, her instinct, and her potential for creatively bringing the two together.

Five months later, the mystery continued to pursue her:

> I'm drawing a bath. The water coming out is murky like that of a pond. I look down. There are long threads or strings in the water. They turn into snakes. Then they turn into more lizardlike reptilian creatures. They come out and start pursuing me. I try to step on one and don't get it.

The recurring image of the snakes or reptiles in water reflected the animal impulses of the unconscious that Carmina had to acknowledge and meet if she was to engage with them in a meaningful way that would lead to independence and full self-expression. Snakes and water were associated with healing in the ancient dream incubation ceremonies. This unrelenting immersion in the world of the snake for Carmina constituted an extended participation in the mystery ceremonies of ancient Greece.

A week later, a dream showed the liberation of positive energy originating in her body in the midst of the fear:

> I am at the beach, in the surf, body surfing. It is an exhilarating feeling. My companions get out of the water as the surf becomes more rough. I feel an enormous wave lifting me and carrying me helplessly toward shore. I am afraid and excited. The wave smashes me down on the sand, but this is part of body surfing, part of the game, and I let the water drag me across the beach.

The Kundalini snake in her spine was beginning to inform Carmina's body and self-image in a positive way. Her exhilaration and excitement allow her to plunge into the sea and undergo another purification. Two years earlier in the first sea ritual, she had been alienated from her shadow, her pregnant double, and dependent on me for the cleansing. Here she is at one with herself, enthusiastically on her own and loving it.

Simultaneously, Carmina consciously felt she was wandering around in hell, in the underworld, with no glimmer of hope for emergence. But, like Persephone, she had tasted the seed, and there was no returning to her previous state of innocence. The central image of the Demeter and Persephone tragedy came up in this dream:

> I am pregnant. I have been abducted, like Kore/Persephone and have been made pregnant by the man. I am writhing on the ground. There is a shadowy older woman in the background doing nothing. She got me into this to begin with. I say something like, "He will kill me." And then, "I don't want this baby" . . . and then something about a heifer or snake or pig. I am convinced that the child within me is a monster.

Carmina told me, "Since the weekend I have felt sterile and papery. At the age of three or four, I spent a lot of time digging in the dirt. When my mother told me about how babies were made, she said that the Daddy planted the seeds. So I went into my garden and put dirt into my vagina." The shadowy older woman in the dream was an image of my role in Carmina's analytic work; she saw her predicament as my fault. In the myth it is Hecate who hears Kore's cries. Eventually, she is the one who tells Demeter what has happened to her daughter. When Persephone returns from the underworld, Hecate attends her. The mystery myth and Carmina's engagement in healing her wounds were fused in this dream.

Carmina's fear of pregnancy was brought into the archetypal realm, where it could be ritually sorted out and understood. She had feared both the invasion of her self-contained femininity by the intrusive masculine and the result of such a union. In reality Carmina was involved with a new man at this time, and her fantasy was, "My lover is a thief, taking me away from you, here." She perceived a man as a threat to the relationship between two women as well as a threat to her self-development. In this attitude she was living the myth of Persephone's abduction by Hades. She needed to learn that she could have all three: herself, ritual intimacy with a woman, and sexual intimacy with a man.

The next dream, two months later, revealed that something had changed. Carmina was closer to embracing her fate:

> I am swimming, floating at the rocky edge of a tiny lagoon. The lagoon feeds into an estuary that eventually leads to the sea. As I am

floating, I notice with fear that there are tiny, yellow-streaked snakes swimming around me in the water. There are also women who are moving out into the estuary, toward the sea. They are going to meet bigger snakes that are swimming in from the sea to meet them. This takes the form of an individualized ritual for each one of them. There is an element of fear in each confrontation, but the fear is tempered by enthusiasm for meeting the challenge. No one is quite sure what "meeting the snake" will mean, but I can clearly see these creatures swimming up the estuary toward the women. My three high school girlfriends are there. One of them takes her shirt off and wades into the water. Even a girl I don't admire is going to meet the snake. I am hanging back, afraid, but I know I am going to go.

The feeling of the dream for Carmina was one of "taking on the snake," riding the rapids. She felt the value in doing this and felt happy when she woke up from the dream. She also said that her period had started that weekend, and as usual she had experienced a profound relief when bleeding began. Some traditions attribute a woman's bleeding to the bite of the snake.[33] The snake is also associated with menstruation; it sheds its skin as a woman's uterus sheds its lining. Giving herself to her moon cycle in a reverent way, Carmina was reconnecting to the prehistoric snake goddess of regeneration[34] and finding a periodic purification and rebirth in her monthly cycle.

As Carmina described the rhythm of her cycle, I remembered a month in Greece when I had spontaneously enacted a ritual of menstrual purification and experienced a mystical sense of oneness with nature. Unexpectedly, unprepared, I had begun to bleed one night. All the next day, I sat on the rocks with Cybele at the edge of the Mediterranean Sea, washing the blood from my body into the sea with every wave. It was a mysterious, moving experience—the unity of my blood and the living waters.

Learning to ride the waves of her menstrual cycle with more equanimity, Carmina's relationship to her inner daughter and to me became more differentiated:

> I am taking care of a little girl, three or four years old, who looks like me. I am taking myself/her to a nice new school, introducing her to a new situation. She is also sick, so I am taking her to the doctor. I tell her that she has a nosebleed, although I don't see any blood. There is no obvious illness. The child begins to cry, because she doesn't want to have a nosebleed. I comfort her as I am getting antibiotics. Another woman with a child is present. There is confusion with the antibiotics.

> At the end you are there. I am sitting in my usual chair. You ask me, "Did you put henna in your hair?" I say no. You say, "It looks really nice." Then I look at you, and your hair is gray on one side.

Carmina said, "You are giving me something, and you have a lot of red in your hair. I feel more equal to you now, but I am aware that we are at different life stages." The nosebleed reminded Carmina of her premenstrual days, in which she craved comfort. Care of the child within was critical to Carmina's healing. "I want to let my heart melt and be open to art." As she mothers her symbolic daughter, she is differentiating from me, seeing me changing as Changing Woman does, seeing my hair turn gray, seeing me as older. This dream heralded our termination fifteen months later.

Carmina's snake energy moved into more accessible form and her tentative yet increasingly successful efforts to make relationships with men also began to support her initiation:

> I'm in an estuary at the point where it goes out into the ocean. I'm swimming out with a man partner through clear water. I want some long, snaky pieces of seaweed that I see. He says, "That's right, fertilizing kelp to take to the delta." I take an enormous rope piece. The ocean becomes frightening. We hold hands. He goes under once, but we get back to shore and at the end are walking over the rocks, holding hands.

Carmina had ambivalent feelings about this dream. She said at first she felt energized when she woke up but then later felt bitter because "I felt I was drowning that day." The positive sense of relationship and self-fertilization present in the dream was not being directly manifested in Carmina's life. She was angry with me for affirming her unconscious process when consciously all she could do was cry, eat, sleep, and feel frustrated. Her state of frozen despair and blocked creativity began to dissolve when she finally asserted that she wanted to go back to school in art and took steps in that direction. Previously, she had not allowed herself to take her art seriously for fear of failing at it. In this dream, Carmina, at home in the purifying waters of her own psyche, is relating to her inner male partner. The snaky, fertilizing kelp symbolized her own regenerative forces at work.

SARAH's symbolic participation in the Mysteries and in the Demeter-Persephone myth was also played out in her conscious and unconscious relationship to her mother and to me. Although Sarah's conscious identification was with her father, early in the therapy she became aware of her unconscious alliance with her mother. She told me, "I call my mother when my husband won't listen to me. I fear a deeper intimacy with him. I depend on my mother's power." Instead of asking her husband for direct, real relationship, Sarah, in a nice but manipulative way, exercised covert power in relation to her husband. She did not feel strong enough as a woman to stand up to him as an equal. Her controlling tendency came, however, not from a wish to dominate but from a feeling of inadequacy in herself.

Sarah had a dream within a dream that expressed the complexity of the mother-daughter relationship in woman-to-woman psychotherapy.

> I have a negative dream in which I am in a mazelike shopping center at night. I am aware of cement everywhere and cold, black, angular shadows. I am upset.
>
> Then I go to see you. You suggest we go to the site of the dream. I drive us there. We visit a small restaurant. You feel it is important that I relive the dream. We talk about the dream in the car.
>
> Afterward we drive back to my parents' house. No one is home. I am trying to decide where we should sit. You say we should sit in my parents' room. We sit on the bed and talk. My parents come home and knock on the door. My mother says, "That woman is in there." We stay a while and talk.

In the dream Sarah initially experiences the dream labyrinth as alien and alienating. I—as her inner therapist—suggest a reenactment of that experience, as if Sarah needs the reality of her unconscious affirmed. I am in control, and that is disquieting for Sarah, who is accustomed to being in charge. In Sarah's parents' home, I suggest the parental bed as the place where we should sit and talk. This showed that our work needed to affect her childhood perception of her parents' relationship. In the dream, her inner mother disapproves of the therapeutic invasion. In our female triangle, Sarah's maternal voice resisted the changes that the daughter was making toward freeing herself from patriarchal identification. At this point I was on the verge of becoming a mother for the first time, so the mother archetype was alive in a new way between us. Previously, Sarah could feel herself to be the older and wiser one of us, because she was already a mother, living into that identity. I had sometimes felt daughterly in relation to her authoritativeness. But different dynamics were now being activated. In the dream, both my voice and Sarah's mother's voice are stronger than Sarah's.

Sarah's reluctance to submit to her own psychological development came up again and again. She said, "I'm afraid of going into therapeutic work deeper. I fear the loss of control. I'm afraid I'll find out that I'm the opposite of the good girl—the bad girl. My ability to function in the outer world is detrimental to my going in and facing the unknown." Instead of taking up her initiation and confronting the snake, Sarah continued to struggle with her relationship to her husband and the male doctors with whom she worked.

A dream about a year later brought up the rape theme again:

> I am in a high-rise hotel complex. There are many swimming pools, as in Costa Rica, but I can also see the ocean. Earlier I have

been raped. I am in my room changing into a bathing suit. I don't have it on yet. A black man with a key comes into the room. I start to scream when we look at each other. The scream doesn't come out loud. But I continue to scream and scream as he forcefully rapes me. No one comes to help me or to stop him. I feel frustrated. After he leaves I go to find help from friends. Then I tell everyone on a loudspeaker in the complex what has happened, publicly asking people for help.

As a single woman before entering medical school, Sarah had spent a year in Costa Rica doing a special studies program working with native women in obstetrics and gynecology. She had loved the work and had enjoyed her tropical stay as a sensual interlude away from her family. On one level the dream referred to the problem of male violence toward women in our culture; on another to Sarah's difficulty with expressing her feelings with her father or her husband, both of whom she felt forced her into being a good girl or a good woman. Also, in her work as a doctor, she often felt forced into a role dictated by the patriarchal power structure of the clinic in which she worked.

Her Costa Rican stay had been a positive journey of self-exploration, in which she had been able to express her sexuality freely in "another land" in a way she wouldn't have allowed herself to do closer to home. But she had compartmentalized her sexuality so that her ego identity as a father's daughter remained unquestioned. Her attempt in the dream to make the rapes public referred to her needing to bring the different compartments in herself into relation to one another. In the process of becoming whole, she became aware of her conflicting attitudes toward men and maleness.

Persephone's fate forces Demeter to come to terms with herself and her motherhood in a different way. In the therapeutic relationship with Sarah, I was the woman/mother/daughter facilitating the change. Although she was fearful of change, Sarah also welcomed it, as the following dream shows:

> I have your daughter with me. I call you and make arrangements to
> bring her back home. You give me directions about a windy uphill
> road. You are comfortable with the situation. The baby is in her infant
> seat in the back. She is wonderfully responsive. We go over a bridge.
> The relationship is very positive.

Sarah was pregnant with her second child, a boy, when she had this dream. But she had wanted a girl. She had never met my daughter, then nine months old. Sarah associated the dream to our previous session, in which we had discussed at length her need to amplify her feminine identity. In the dream my daughter symbolized the infant stage of her femininity that she was developing a relationship with through the therapeutic work.

It was apparent to Sarah that her wish for a girl child included her own longing to feel like a woman. And she thought that having a second son would give her the opportunity to nurture her femininity in a different way, without projecting it on a daughter.

Sarah named and defined her inner daughter when, five years after she terminated therapy, she gave her consent to be part of this book and took the name of Sarah. According to Robert Graves, "Since Sarah was a Laughing Goddess and her progeny was destined to be 'like the sand of the sea shore,' she was evidently a Sea-goddess of the Aphrodite type."[35] Unknowingly, Sarah chose a Goddess power of beauty and sexuality, a variation of her Mary Magdalene shadow, when she assumed this name.

Sarah had been aware of a little girl, her inner daughter needing to be cared for, from an early dream:

> A little girl is in a room in bed with the lights out. I am watching from a distance, but I am also there. I see a shadow under the door. Someone is pacing back and forth in front of the door. I am afraid for the little girl, but I feel helpless. I know a dirty old man is out there. Finally he tries to come in. I grab the girl's hand and run away with her to the other end of house. Her mother runs and tries to delay him. Then I look back, and her mother is fighting him. He is fat and drunk, despicable. More and more of the mother is disappearing into or underneath him. I keep saying, "Run, run." But *I* have to run to save myself and the little girl.

The dream evoked Sarah's memory of hearing her brother outside her bedroom door. She had felt in control of the sexual play with her brother, but in the dream she feels helpless and has to flee to save the child. Sarah is mother, daughter, and little girl here. In reality, Sarah's mother had known nothing of the relationship between Sarah and her brother. She and her brother were acting out the repressed sexual shadow in the family. The mother in the dream is left to fight the lecher and be raped. This corresponds to an element of the Homeric myth in which Demeter tells a story of her own rape when she arrives in Eleusis.[36] The mother-daughter mystery involves the empathy and participation of each in the other's experience.

A year later, home on leave with her new baby and school-age son, yet attempting to keep up with her endocrinological research, Sarah had a dream in which the mystery snake briefly appeared.

> A woman is being dragged along by a man and then pulled downstairs. He shows her a snake closeup, and she throws up.

Sarah said that she liked snakes and had wanted to be a zookeeper at one point in her childhood, but she recognized her revulsion for the snake in this dream as her fear of the psychological descent. The abduction referred both to her patriarchal identification and to the potential for a deeper experience of the mystery. But her fear, her responsibility for her young children, and her professional life now prevented her from letting go to the unconscious. The combination of demands was absorbing all her energy.

Sarah's deeper experience of the mystery came through the recurrence of Crohn's disease symptoms, which finally forced her to stop work altogether when her second son was two years old. After a painful, invasive medical procedure she dreamed:

> I am walking somewhere. A woman comes up and says a plane has crash-landed. Two other planes are available. She says she will fly one, I the other. She leaves me with my plane. I am standing inside near the cockpit. A cupboard falls open, and bricks fall out. I run over, shove them back in, and close the door. The sign reads: *radioactive*. In a sudden rush, I fear uranium, cancer, and terrible long-term consequences. I run to find my husband. I want to wash my hands.

Sarah felt terrible after the diagnostic procedure, which had been performed by two insensitive male doctors. The dream reinforced her sense of contamination and violation. Sarah did not believe she had a right to feel humiliated; she felt she was somehow at fault for reacting to the procedure with horror. At this point in her life, Sarah crash-landed. Besieged by the symptoms of her disease, she was being forced to abandon her work. She could not simply take off on another mission—her symbolic contamination by the procedure could not be ignored.

Sarah called me after the medical test and the dream, asking for help to contain the horror of what she was going through. I was struck by the dream wish for a purification: "I want to wash my hands." She felt polluted. Sarah and I had been working together for nine years. An impulse arose in me—similar to the one that had arisen eight years previously when I had found the silver charm of Kuan Yin—to enact the dream message for Sarah. Before the next session, I prepared a cleansing ritual for her, which we performed in the first ten minutes of the hour. It was a simple ritual involving the lighting of candles, a blessing with water, and an invocation to Kuan Yin. The enactment symbolized renewal of both body and soul. The purification paralleled the first stage of the Eleusinian mysteries.

Enacting the dream message was renewing for Sarah, but she also had other responses. The cleansing ritual brought up her feelings of loss about the miscarriage between her sons' births. She wondered again if the baby had been a girl. She said, "I try to deny that there is anything wrong with me. You take me to a dark place, the shadow of the father-identified daughter. Your visiting me in my home and doing the ritual makes me feel more vulnerable. It validates my having to take leave." Ritual creates internal space for a woman. In that internal place she finds feelings and experiences that she never has room for in her busy external life. It opens a woman to her own depths. This purification ritual opened Sarah to her own vulnerability, which then allowed her to submit to her fate with a new attitude that included the value of her inner world.

BEATRICE had lived out the myth of Demeter and Persephone in her waking life. In her case, however, her mother had given her over to the strange man, the first of many men who had led her into an underworld existence. Beatrice's seduction at the age of seventeen by the American journalist who took her to Vietnam had been only part of her descent into the land of the dead. When she met me, Beatrice was pulled back into the mother-daughter relationship in our therapeutic container. She was also drawn immediately into her feelings about being pregnant and undergoing an unwanted abortion. While trying to integrate the meaning of these events, she became pregnant again, married, and bore her daughter. The biological definition of her womanhood continued until her baby was weaned. While she was living the early symbiotic stage of motherhood, finding her lost mother in her own daughter and in me, she was protected from facing the terrors of her past. But the terrors lurked, waiting for her energy to be freed. Two years before Beatrice terminated her work with me because she moved away, she had a disturbing dream that showed her work was not at an end:

> I am lying down. A snake crawls underneath my back to bite me. First it comes at me from the front, but when it realizes I can see it, it goes behind and under my back. It has black wriggles on it.

Beatrice regarded snakes as "evil, vicious, and representative of false hopes." She had an image of snakes rushing into the shrubbery in Asia and Vietnam. But most telling, she said, "This dream is about my experience of self-rejection, my emptiness. My grandmother made the greatest impression on me. She was a strong matriarchal figure, feminine and vain. But I don't know what it means to be feminine; I have modeled myself after men in business." The dream said that Beatrice could not avoid confronting her own demon snake. Although at this point she is refusing to engage with it eye to eye, it finds an unseen way to get her. The black wriggles on the snake are the zigzag pattern of the waters of life, represented at Çatal Hüyük. Although the snake threatens evil and death here, the energetic wriggles show that rebirth is also possible.

Beatrice's daughter was almost two years old when she had this dream. Beatrice had found much healing in her relationship to her daughter and to me as symbolic mother. But she could not continue to avoid confronting her deeper wounds. Her feelings of emptiness and self-rejection originating in her mother's rejection of her as a child had to be met psychologically with the same intensity and depth that the biological synchronicities of our pregnancies had engendered.

In the downgoing and uprising serpentine spiral of the psychotherapeutic ritual, resistance must always be respected. Fear of being bitten by the animals of the unconscious, of making the dark descent, always serves a psychological purpose. A woman has to make this journey at her own pace, in her own way. It is essential that she be grounded in her external life of friends, family, and work. Her ego's resistance provides the necessary restraint to protect a woman from an overwhelming flooding of unconscious contents and to make the work progress in a slow, self-controlled way. Beatrice had good reason to fear the impact of the cumulative collective evil she had been subjected to in her life. For Sarah, the denial of evil in her Catholic family and schooling had created an enormous shadow problem in the unconscious. And Carmina's repression of the negative aspect of her relationship with her disabled brother had festered as a huge, dark wound in her psyche. I was always grateful for the internal barriers that monitored the pain each woman could endure as she was forced into the underworld by her own Self-motivating forces.

As each of these three women met the snake, the mother-daughter mystery was being enacted in our relationships. Merging and separating, we drew on the feminine source of life in ourselves through the Eleusinian mysteries. Elements of the Greek rites appeared in our work: purification, sacrifice, and withdrawal from the world. Separation from the mother was effected by a dramatic, dark, other force, often represented by an actual man. Reunions occurred with literal mothers, with archetypal or spiritual figures in the unconscious, and with me. As Carmina separated from her mother, she came closer to me and then moved toward separating from me as she realized her vocation in art. As Sarah separated from her mother, and longed for her lost femininity, her psyche reached out to the symbol of my infant daughter for renewal. Beatrice merged with me in the interest of her own survival and relived her mother's abandonment in the need to separate from her baby daughter. Each separation and reunion roused the regenerative mystery snake. As each woman struggled with her separation from and reunion with her inner and outer mother, I served sometimes as mother, sometimes as daughter, in her drama of self-discovery.

Figure 12.

9

Emerging Through Ritual Separation

A woman emerging from the enclosure of psychotherapy both celebrates her transformation and begins a new phase of life based on an initiated state of consciousness. The inner light she has created reflects a different vision. If a woman's emergence evolves organically, it flows out of a reconnection with her feminine heritage and a deep healing in an encounter with the divine feminine. She has become a woman-identified woman and assumed her individual authority. The enclosure has served its purpose; it is now a part of her. With her enhanced sense of self-esteem and self-reliance, she feels increasing independence. Through her intimate relationship with her therapist as sponsor, midwife, priestess, mother or daughter or sister, she has found ways of relating to her own inner feminine guides. Her autonomy includes the capacity to relate to her inner life without the presence of the ritual container. It may also include an awakening spiritual life, a realization of the divine in everyday life.

In terminating her work in the woman-to-woman container, however, a woman is forced to reenact the mother-daughter mystery separation again. Emergence is therefore both an end and a beginning. When termination comes about through the natural evolution of healing, the work of the emerging phase then becomes a delicate process of separating our psyches, which have become intermingled during the containing and transforming years. In that case I am glad to send a woman on her way, knowing that my role in her life has been fulfilled. The possibility of her returning in the face of a new problem or at a different stage of life allows the relationship with me and the container of the therapy to serve as a symbolic touchstone in her psyche. But when an external reason, like a move, prematurely brings about termination from therapy, I and she always feel a sense of regret about the process being aborted. In that case, I try to bring about a graceful suspension of our work, acknowledging the feelings of sadness or anger and affirming the loss. If possible, I also refer the woman to a therapist in her new location. The transformative energy of an initiation continues until the end, whether timely or premature. The dark labyrinth of the unconscious, a maze always pregnant with death, continues its quest for healing.

BEATRICE's termination in therapy occurred prematurely, because she suddenly had to move back to England. During her pregnancy and the early months of her baby girl's life, the ghosts of her past had retreated. But when her daughter was four months old, they reappeared, and she found herself in the underworld once again. She dreamed:

> I am looking for my stepmother's house in London, but I don't want to find it. I find myself in an underground maze, a library or bookstore. A European man is standing there. He says he will help me, but I know we are going the wrong way. The Chinese man appears, and I turn to the other man and say, "See, I knew he would help me." I know I don't want to find the house. I keep taking the long way around in the maze.

Beatrice was afraid to find the center of the maze or labyrinth where transformation takes place, for the central place is also the heart of the wound. Even the helpful Chinese man could not make her feel safe in this. Because her stepmother had denigrated and hidden Beatrice's Chinese ancestry, Beatrice had not consciously developed a relationship to her heritage. But it was alive in the unconscious. The dream suggested that Beatrice had to go back to the stepmother, at least psychologically, to complete her journey, even though she was still resisting that confrontation. In order to illuminate her Chinese identity, mostly hidden by her adaptation to Western culture and her Eurasian mien, she had to find her power as a woman and redeem the wounded masculine element in her psyche. With no father figure and many victimizing experiences with men until she met her second husband, the yang energy in her psyche had to come from an unknown place. The Chinese man in the dream seemed to be a hopeful sign.

Beatrice's psyche took up the problem of her wounded inner masculine energy as it was intertwined with her infant daughter's development. She dreamed:

My baby is in danger. Her crib is on fire; she is on fire. A man is standing next to the crib with a big ax. I can't do anything about it; I can't move to help her. I am powerless.

Beatrice said that once in the middle of the night she had found herself standing next to the baby's crib; she had been sleepwalking. "I was freezing cold and shaking. I'm worried about doing something in my sleep like picking her up and dropping her." Beatrice doubted her capacity to be a good mother. She and her husband were having another financial crisis. Without her steady income, his intermittent work as a musician barely kept them solvent. She was contemplating going back to work when her daughter was six months old. Symbolically, in the dream, her daughter is also herself, the new life she has touched in her therapeutic work. That baby too is fragile and needs protection; it is threatened by violent male forces.

As she worried about being able to provide for her daughter, Beatrice's Vietnam War experience and her relationship to Kuan Yin came up juxtaposed in a dream:

> I have been asleep. Someone is calling to me from outside. I run out to look. A great crowd of people is gathered in front of the building, saying, "Oh, it's up there, it's up there." The building is shaped like a Chinese pagoda, with a winding staircase inside. My white yak is climbing the staircase. The people all want to shoot her. I get desperate and start pushing through the crowd. Helicopters with guns are circling the building. Kuan Yin is standing there showing me the direction the yak went. Kuan Yin woke me up as I was saying, "Let's save her, let's save her!"

Beatrice associated the yak, a working animal that provided both wool and milk, with livelihood. The yak represented an instinctual mothering that existed through Beatrice's Chinese blood. The building was similar to the one she had lived in as a child in Shanghai. A simple but strong beast of burden, with its life-giving milk and wool, is in danger of being killed by the impersonal forces of male aggression. The helicopters and guns indicate the power of men and maleness over Beatrice and the mechanical aspect of her psyche that she used to distance herself from traumatic experiences. But the goddess of compassion is trying to help her.

Nightmares of her Vietnam trauma continued to plague her:

> My baby daughter is lying in a custom-made glass coffin. She is dressed in a bridal gown with a garland of flowers on her head. She looks like a wax doll. I have a dreadful feeling of loss.

> I am watching a Marine friend crying at the landing strip in Vietnam. As he cries, he pulls another Marine's body out of the helicopter.

I walk over and ask him to do it again because I have forgotten to put film in the camera. I feel ice-cold and very calm.

I am putting the plastic bib on my daughter. She starts to cry and looks at me in pain and fear. Suddenly her head falls off.

Two of these three dreams referred to actual experiences that Beatrice had had in Southeast Asia. She had photographed her friend's body as it was taken out of the helicopter. She said, "If I hadn't had film in the camera, it would have happened exactly as it did in the dream. I was removed from any normal reaction to death; I was defended by the camera." The plastic bib was an allusion to a device used during the Pol Pot regime: it was a portable guillotine used to punish children in the fields who refused to work. It consisted of a round wooden disc with ropes, which the other children pulled to cut off the miscreant's head.

The central dream of her daughter's little corpse in a glass coffin carried the immediate feeling for Beatrice. This dream referred to her numbed emotions, which threatened to cut her off from the direct feeling relationship her daughter needed. The dreams brought her past trauma into her current life. As she felt the first stirring of separation from her infant daughter, Beatrice's unconscious brought up the past with the healing intention of making her recognize her emotional alienation from herself and potentially from her child.

On the positive side, the nursing relationship with her baby continued in part the fusion between them that had existed *in utero*. It allowed Beatrice to participate directly in the powerful, primal process of nurturing new life. In this state, her reason for being, her identity, was given. I was astonished at her capacity for letting go and immersing herself in the pregnancy and delivery. The internal pull toward having a child, crystallized as it was around the image of Kuan Yin, was incarnated in a beautiful surrender of her own ego to the process of becoming a mother. In the early months, she devoted herself entirely to the baby. When her daughter was seven months old, Beatrice had the following dream:

I come home and pick my daughter up. She is wearing a long, blue gown, like a christening gown. It is bordered by a dark brown band at the base with green on the top. It looks like blue sky, ocean, and land. It is like watching the earth moving, Mother Nature in the raw.

Beatrice said, "I am basing my life on her." Through the nursing relationship, Beatrice had touched back into the primal Mother/Nature archetype and was healing herself in the relationship with her daughter. Given Beatrice's history, and her own deep need to experience the oneness that she had apparently lacked as an infant, she understandably erred on the side of giving up too much of her identity to her daughter in the early months. Seeing them together in my office, I observed that Beatrice used nursing as the main definition of her role with her daughter. Instead of making an attempt to differentiate and interpret the baby's needs, she automatically put her to the breast. For Beatrice, the nonreflective merging was wonderful, but the baby increasingly required more differentiated responses from her mother. Beatrice's development of her own yang energy would help her in this respect. In Jung's view, differentiation, discrimination, and separation are seen as part of the masculine principle of *logos,* as opposed to the feminine principle of *eros,* relatedness.[1] Although this distinction has been widely debated by Jungian-oriented feminists in recent years, I continue to find the terms useful in describing what is happening in the male-female polarity in the psyche.[2]

At this point my psyche took up Beatrice's task in relation to the masculine. The same month that she was struggling with her demons, I dreamed that I was attending her as midwife in a new pregnancy and delivery that culminated in the birth of a baby boy. I understood the boy as a psychological child we had conceived and been gestating between us. The baby symbolized her missing logos energy. One of the mysteries of feminine creativity is that a woman can give birth to her opposite, to maleness. In woman-to-woman psychotherapy, the mystery is symbolically enacted as two women conceive and give birth to a new way of being. In the Eleusinian mysteries, the culminating announcement is "The Mistress has given birth to a Holy Boy." The child that Persephone births in the underworld promises rebirth for the Eleusinian initiate. The baby boy in my dream also alluded to a cultural rebirth of positive masculine energy that is not part of the patriarchal power structure.

The Chinese term *yang* speaks to basic oppositional forces in human beings, rather than reflecting the patriarchal male role in our society. The changing image of yin and yang combined in a circle symbolizes the complete individual psyche. The psychological impulse toward wholeness makes it imperative for women to realize the yang energy in themselves, but yang and yin, logos and eros, have been so distorted and split in patriarchal culture that it is very difficult for a union of opposites to be accomplished. Men eschew the female/eros/yin, which they equate with weakness; women resist the patriarchal dominance and control that they associate with male/logos/yang. For wholeness, men need relatedness; women need differentiation.

Male and female energies in the Tiyyar tribe of the province of North Kerala, India, are clearly delineated.[3] The Tiyyar girl becomes a woman by being ritually "defined both in opposition to and in union with male elements." Unlike the Navajo girl, her ceremony, the Talikettukalyanam, or "*tali*-tying marriage," takes place prior to her first menstrual period. But like the Kinaaldá, the Tiyyar initiation lasts four days. The initiate is secluded for three days to observe the usual taboos on menstruating women, "as if her first menses had taken place." On the fourth day, she receives elaborate purifications of bathing, dressing, and ornamenting.

Throughout the *tali*-tying ceremony, the initiate comes into contact with symbols of maleness. She is sprinkled with rice, symbolic of semen; presented with a phallic upright arrow planted in the earth by her brother; and given an arrow during her seclusion said to be that of Kama, god of desire. Finally, she is brought into relation to the sun by lighting a coconut lamp.

At one point in the Tiyyar ritual, the initiate breaks a hole in a leaf covering a clay pot and extracts one of the small objects placed in the pot. This divination is said to predict the number of children she will bear. According to Bruce Lincoln, the pot that contains the objects symbolizes the womb, and the leaf covering it the woman's hymen; by piercing the leaf she enacts her own symbolic self-defloration.

Psychologically, this indicates the girl's control over her own body, sexuality, and reproductive choice. Several women I have worked with described selecting the man with whom they first had intercourse not for his qualities as a potential mate but, quite the contrary, knowing that he could never become a mate. A man chosen in this way serves as the instrument for the woman's rite of passage, her induction into sexuality. Personally, such a ritual choice affirms that the woman's sexuality belongs to her, not to her mate; archetypally, it constitutes a dedication of her sexuality to the Goddess, to serving life.[4] By contrast, Beatrice's early experiences of sexuality were degrading and abusive. She was utterly without a sense of the value inherent in her feminine sexuality. Instead of feeling that her sexuality was hers to enjoy and fulfill, she had seen it as a way of earning affection from the men she was involved with.

The name "the *tali*-tying marriage" derives from the high point of the Tiyyar ceremony, when the *tali*, hung on a white silk thread, is tied around the girl's neck. The *tali* is a small golden ornament shaped like a leaf of the pipal tree. The tree is worshiped as an embodiment of the god Vishnu and is said to symbolize male creative power.[5] By this simple act of adornment, the Tiyyar girl becomes a woman, a change effected by ritual rather than by physiology. The marriage celebrated is a union of two opposite forces that are felt to be male and female. These opposites are joined to create wholeness out of separateness. At the end, the initiate holds a coconut with a flame, a solar image, affirming the sun's power. Then she pours water on the roots of the coconut tree, bringing her fructifying femininity to her people's cosmic tree.[6]

In the Navajo and Tukuna puberty rituals, the girls are also brought into relation with the sun as a masculine force opposite to their femininity. Changing Woman is impregnated by the Sun, who, along with Dripping Water, fathers her twin sons. The Kinaaldá girl runs toward the sun three times a day, and her cake is a solar symbol. The Tukuna *vorëki* is initially hidden from the sun, then brought into full sunlight when she emerges from her cocoon. She also emulates the mythic heroine Ariana, who plucked the sun's hair. But in these two rituals, unlike in the Tiyyar ceremony, there is no internal union of masculine and feminine accomplished. Rather the woman's femininity, her oppositeness to the masculine, is emphasized.

Unlike the Tiyyar girl, for whom the union of opposites is accomplished ceremonially, Beatrice had to attempt an inner union through psychotherapy. My dream of birthing Beatrice's symbolic boy child was a ritual response on the part of my unconscious to provide the healing element in her psyche. Beatrice's bond with her infant and with me in therapy had recreated the threefold feminine vessel of her early childhood. In the therapeutic container, I was the wise crone, she was the mother, and the child was the daughter. Symbolically we each contained all three aspects of the feminine trinity. With the archetypal energies of Kuan Yin, the Virgin Mary, Hecate, Demeter, and Persephone activated at a deeper level, we had a multifold feminine constellation between us. The restoration of the old matriarchal pattern proved to be healing. But just as the pattern reached its perfect re-creation, a baby boy was born in the unconscious. The absence of the masculine in Beatrice's early upbringing had left her abjectly susceptible to men and unbalanced psychologically. She had to move on to develop the yang energy that would allow her to differentiate and empower her to nurture herself.

In the context of our work, that differentiation was also needed in order for her to separate from her daughter, to begin weaning, to go back to work. She gradually had to withdraw from the symbiosis with her baby and reconstitute her own identity, in order to foster the child's healthy development and her own. For Beatrice, reconstituting her own identity meant returning to, reexperiencing, her traumas of abandonment and isolation and her brutal war experiences.

Weaning is a powerful emotional and physiological event; a mother has to hold the archetypal and instinctual forces that arise for herself and for her child. As Beatrice began to think about weaning her daughter, anxious memories of her own mother surfaced as they had at the beginning of her pregnancy. "I can't stand to hear the baby cry, because I never got to say good-bye to my mother," she told me. Beatrice emphasized that she could not get past the question of why her mother had not wanted her. Having had her own child, she could not imagine a mother not wanting a child near her once she was there.

During these difficult months, in which the separation motifs with her daughter were resonating with Beatrice's forced separation from her mother and grandmother, I felt as if my sole function was that of compassionate container for the streams of conflict and sorrow that were converging and dissolving. I can only postulate that the merciful archetypal feminine, Kuan Yin herself, was incarnating herself between us to receive the deep pain and the search for peace of the woman across from me. How else to explain her trusting me with tending her primal wound in spite of having had trust betrayed at an early age?

The physical weaning of her daughter provided a counterpoint to Beatrice's separation from a safely defined symbiotic role. In our sessions, we discussed the many times a night the baby woke her mother in order to nurse, her husband's role in the weaning process, and the overall demand on her emotional and physical resources as Beatrice began part-time work. Her dreams took up the issue of her personal identity as a mother and wife and its relationship to her wounded yang energy. During this time she regained her connection to the enduring quality of the yak that had been in her dream: she began to work free-lance for software companies and contributed to supporting the family. She dreamed:

> My husband and I are walking down a city street. I am pushing a
> pram. He is pushing our daughter in the stroller. I'm pregnant. The road
> forks; one is dirt and goes toward the beach, the other path is concrete
> and near houses. A woman is coming up the concrete road. I don't like
> her. I am pinching her, being horrible, speaking snidely to her. She says,
> "I just want to find something to eat." I feel sympathy. She has twin boys
> in a pushchair. My husband says, "Hurry up, or we'll never get there." I
> say, "Go ahead—this woman is coming with us." I look down at my
> pram and see triplets, two of them aggressive, bright, cheerful; one shy,
> clinging, unsure. We're all going toward the restaurant.

Beatrice described her shadow figure in the dream: "She had dirty blonde hair and was covered with bruises, marks, and scratches. She is another me, the unmarried Beatrice left behind, the creative me." Beatrice asserts herself in an uncharacteristic way by telling her husband that this woman is coming with them. She takes responsibility for her abused, hungry, unkempt shadow. In the dream, Beatrice is pregnant and mothering triplets. She identified them as her husband, her daughter, and herself; the first two bubbling over and uncontained, herself the shy, clinging, unsure one. In daily life she was overwhelmed by the symbiosis in which she was immersed; the weight of her past and her own mother-daughter problem was adding to her inability to separate from the three-way dependence in her family. The dream insists that she needs to nurture herself at the most concrete level and that in doing so she would address the deep wound with respect to the masculine. The infant twins are healthy here. Perhaps the mute, retarded state was being supplanted by a new yang potential. Changing Woman gives birth to twin boys who slay the monsters threatening her people.[7]

It was reassuring to both of us that this dream dealt with ordinary human experience. It addressed her personal identity in the context of the current reality in her life. This contrasted dramatically with the previous onslaught of repetitious nightmares, suggesting some healing of her traumatic war experience was taking place. Here was a shadow figure of ordinary proportions with whom it might be possible to interact.

A month later I dreamed again about Beatrice's male baby:

> I am nursing Beatrice's child, a boy. He is lying across my chest, a
> dead weight, sucking voraciously at my right breast. He is so heavy
> that I finally disengage him and give him back to her.

The dream made me conscious of how important my fostering this masculine principle was in our therapeutic work. It showed me giving her the yang energy she needed to support her individuality as a woman, to counteract the destructive masculine forces of war. A victim all her life, Beatrice needed to assert herself, to realize her authority in relation to her husband and the men she worked for.

When she was able to wean her baby girl at twenty months, Beatrice found herself in a quandary of depression and disconnection. "After weaning I don't know my role. Why do I support men's delusions? Now, again, everything seems transitory. I never before made a choice, a commitment; everything was circumstance, either the man or the situation. But I made a commitment by becoming pregnant and having a child. And I'm wishing for another baby." Beatrice's state of acute disorientation reflected both her past identity confusion and the bewildering rapidity of the changes she had undergone in her relatively short time in therapy.

Cut off from her feelings at an early age, she had not truly grasped the reality of the roles into which she had been thrust since being abandoned by her mother. Each situation had demanded a different role: the orphanage, her adoptive father and stepmother, her journalist lover in Vietnam, her first marriage to a disturbed man. Her work identities had depended on the current boss or company that employed her. In a way, her history had consisted of a series of false identities, none of which were congruent with her own internal feelings.

The reality of her present identity as wife and mother was apparent to me. But given her history, I could see why she might wonder, in her postweaning state of loss, if it had been any more real than any other role she had previously played. Her wish to become pregnant again was also a wish for biology to define her identity again. A genuine relationship with her child had been established. "In relation to my daughter I feel I'm not role-playing the way I always did before," Beatrice told me, "This is new to me; there is substance to me with her." Motherhood had challenged Beatrice to relate to her immediate reality through feeling, and that persisted even during her extended depression.

Beatrice had not yet emerged from her depression when fate abruptly forced her to abandon the container of her therapeutic work with me. Her stepmother had a stroke and pleaded with Beatrice to bring her family to live in England. At about the same time her husband received an attractive offer to play with a band in London. With the combination of events, Beatrice felt a sense of urgency and inevitability about returning. She said, "I never separated from my mother. I'm still looking for her and for resolution in my stepmother; I don't know why. I have to reconcile the person I was in England with who I am here, who I was fifteen years ago with who I am now. I become the dutiful daughter in England, agreeing to everything, seething inside. Yet I still feel responsible for my stepmother." Within a month Beatrice left the therapeutic enclosure that had contained her for five years.

In the few weeks remaining before she returned to England, Beatrice's difficulty with emerging from the nursing relationship with her toddler daughter was compounded by the anguish of our premature termination. Facing confrontation with her tormented past, she became increasingly anxious and fearful. She dreamed:

> The witch Grunella is leaping out at me from every door in the
> house wherever I go—the bathroom closet, the bedroom, everywhere.
> I open many doors; she is always there.

Beatrice and her husband were again suffering financial difficulties, which had her constantly worrying about paying the rent and brought up her old fear of going hungry. The invitation to move to England promised financial relief but necessitated confronting her stepmother's destructiveness, one part of the archetypal evil that haunted her psyche.

Beatrice's approaching separation from me reopened the old wound of her forced separation from her grandmother and mother in China. In the unconscious, Demeter and Kore's separation was also powerfully alive. Shortly before leaving the country, Beatrice had a dream that poignantly expressed how drastic the loss of our relationship and her therapeutic container threatened to be for her:

I see a hearth with a fire that is almost out, dying logs and ashes. Every now and then I look back at it, and it flares up again. I know something spiritual is needed, and I remember that Kuan Yin died by burning.

Beatrice told me, "I'm anxious about this threshold. I don't know what will happen. I feel sisterly toward you. I think I'll be bereft without you." I felt bereft for her when she told me this dream. I had strong feelings of caring for this courageous woman whose fate had crossed mine in such a profound way. The dream reflected the depth to which our work had affected her; she feared the death of her soul image and of her spiritual life.

The premature termination with Beatrice did abort her therapy. We experienced Hecate again, as the goddess of transitions. Our work had also affected me deeply. I told Beatrice that our being pregnant at the same time had been important to me in my own exploration of the feminine. We discussed a referral to an analyst in London to continue her analytic work and affirmed the possibility of staying in touch if and when she felt like writing. I could only hope that Beatrice's reunion with her aged stepmother, to whom she felt grateful for giving her a home, and the return to the place her mother had sent her thirty years before would be a healing integration for her. I prayed that the spirit of Kuan Yin, rekindled in our work during our pregnancies, would remain alive in Beatrice's relationship to her little daughter. I did trust that if she followed up on consulting an analyst in London, eventually she would be able to complete her journey. But knowing that my father's wounds of war had eventually led to his suicide, I feared for Beatrice, whose life had been one archetypal trauma after another. And I felt her loss and mourning as my own when she left that final session. The memory of my ritual visits to Beatrice in the hospital and at her home remained as touchstones of our therapeutic work to me. The archetypal feminine dyads moving upward from the unconscious in our relationship had called to be met. She and I had answered the call with fitting ritual actions.

SARAH's emergence from the therapeutic container was also precipitated by her family's decision to move away. But in her case the time was ripe for terminating her work with me. Sarah could look forward to a move out of state, where her husband had been offered a promotion in his law firm, because she had experienced an internal equalizing of masculine and feminine modes in herself. The recurrence of the Crohn's disease symptoms that required her to stay at home with her sons had freed her to be with nature and to explore her own nature. Years of couples therapy with her husband had provided a container in which their relationship also grew.

She had two dreams that helped bring her into positive connection with her husband:

> My husband and I are on roller skates. At the beginning it is like a hockey game, confrontational, hostile, and tense. At the end we are almost dancing.

> My husband and I, you and your husband are having a meal together congenially.

Spurred by this image of harmonious relationship between masculine and feminine, Sarah was motivated to have the diamond in her wedding ring replaced. She regretted that her move would cause her to stop our work together, as well as to leave friends and family. But she also felt that the new environment would give her an opportunity to establish different patterns based not on her career but on devoting herself to her own deeper needs and those of her immediate family. Sarah continued to have special physical needs, so she planned not to work for at least a year after the move, even if her symptoms continued to improve.

In the second dream, Sarah created a fourfold *coniunctio,* a double dyad of masculine and feminine.[8] In her unconscious, my marriage supported and completed hers. She and I with our husbands were sharing a ritual feast. Sarah accomplished psychologically the union of opposites that is accomplished ceremonially for the Tiyyar girl in her ritual.

Sarah had a year in which to terminate therapy and prepare for this major change in her life. During that year, her unconscious revealed a gradual movement toward a ritual ending to our work together. The psyche recognizes itself in ritual—once the impulse has arisen, the whole psyche of the woman becomes preoccupied with accomplishing it. The extended preparatory period allowed the psychological power to accrue. Over the years Sarah had several times spontaneously enacted her fantasy of our relationship, thereby creating a ritual. She appeared at one session four years into our work with a chocolate truffle for each of us. The occasion was a rare hour in which she said, "I had time to do things for myself." In a celebratory spirit Sarah wished to acknowledge our feminine dyad for its part in her being able to carve out a little precious time. Sarah spent that hour affirming the fruits of her psychological labor. The couples therapy with her husband was going well; she was able to assert her needs more than in the past. She told me she was also appreciative of "having had the calm container and the consistency of our relationship as well as the therapeutic process itself."

While we ate our truffles, Sarah mentioned that during one session with me some months ago, when she had been very upset at having let down one of her male superiors at work, I had absentmindedly picked up the pearl she had given me and held it for the rest of the hour. She said, "It was soothing to me that you did that; it meant so much to me." Although unconscious of it at the time it occurred, I realized when Sarah told me about this incident that it had been a meaningful ritual action on my part. She had been mortified and ashamed at having forgotten to do what the older male doctor had requested of her, and I had intuitively held the pearl, her own gift to our *temenos,* which embodied for her a deeper wisdom. Kuan Yin is called "Bestower of the Wish-Fulfilling Gem."[9] Sarah's forgetting to execute the doctor's command was, in fact, an intentional act of her unconscious that was part of her moving away from her father-pleasing mode into a more authentic womanhood. Forgetting to serve the patriarch represented a deep affirmation of her own psychological development.

On several similar occasions when she took some time for reflection before our therapy hour, Sarah arrived with tea and milk in styrofoam cups for both of us. She said that having tea emphasized taking time out for herself from the normal course of the day or week. This was another unplanned ritual that incarnated feminine sharing. On one of these occasions I had on my desk a slide projector and slides of birth-giving Goddess images for a class I was teaching. As we drank our tea, I offered to show Sarah the slides, because she worked with women's fertility as a doctor. She was delighted to see them and commented that she appreciated the way I had been able to speak about my pregnancies and miscarriage. She felt that I had been a model to her for reflecting birth and death as natural processes to her women patients.

Out of Sarah's individuality and her relationship to me, a ceremony of bonding emerged. Her ritual expression of "having tea" echoed for me my analysis with Barbara Hannah in Zurich. There, when my analytic hour fell at teatime, the maid brought us tea and cookies on a silver tray. When I terminated with Miss Hannah to return to California, after our last hour, as our ritual good-bye, we adjourned from the consulting room to the drawing room in her home for a glass of sherry.

These quiet ritual moments with Sarah in her eleven-year-long analysis honored the initiatory work of the woman-to-woman container. At those times the labyrinth of the unconscious moved from darkness into the light of consciousness. Six years into her therapy with me, Sarah dreamed:

> I am walking through an involved garden. You are there with me.
> You are the guide. It is mazelike, formal, domesticated, and low like an
> herb garden.

Sarah said that I was there in the garden for different reasons from hers, that I had a different role. She had been reading to her older son about the

Cretan labyrinth and the Minotaur. The intimacy of their mother-son relationship was contributing to her psychological awareness. At this point Sarah had been in a maze of indecision about external events to do with her job at the clinic, her physical well-being, and her husband's commitment to his law firm. But on a deeper level, the dream asserted ordered meaning by combining images of her love of gardens with the formal process of psychotherapy and its archetypal foundation in the labyrinth of dream incubation.

A week later Sarah had a dream in which she was gripped with fear for her son:

> My son and I are standing on a dock. He falls into the water next to a ship. I am afraid the ship is going to crush him as he bobs up and down. At first I think I can hold the ship back. But it is an ocean liner, and I can't. So I jump into the water on top of him and push him under so we can get under the dock. I don't know if there is a breathing space. I am pregnant and don't know if I am strong enough to take care of it. Finally, under the dock, the tide is going in. We are floating with him holding onto me. I wake up still floating away, not able to get back to the dock area because of the strong tide.

Sarah had gradually become aware during her therapy that denial of the shadow was injurious for her child. I was relieved when she had this dream, because I had had previous dreams in which her older son was in danger. In one of them he had been hit by a tidal wave and knocked unconscious. I felt that I had carried this awareness for her for years at the beginning of our work. As we moved toward termination, we were able to reflect on the changes in her that had taken place during her extended initiation. Even the recurrence of Crohn's disease symptoms, which forced her suspension from work, had been an opportunity for her to indulge in motherhood and eventually to take up the challenge of moving with her family out of state.

One of the images that recurred during this year devoted to emerging and ritual separation was that of an oak secretary that Sarah had had since she was a little girl. This desk had appeared in her dreams repeatedly, mildewed and moldy, covered with ugly paint, belonging to someone else, at a garage sale. For Sarah, the lovely oak desk represented an internal organization and peace of mind that had remained elusive in her everyday life. Sitting at that desk, with all its cubbyholes for special things, organizing her life, was the image of self-realization for her. The move, although it necessitated leaving the home she had created, with her spring flowers, promised to make possible the symbolic restoring of the oak desk. She envisioned a small room all her own where she could put the desk and her things and be with herself when she needed to be alone.

Another theme that became amplified during this period was her relationship to her own spirituality. Toward the end of her work she dreamed:

> I come to see you for a regular session. You are wearing a creamy
> beige silk man's tie with a small reddish burgundy design on it. Then I
> see you socially. You are living with a roommate, a woman. You invite
> me to dinner with some other people. You get home after we arrive,
> and you ask for help moving your sewing machine. The roommate is
> cute, wears knickers, overalls, both stylish and unusual. She is light-
> haired, opposite to you. We eat dinner.
> After dinner, you and I go for a walk. You ask what I thought of
> the tie you were wearing in our session. I don't want to answer, but
> after you ask several times, I say, "I like the design, but I'm not used to
> you in a man's tie." Then I ask if I can try it on. I have to ask how to
> tie it, because I've never worn one. We continue our walk and meet my
> father's partner. He says, "You will never make it on that road, because
> you have sandals on and it's cold."

Sarah associated the man's tie with silk scarves that I often wore to work. "Your scarves have always reminded me of priest's vestments; you hold them like the priest does during the Mass. I think of goddesses and witches. I don't like women wearing men's suits and ties," Sarah told me. She felt she could not separate her personal and professional life; she always brought work home. In the dream she sees me as being able to differentiate the two: I wear the man's tie at work, while at home I have a frivolous, light-haired shadow. The tie alluded to the authentic image of the yang in the yin design, a discrete masculine force in the field of the feminine. Sarah was looking for a different place in her home to keep her sewing machine, which she was currently using to make a quilt.

On a deeper level, however, the dream brought up Sarah's emerging sense of the power of feminine spirituality and its threat to patriarchal dominance. The visit to my home in the dream revealed me as a woman-identified woman. Sarah had joined a woman's spiritual group. She told me that she was learning that "woman's wisdom is in myself, not outside me." Sarah's positive association to the tie, my scarves, and the priest's vestments belied the inhibiting father complex in the dream. She had developed a true spiritual connection to Kuan Yin and been deeply moved by the other archetypal feminine figures of Atalanta, the Queen, and Demeter/Persephone in the course of our work.

Though Sarah felt a new sense of spirituality, grounded in the feminine, she also doubted her feelings. In her experience the spirit came from a male God through a male priest. For her to move away from that religious authority was a huge shift. It took place gradually as she discovered that she could live more naturally and felt more balanced when drawing on her own inner sources.

Near the time of our termination, I dreamed about the mantle of feminine spiritual power that Sarah had seen in my scarves:

> Sarah is asking me if I can bring my brown silk shawl to a session for her to try on, because I had once offered to do so. I wonder how and why I had offered.

I knew the answer to the dream question in the context of Sarah's approaching termination. It was my responsibility to give back to her the power and authenticity she had projected on me. Our ritual separation would include my clothing her in the mantle of the priestess. Adorning Sarah with a sacred shawl touched on the archetype of Changing Woman when the Navajo Kinaaldá girl is adorned with a shawl and prays over the corn pollen just before blessing the cornmeal cake. When the initiate takes on the mantle of the mythic heroine whose gifts and grace bless her people, she herself is imbued with that feminine power.

Sarah, through her difficult journey in psychotherapy, had become a cultural heroine. Wearing my shawl was a symbol of that accomplishment for her, because I was her sponsor in the initiation process. "You have taught me to take care of myself," Sarah told me. Before she was forced to stop working, the influence of Sarah's new feminine perspective was permeating her medical treatment and influencing every woman she saw in her office. Unlike her male colleagues in the clinic, Sarah spent time listening to her women patients and responding to their concerns. She empathized with their fears of infertility as a result of endocrinological disorders, talked to them about their feelings and their bodies, and understood the pervasive quality these issues had in their lives. Most women Sarah treated had already been hurt—emotionally, psychically, or physically—by treatment from male physicians. Sarah's receptivity, attentiveness, and caring had a healing effect in itself. Further, she acknowledged the deep archetypal nature of the forces of birth and death working through a woman's body: she could honor a woman's need to ritualize her feelings about having to give up her fertility or saying good-bye to a miscarried baby or naming a stillborn baby before burial. In her own way, Sarah was serving as midwife and priestess to her patients.

My symbolic gift of adorning Sarah as a nearly accomplished initiate was inadvertently echoed in a gift to me a few months before our termination. Sarah brought me the painter Meinrad Craighead's book *The Mother's Songs: Images of God the Mother.* The book had caught Sarah's eye in a bookstore and had somehow reminded her of me. I had never before seen this artist's work but immediately found in her paintings images from the unconscious similar to those I presented in seminars I was teaching. I began using slides of Meinrad's paintings in these seminars. Through a series of synchronicities I met Meinrad just before Sarah moved away, and Meinrad indirectly, sibyl-like, influenced Sarah's ritual of termination.

The last dream Sarah had before our closing session was the following:

> I am selling things in a bazaar. You come in, look at the handmade
> articles, and compliment the fine work. I feel a sense of approval for
> my work.

Sarah's dream reassured her that the work she had done and was now disseminating was worthwhile. She needed to be reassured because she felt discouraged by how little progress she had made over the years in being able to equalize her work and her family life. The dream affirmed the importance of the psychological work she had done and the value of her feminine creativity now in staying home with her children. The past and the present had meaning; the future would be woven out of that.

Only after Sarah emerged from the enclosure of analysis, terminated her work with me, and went her own way was she able to find the balance between personal and professional life that she sought. It was as if she had to resume her own authority, separate from me and the inherent conflict in having a sponsor or role model who was balancing family and career while she had to stop work in order to find her own feminine source. She emerged into a new life away from all that was familiar, knowing her task and able to do it because she had a whole new environment in which to create herself anew.

CARMINA's emergence from the labyrinth and from our container came about slowly as she allowed her art to take precedence in her psychic field and became more comfortable in her relationships with men. Several years before she terminated, she dreamed about a ritual ending for which she felt unprepared:

> We are here, you and I, but the room is different. We are doing an
> elaborate ritual, a leave-taking. I have my purple coffee cup, and we
> have lots of herbs and flowers. But I don't know who is giving what to
> whom. I am a little girl named Gina. I/she am/is a baby kindergartner.
> You are putting my shoes on me and saying that I am leaving. Every-
> thing has to slow down and wait for me/her.

Carmina's inability to view herself with compassion has changed. She said to me about the dream, "I am worried about leaving." This beautiful dream was a reflection of her capacity both to imagine terminating in a lovely, orderly way and to feel and acknowledge her psychological age of five in the therapeutic process. Here she is able to express her need and feel met in it. Developmentally, a mother ties the daughter's shoes until the girl can do it herself. Carmina needed me to continue to sponsor her, to adorn her until she outgrew that need and her initiation was completed.

The urge to create art was undeniable in Carmina, yet that energy had been frozen. One of the signs of her heart melting in her dreams was the appearance of the magic isle, Avalon, she had briefly glimpsed in her early purification dream.

> I'm leaving a room in a museum. An older curator, a man, is block-ing the exit. He's grumpy and doesn't want me to move behind the curtain. I push past him, where I see men's clothes hanging, coats and vests. On the table next to them are ritual objects, of patriarchal im-portance, from the Episcopal church. One of the objects on the altar has to do with the altar boy. I leave the little warren and go out into the open space onto a terrace.
>
> I'm with my mother and my younger brother, looking at a tinted photograph of a family sitting in their house. The family group is smug and pleased with themselves. Looking across the street I see trees planted, prehistoric-looking, a tropical plant with palm fronds going up. We're on the edge of a chasm. I look down and see "my middle is-land"/Avalon, a magical place. The landscape keeps bending and fold-ing, giving me pleasure. I point it out. "Look, see, there is this incredible place!"

In this dream Carmina moved beyond the burden of her patriarchal personal history in which the museum and the church were one. The cura-tor, denoting a conventional patriarchal attitude, is blocking her from ac-knowledging her own creative impulses. Pushing past the persona, she finds the vestments and then leaves the all-male church. Outside on the terrace, the conventionality of the family group is revealed in the photo-graph. After seeing how the church and family of her past bound her, Carmina was able to see her special place, her inner feminine self, symbol-ized by the mystical isle of Avalon, where the priestesses of the old Celtic religion, devoted to the Goddess, were trained.[10] One of Kuan Yin's em-blems is a palatial pavilion that suggests a blessed afterlife.[11]

In the next dream Carmina had further freed herself from convention and found her creativity again:

> I am following a woman down a path. We are walking near the water. It is approaching evening as we come down near the shore. With a great feeling of relief, I see that I am back in the land of the pavilion. The water stretches away from the twisting shoreline. There are tide pools full of live things.

Carmina has surrendered herself to following her own femininity and finds her magic land and tide pools teeming with life. Initially, her tears flowed in sorrow at not being able to draw or paint. Then tears flowed with compassion for herself, melting her frozen heart. The tears have gradually pooled to create a fertile, healing environment.

As Carmina opened to the possibility of applying to graduate school in a master of fine arts program, her unconscious began to affirm her work in new ways:

> I'm moving a stack of empty white canvases because I'm going to restore them. I have a choice between a large piece of wood and a smaller, flimsy, less expensive piece. A voice in the background is encouraging me to get the smaller one, but I say, "No, it's very important to have the best material."

This dream followed an hour after which Carmina had felt much better, because she had allowed herself to feel compassionate toward her inner daughter. She said she had mistrusted herself and her intuition but now felt confirmed because of her intuitive connection with me. The self-critical, cynical voice that devalued her talent is absent here. Restoration of the empty canvases symbolizes restoring the value to her art and herself, which she had previously denigrated.

In the next dream she appeared with her double, using her drawing to go back in time in a way that is similar to the analytic process:

> I'm sitting with myself, two of me. We are sifting through a pile of drawings, going back in time, older and older. Then, as I do it, I go into a trance, scribbling and drawing. Someone says, "Yes, keep going, the more you scribble, the farther back you go."

In this dream Carmina and her shadow or double are at one in the creative process, which is now also her therapeutic process. The energy is intensified by the doubling. Here she goes into a trance of her own making, letting the creative muse take over in order to regress freely and easily. The negative voice is gone; a positive, encouraging voice is there instead. As Carmina came together with her own shadow power, she separated from me on a new level. A month later, she dreamed:

> You are giving me maps, round paper descriptions, each one a history of your life, what you have been doing, perhaps each one a year. While you are giving them to me, I think, "I don't want to see these; it's too personal." But when I look at it, I can't read it. It is in your peculiar script, your set of symbols, idiosyncratic, so I cannot read it.

Carmina was concerned with boundaries again in this dream. She was reassured when she discovered that she couldn't unlock or unravel the language of my identity. My experience provided her with the means to map her own unconscious. She didn't have to understand the words or the details, because she was not meant to imitate me. She simply needed to map herself out of the labyrinth with my help. In the dream my idiosyncratic handwriting symbolized my uniqueness. Carmina had also dreamed, "You tell me that I am unique." Her individuality, my individuality, and our relationship were alternately confirmed as she moved toward integration and termination.

Scribbling her way into the past produced an unmistakable consolidation in Carmina's psyche:

> Someone is coming home. This is a great moment, full of excitement and expectation. I can't tell who is returning; it could be me, or my cousin or friend. Am I meeting myself as I walk in the door? I'm apprehensive at first about this meeting. What if I don't measure up to the one returning? But as she/he comes through the door, I run and throw my whole self into their arms and wrap my legs around them. I feel uniquely centered in my body.
>
> I have the clear thought, "The parts are back together, and 'everyone' has been waiting to start until my return."

After Carmina's disintegrative depression of several years' duration, this reunion with herself was welcome to both of us, even if it was visible at first only in the unconscious. Her painting began to be a bridge between her conscious and unconscious life.

In the next dream, her painting took her into conscious ritual space:

> I am painting squares of women's rituals and images. In the painting there is a line of women going down to the water. I decorate them with jewelry in gold pen. I dream that I am one of these barbaric women with gold lines coming off me.

Carmina has entered her own painting and been amplified and endowed by her own hand. She has dressed and adorned herself with gold jewelry, dreamed herself into her own fantasy. By objectifying the feminine image, she also internalized it. She told me, "I am trusting, letting go, allowing things to happen instead of making them happen." The dual Demeter-Persephone interaction between herself and her inner daughter, and herself in relation to me, freed enough energy for her art that she began applying to graduate school.

As Carmina's trust in herself grew, her fear of men diminished, and her internal identification with her disabled brother dissolved. My husband appeared in a dream in a different guise than in dreams of earlier years:

I have come to see you. You are not there. You have a substitute. Your office is big and dark. The substitute is a homosexual man or woman, but I can't tell which. I think, "Maybe it's her husband or wife? No? Which one has children? Who has which job?" The substitute looks like a forty-year-old lesbian with glasses. I go along with it, showing this person drawings of dreams. She says, "I'm glad you are doing them. Good."

Suddenly, you come in with your husband. The office is now your home. You have a nimbus of beautiful reddish hair and are wearing a beautiful white dress. You sit next to me. I am sorry not to show you the pictures. I don't want to leave. You are blazing, intense.

Carmina's dream revealed a fear that in her therapy she would fall back into a lesbian affiliation. She needed the vision of the idealized marriage, projected into me and my husband, that she created in the second half of the dream. She no longer rejected my husband or ran away, as she had in earlier dreams. She had never met, nor did she know anything about, my actual husband. But the knowledge of his existence, manifested in the dream, symbolized hope for her future with a man.

For Carmina, metamorphosing into conscious relationship to a man included merging with her double in the form of her beautiful cousin:

I see my cousin with her hair blowing, and it strikes me how beautiful she is. All her clothes have minerals and metals sewn into them. It makes me feel deflated.

Now I'm in a room with strange creatures, all women, primitive Venus figures, almost spherical, breasts, bellies, no personality, all sexual. Beads are sewn into their skin/hides. They watch men come in, randomly pick one, and have sex. Then I'm one of them, but I don't know how I know. Someone grabs me from behind, and I say, "Who is it?" A man says, "It's all right, Carmina," and I relax, recognizing a good friend from high school.

I'm with a man who has a cult hero quality, relaxed, spontaneous, removed. We are floating around at a party. He finally indicates the two of us are going to leave, which is what I wanted all along. He is standing on the porch waiting for me, no shoes, hair blowing, a large shirt, a sweater without a button. He is completely loose, radiating sexual awareness. He comes, and we go off, a ritual going off, a marriage. I want to be seduced by him. We're drinking champagne and spilling it all over us. I wake up laughing.

In the Navajo, Tukuna, Tiv, and Tiyyar rituals I have discussed, elements of bodily mutation effect the transformation from girl to woman. All four initiations include bathing or cleansing as purification, adornment of the initiate's body with jewels, and the presentation of new clothes. In the Kinaaldá, the bodily mutation is effected gently in the form of the molding and massaging and finally painting with clay; in the case of the Tukuna, after the girl's body is painted and adorned, she is altered by a painful process of hair pulling. In the Tiv tribe, the girl is scarified; in the Tiyyar ceremony, the gift of the gold *tali* tied around her neck marks her as a woman.

In these dreams, as in the analysis, Carmina moved from feeling inadequate as a modern woman through psychological stages of transformation into womanhood. The changing begins with her envy of her beautiful cousin or positive shadow, whose clothes, ornamented with minerals and metals, suggest an initiated woman. Then Carmina returns to prehistoric times and identifies with fertility figures whose skin is decorated with beads. These women are like clay figures found in Neolithic Europe into which grain has been pressed to invoke fertility.[12] Carmina's experience of herself in the dream as a primitive fertility goddess in relation to anonymous men takes her back into a revitalized adolescence. Her beaded skin also suggests Changing Woman, who in one tale is said to have white beads in her right breast and turquoise in her left.[13] Finally, in the dream, femininity renewed, Carmina has become an individual modern woman, able to enjoy a wonderful seduction with an individual man of her choice.

Just before her trip to Spain, another series of dreams manifested the continuing integration of her femininity and her sexuality with men.

> I am traveling with a group of people. I am one of three prostitutes. Some men are there. We stop at a resting place. I go off with one of the men. I say, "This is fine, but make sure I don't have to do this with anyone else." We try to climb over a wall, but there is not much privacy.

> I am eating a meal. A black woman starts singing Nina Simone blues. She has ritual paint on her face; she is a priestess. She says, "I am singing this for priestesses." Men disappear. The women are moving in patterns. I am in a group of girls trying to learn the paces. It is an all-women's ritual, an initiation. We're laughing, traveling on a road. I keep wanting to plant trees.

> I am back home. I find a gold leaf earring on the ground, a little bent. I know it is leftover from the ritual. In my mind the earring belongs to a goddess. I can't remember which one, which cult. I put it on. My mother looks at it. She says, "Why are you wearing that?" I'm upset because she doesn't know.

Carmina assumes the role of the sacred prostitute at the beginning of the dream and dedicates her sexuality to the Goddess by giving herself to one man. After that ritual, the group feminine initiation is asserted once again. As a modern woman she re-creates herself in ritual bonding with other women alternately with relating to men. The gold leaf is the *tali* that defines a woman as ready to mate. Carmina had realized her own instinctual power before finding a real relationship with a man. In the dream her mother does not recognize the daughter's initiation, and has yet to realize her own.

Returning from Europe, where she had tentatively reconnected with men, Carmina realized that she had to sacrifice her old expectations of men being either inaccessible, damaged, or violent if she wanted to give a man a chance to relate to her. She dreamed:

> I am with a group of women performing a ritual. Each woman has a paper tag that represents a man in her life, husband or lover. At a signal, the women throw their paper bits in the air. One piece of paper will be caught, and that man will be "brought to earth" or killed. It is like John Barleycorn. He will be sacrificed for renewal or fertility of some sort. It isn't grim.

This dream is cultural as well as personal. It shows a group of women gathered with the common goal of sacrificing their patriarchal identification in the interest of their own femininity and real relationships with men. John Barleycorn represents the patriarchal view that women are inferior, that men are godlike, that life and culture are to be determined by men. The result of this sacrifice for a woman is to realize her feminine power. The meaning of the word *sacrifice* is "to make sacred." When a woman sacrifices the patriarchy, she makes her own nature sacred. As a woman changes, so do the men around her. In her new womanhood she creates sacred relationships with men. Carmina, as cultural heroine, was participating in the sacrifice of renewal for herself and others.

A few months later, Carmina dreamed:

> I am watching a man and a woman making love. I believe I am the woman. My relationship with the man feels unbalanced initially. This is not unusual. It feels as though I am under his power, as though I belong to him, that I have no power of identity in relation to him. But as we make love I identify more compassion than I expected. The relationship begins to feel more balanced.
>
> In a later sequence, I am watching the lower right hand square of my Barcelona painting being removed and hung in a frame on the wall. I am amazed at how beautiful it is. The picture plane is split down the middle—one color on one side, and another on the other.

Significantly, the power issue with the masculine in this dream is equalized by Carmina and her lover's compassion during lovemaking. Sexuality in itself provides the medium of sensitive, related communication. Positive feeling toward the "other" also supported Carmina's appreciation of her art. Like the male-female couple in the dream, the painting is an image of duality, two colors split on a single canvas together making a beautiful whole. Opposites were coming together.

Eight months later, Carmina's capacity to feel in relation to a man or maleness was further liberated in her rapport with the new man in her life:

> I have a constant sexual fantasy in the back of my mind. I'm making love to a man; then we are lying next to each other. I feel the sensation of being in love while making love, open, poignant, and I start to cry. I say, "I'm melting." I melt into him.

Carmina's growing trust and serious involvement with her new lover was dissolving her negative father/brother complex. As her relationship with this man developed and applications to graduate school were completed and filed, Carmina dreamed:

> I am enacting a ritual with my three girlhood friends, now women. A group of people are standing in a circle watching. One of the women is nude. Another is bathing her with precious liquid. The liquid is champagnelike. Each one of us undergoes this ritual.
>
> I am talking with the three of them. We are talking about the problems going on in their lives. One of the women says, "Carmina is the one who does this work for us." It is like the child in the family who has the therapeutic role. I feel good and proud. It is true. There is nothing unusual about it.

Carmina had grown up with the three women in the dream. In the course of her therapy, they had often appeared in her dreams as a group from which she felt excluded by her suffering. She had just turned thirty knowing that she was first in the group to do so. Now, moving toward completion of her analysis, Carmina is acknowledged by the group in the unconscious as having accomplished something for each of them as well. The inner ritual celebration has begun.

As she and her lover began to talk about moving in together, Carmina dreamed:

> I wake up in bed with my lover. I've lost an earring in the bed. I look down and find many earrings and other jewelry in the bed. Then we're outside digging a hole in the ground, finding potshards and bones, doing archaeology.

The dream showed that Carmina's sexual relationship with this man was helping her retrieve her femininity. She finds her lost jewelry—symbol of the enduring value of the feminine—in their bed. This was her inner archaeology. Externally, together, she and her man friend were also unearthing the past, digging up our patriarchal history, examining it, classifying it, and trying to re-create male-female relationship.

Carmina, living the Demeter and Persephone myth, however, also continued to experience the man's intrusion into the feminine container:

> I am preparing to go to a party, but I don't have anything to wear. All the other women have gowns or something unique to wear, but everything I try on is dirty, inappropriately casual, or doesn't fit because I am too fat. My cousin is going to the party, and I see her dress hanging in the closet. I feel left out—as if I will never have "the right dress." At one point I am sitting on a bench, and I realize that my lover is hiding under the bench. At that moment I am wearing a particularly "wrong" dress that people have been making fun of. He says something like, "Don't worry about it. You look fine no matter what you wear." Naturally this doesn't make me feel any better, although I know he is trying to be helpful. And besides, what is he doing under a bench in a clearly feminine situation?

This dream returned to the initiation motif of adornment but now in the context of Carmina's relationship to her lover. She asserts that adorning herself belongs to her feminine identity; she is not doing it *for* him. In the next dream, adorned as a woman, she is able to relate freely to a man:

> I am with a group of young women, riding in a carriage. We are all wearing dark glasses. We are going to the beach. A group of young men go by and begin to flirt. But it's cool flirtation like high school; no one actually looks at anyone else. All of a sudden I turn around and boldly stare at the group of young men. I look them in the eye. All my female friends get mad at me because I'm not playing the game right. I say I don't have to. . . .
>
> The girls and I are now transformed into a group of women in exotic Middle Eastern dress, heavily embroidered garments and lots of jewelry. We are being chosen to be brides to these young men, who have become bandits or tribal or something wild like that. The other women are laughing, and each goes with a man. I am waiting. Finally some women come running in and say that one of the bandits has come for me. They are teasing me and ask me if I like him. I say, "I don't know yet. I haven't met him, but I think I will." I go out onto a balcony and look down. I can see the bandit coming for me. I have a Guatemalan jacket that belongs to a woman friend. It has a pin on it with a whirlwind design. I take the pin off the jacket to put on my dress, but it gets lost in all the fabric. Finally I find it again; it has turned into a shell. I pin the shell on my dress.

Carmina returned to high school again in this dream to consolidate her sexual identity. Her individual maturation is symbolized by her insisting on meeting the men eye to eye. When she returns to a tribal setting, she has incorporated her double: she is wearing the beautifully adorned garments that she envied her cousin in the earlier dreams. Secure in her beauty, her sexuality, her sense of Self, she is prepared for her union with a man. All the women are waiting to be taken. Part of the experience is to be separated out from the female group, as Persephone was. In the process of transferring her friend's pin to her own dress, the piece of jewelry is transformed from a whirlwind into a shell. The wind was Carmina's chosen weapon; the shell symbolizes female genitals. The wind, the shell, and the decorated garments also evoke the presence of Changing Woman and her doubles, White Shell Woman and Turquoise Woman.

Carmina's dreams of abduction referred to a call to another stage of individuation. Fascination with an unknown "other" compelled her to take up her own fate, her own development. For Carmina, as with Persephone, the irresistible inner "other" was maleness. But Carmina's dreams showed a continual return to a female community—renewing herself in feminine rituals and traditions—alternately with relating to men, both within and without. This is an important lesson for a modern woman to learn, because patriarchy has isolated women from one another. A woman in our society must both individuate and reestablish bonds of community with other women in which to affirm herself and realize her power.

Carmina's fate was to be accepted into three graduate school programs in art while making plans to live with her lover. She decreased her therapy hours to twice a month as we prepared for termination. Three months before we ended, she dreamed:

> You and I are together, the two of us. Initially it is in a very small space with a pallet to sit on. There are small objects and very old things around. It's an interpretation of the space and objects here in your office. You say to me, "There are two things you needed to realize, and you have realized them." I feel I am getting it.

> You walk in with a baby. Your husband is with you. You look radiant.

Consciously Carmina couldn't embrace the joy and realization implicit in this dream because she recognized that her initiation and healing were drawing to a close. After years of intimacy with me, she had to separate, to emerge from the container of analysis. But these realizations were the beginnings of the fruit her labor of life was to bear. And she was ready for her independence even though it made her anxious.

A few weeks later she dreamed:

I forgot my birthday.

Snakes are biting my fingers.

Carmina associated these dream fragments with her need to be painting regularly. Forgetting her birthday was forgetting to honor her own life force. The snake bites were awakening her fingers to paint. Having snakes in her hand could also be a tool, she felt, if she learned to use it. This dream asserted the objective nature of her therapeutic work, of her initiation, of the mother-daughter relationship. The mystery snakes were in her hands now. She was prepared to exercise her own power and autonomy. Carmina's final dream image in her analysis was this one:

I have a battered ancient snake that has been through a lot but is still alive.

In these months, while Carmina was preparing to terminate, I was planning an odyssey back to Greece with my children, then four and seven. I had grown to appreciate the garter snakes and occasional small rattlers that lived near my home. I cherished the snake that lived near the steps in the front garden and felt blessed when it showed me a glimpse of itself as I left the house each day. I recognized it as a guardian spirit.

In anticipation of my return to Greece I telephoned a Greek friend, only to hear that Cybele had died the previous month. Although I had seen her infrequently, I was deeply shaken. She had initiated me into the dark side of the feminine, and I loved her. The morning after I learned of her death, as I was leaving the house to take my four-year-old daughter to preschool, I found our house snake dead. I burst into tears, irrationally knowing it had died because Cybele had, and that in some way, her death had carried her into the arms of the Snake Mother she had feared. My little daughter said, comfortingly, "Don't worry, Mommy; maybe another snake will come."

Carmina and I were connected at this deep level of chthonic life energy, and I shared this loss with her as the time for her emergence drew near. Our termination ritual was pregnant with the depth of meaning that had accrued over our ten-year process together.

After the many years of work with Carmina, Beatrice, and Sarah in which a unique analytic cosmos with each developed, the impulse with each to enact a termination ritual spontaneously arose. Dreams, fantasies, and the relationships themselves had all betrayed a ritual intent. We observed the unconscious while its purpose unfolded and listened carefully to the dreams both for affirmation that a ritual should be enacted and for information about its content.

As the preparation for the ritual evolved with conscious attention to unconscious intent, each woman selected familiar ritual acts or created new
ones that had meaning for her to be used in the ceremony. I chose elements
for the enactment keyed to the individual woman's unique psychic constellation as I knew it from her dreams and analytic process.

My role in the rituals was an extension of my role as analyst. At times it
was the equivalent of what the Ideal Woman represents for the Kinaaldá
girl undergoing her initiation. Other roles were midwife, teacher, or priestess. I was the human ally, the mediating woman, in the ceremonies. The
presence of a higher being was also necessary to carry the transpersonal or
archetypal energy. We invoked a goddess or other feminine deity, inviting
her to bless us. The choice of deity was determined by the potentiating archetype activated within each woman's psyche, activated in the interest of
furthering her development or her initiation into womanhood, or simply
activated toward healing one aspect of her wound. Positive spiritual energy
that manifested itself during the analysis took form in this choice during
the creation of each ceremony.

When a woman chooses to enact a ritual in psychotherapy, the female
deity is the central presence on the altar that we create. In every ritual the
altar holds the timeless mystery of transformation. Candles, flowers, and
other objects placed there are material images of the woman's prevailing
psychological dynamics. Salt and water or incense may be included for a
purification. The woman brings and offers a sacrifice to symbolize what has
to be left behind for the sake of maturation. Earth, air, fire, and water, with
their separate energies, are represented for the invocation of the four directions. A simple communion meal, bread of earth grains or some fruit together with a drink, is also arranged on the altar. Clothes and jewelry are
carefully selected. Each color, flower, food, and element is chosen for its
specific meaning within the larger context of the ritual's design. Whereas
the Navajo, Tukuna, and Tiyyar rituals have a collective, mythological
meaning, here the individual significance to the woman is elaborately amplified. Both who she has been and who she wishes to become are symbolized on the altar. The rite and its symbols enact her ego's descent into the
labyrinthine depths of the unconscious, its passage through death, and its
return. At termination, they also express the separation of our psyches and
the opening of the container. The effect for the woman is a rebirth into a
state of feminine grace, with a renewed capacity for life.

The climax of the Eleusinian mystery ceremony came when Kore,
now renamed Persephone after her sojourn in the underworld, was called
up by the deafening otherworldly gong. The three women initiates whose
stories I tell here experienced a similar emergence in seeing their work

given another life, independent of them yet a part of them, for the purpose of this book. In choosing their book-names they also experienced a ritual renaming.

Carmina, Beatrice, and Sarah know that the central mystery of their analytic work can by nature never be revealed. It is this knowledge of the ineffable core of the initiation process and the analytic relationship that has allowed them to share their work with others in this form. In ancient Greece the mystery personages of Demeter, Persephone, Hecate, and Hades were repeatedly depicted in art. The attributes or sacred objects used in the ritual were likewise engraved on triglyphs and metopes and memorialized in paintings. These were the public aspects of the figures and objects shown outside the mystery proper. They were no secret. The mystery lay in the enactment of the ceremony, as the mystery of the psychotherapeutic process lies in its enactment.

In woman-to-woman psychotherapy or analysis, I symbolically serve the Goddess. Many roles fall to me throughout the ritual phases of containment, transformation, and emergence. As sponsor or Ideal Woman, I uphold the values of the newly emerging feminine identity and power in individual women and in our culture. As Hecate's handmaiden, as midwife, I guard the boundaries, the crossroads, the edges between life and death, death and rebirth. As priestess of the mother-daughter mysteries, I preside over the sacred rituals as they emerge from the unconscious of the women across from me. I am the liminal presence, the facilitator, guide, or catalyst. I sit between inner and outer. I hold the tension between the opposites. My place is in the shadow, always transitional. When a woman accomplishes her initiation, becomes herself, and terminates with me, I recede from her life. My service is done. She emerges, a woman who walks in beauty, carrying a torch, radiating light.

Containment, transformation, and emergence form a ritual pattern of renewal for women. The pattern has both an inner and outer place in women's lives. In her moon cycle a woman experiences that pattern recurring in her own body throughout her lifetime. Initially, as a girl child, she is self-contained. Her body is hers and closed to the world. Menarche "opens" her physically, emotionally, and psychologically to external influence or intrusion. With each menstrual cycle, she undergoes a bodily transformation. Each month brings periods of containment, changing, and emerging. Her sexual receptivity fluctuates with her changing moods. During pregnancy a woman finds herself in a deep state of inner-containment while creation and transformation take place in her womb. Emergence comes when the blood flows in childbirth and the baby is born. During lactation her milk flows, opening her physical boundary into the world, into relationship in a new way. Later in life, when her blood ceases, she returns to another state of self-containment. Transformed once again, she emerges into old age and an identity as a grandmother.

In woman-to-woman psychotherapy, a woman is enclosed, contained by her therapist in a process of dream incubation and ritual transformation whose essence is change. There, a woman evolves an awareness of the psychological and emotional corollaries to her inherently changing physiology. Initially, she chooses to withdraw from the world and introvert her energy in order to seek healing. Along the way, she submits to initiation. The ritual of her changing will include many other symbolic rituals that arise in her dreams and fantasies. As her transforming intensifies, she may feel the urge to enact what she sees or feels in her inner world. If she dreams about a restorative bath or swim in the ocean, she may wish to enact a ritual of purification by taking a special bath or visiting the seashore. If the inner image is that of sacrifice, she may feel the need to burn a token that symbolizes the painful giving up of cherished ideals or obsolete attitudes. If she dreams of a ritual feast, she may create an intimate meal for herself and other women to celebrate the festival or rite of passage to which the dream alluded. The enactments may contain elements from ancient or tribal rituals that have arisen in her psyche, or they may be entirely her own creation. At times she may be moved to invoke the Goddess or other particular feminine guides who have appeared in her unconscious to help her. She may ask for their blessing or protection or for aid in warding off a threatening complex. The double feminine container is an intense matrix for the evocation of the power of feminine deities. These deities encompass earth, sky, and underworld; the waxing, full, and waning moon; water, fire, and air— the archetypal sources of the divine feminine within her. If a woman responds to the impulse to enact her inner truths, even in small ways, she enhances her capacity to access her own wisdom. Taking her unconscious, her dreams, and her Self seriously, she creates a dialogue between her ego and unconscious that produces an ever-changing flow of creativity between inner and outer life.

A woman finds that this knowledge, instead of making her a slave to her own biology, has far-reaching ramifications in her external life. By turning inward to differentiate the shifts in her emotions, thoughts, and perceptions, she gradually frees herself from the patriarchal messages, within and without, that restrict her fullness as a woman. By reconnecting to her ancient feminine heritage, she births an individual voice and identity as a modern woman: embodied wisdom. Using the past to create a feminine identity in the present includes valuing herself and other women in their own right, not as adjuncts to men. Her new womanly self-consciousness also affects men's awareness of their stereotypical attitudes toward women. Valuing the feminine, she becomes a cultural heroine, a model for other women to follow.

When a woman emerges from such a ritual of transformation in psychotherapy, she is self-aware and self-confident. She is able to put into practice the insights and realizations about herself and the feminine in our culture that will help shape the lives of women and girls in the future. She is prepared to assert and, if necessary, fight for the values that she has embraced as her own. And she is willing to bond with other women to support, disseminate, and bring to consciousness those values in both men and women in the culture at large. She continues to draw comfort, inspiration, and knowledge from the source of the divine feminine in herself that she touched during her initiation into womanhood.

An initiated woman can consciously create a renewing pattern of containment, transformation, and emergence beyond the enclosure of woman-to-woman therapy for herself and other women. She may choose to make periodic ritual retreats alone. Withdrawing from the demands of everyday life to reflect on herself, she may develop a pattern of seclusion in conjunction with her moon cycle, either before or during menstruation. Or a special time of the week, month, or year may better suit her lifestyle. It may be an hour, a day, or a week. A woman may choose a grand setting in nature, an intimate room in her home, or a beautiful place in her garden. Whatever the timing or the place, then and there she is able to drift into her own being, listen and hear her own voice. Whether it speaks in whispers of love, in screams of pain or anger, in shouts of joy, or in silent thanksgiving, the voice is hers, hers alone. She finds the depths and limits of her emotions, the clarity of her thoughts. She finds courage in her strength and ebullience and resolution to inner turmoil. When a woman emerges from such a retreat, she is grounded again in the reality of her feminine identity and resistant to the pervasive patriarchal injunctions in our culture. Wisdom gained in this quiet, powerful way will influence and subtly change her relationship to her partner, her job, her parents or parenting, and her political and spiritual life. And women who create such ritual retreats together, listening thoughtfully to each other's voices, have the transformative potential to change the world.

Notes

Shortened references are given here for works that appear in the bibliography.

PROLOGUE

1. Wyman, *Blessingway*, 32.
2. Wyman, *Blessingway*, 32–33.
3. Wyman, *Blessingway*, 32.
4. C. G. Jung distinguished between the personal unconscious and the collective unconscious levels of the psyche. The personal unconscious in each of us consists of repressed or forgotten personal experience. The collective unconscious consists of archetypes—contents having a "universal and impersonal nature identical in all individuals." Archetypes are preexistent, psychic forms or primordial images. "Concept of the Collective Unconscious," 42–43, pars. 87–91.
5. The word *dyad* is used to describe the dynamic relationship between two people.
6. Rich, *Of Woman Born*, 20.
7. John Noble Wilford, "Critics Batter Proof of an African Eve," *New York Times*, May 19, 1992.
8. *Container* is used to refer to the psychological enclosure of therapist and patient and also includes the physical space in which the work takes place.
9. Lincoln, *Emerging from the Chrysalis*, 101.
10. See C. G. Jung, *Psychology and Alchemy*, for an extensive treatment of analytic work and the symbolism of alchemy.
11. Carol Christ wonderfully describes the importance of story telling for women's spiritual awakening in *Diving Deep and Surfacing: Women Writers on Spiritual Quest*.
12. Jung, "Psychotherapists or the Clergy," 331, par. 498.
13. Wyman, *Blessingway*, 32.

CHAPTER 1
Creating the Feminine Container

1. According to Jung, the *Self* is the "supraordinate personality" in the psyche, which is ever striving to be realized through the ego. The Self often manifests in dreams as a same-sex figure of supernatural proportions. "Psychological Aspects of the Kore," 182–83, pars. 306–10.

2. Meier, *Healing Dream and Ritual,* 1, 53, 20.

3. Meier, *Healing Dream and Ritual,* 10.

4. For a discussion of the complexity of the analytic relationship, see the introduction to Jung's "Psychology of the Transference."

5. Jung, "Psychological Aspects of the Kore," 188, par. 316.

6. Wyman, *Blessingway,* 46.

7. Jung, "Woman in Europe."

8. Miller, *Toward a New Psychology of Women.* It was affirming for my work to attend a conference in May 1991 at Mills College on the Stone Center research led by Jean Baker Miller, M.D., Janet Surrey, Ph.D., and Judith V. Jordan, Ph.D. The three tenets of the Stone Center relational perspective are that we grow in, through, and toward relationship; that for women, especially, connection with others is central to psychological well-being; and that movement toward relational mutuality can occur throughout life, through mutual empathy, responsiveness, and contribution to the growth of each individual and to the relationship. A collection of papers on this model can be found in *Women's Growth in Connection: Writings from the Stone Center.*

9. Gimbutas, *Civilization of the Goddess,* 8–9.

10. Cameron, *Symbols of Birth and of Death,* 18.

11. Cameron, *Symbols of Birth and of Death,* 27–43.

12. Moss and Cappannari, "In Quest of the Black Virgin," 61.

13. Corn is the generic term for grain in Greece and Western Europe. It is not the Native American corn now in common use.

14. Boer, trans., "The Hymn to Demeter," in *Homeric Hymns,* 91–135.

15. Neumann, *The Great Mother,* 308.

16. Harrison, *Prolegomena,* 272.

17. Harrison, *Prolegomena,* 272–76.

18. Harding, *Woman's Mysteries,* 113.

19. Keuls, *Reign of the Phallus,* 110. Ms. Keuls, a professor of classics at the University of Minnesota, examines the cult of male power and violence that existed in Athens during the Age of Pericles c. 430 B.C.

20. Henderson describes the cultural unconscious as "an area of historical memory that lies between the collective unconscious and the manifest pattern of culture." "The Cultural Unconscious," in *Shadow and Self,* 103.

21. Jung, "Anima and Animus," 208–9, par. 336.

22. Men experience a similar fascination in relation to the *anima.*

23. Spretnak, *Lost Goddesses of Early Greece,* 98–111. Ms. Spretnak offers a version of the myth in which Persephone chooses to go down to the underworld.

24. Perera, *Descent to the Goddess;* and Betty Meador, *Through the Gates of Wonder: Inanna's High Priestess, Enheduanna* (forthcoming).

25. Matthews, *Sophia: Goddess of Wisdom,* 62. In this version the goddesses have Roman names, Ceres and Proserpina, Venus, Minerva, and Diana.

26. *Temenos* is a Greek word meaning temple.

27. Wyman, *Blessingway*, 32.

28. Wyman, *Blessingway*, 420.

29. I have drawn on two major sources for the elements and order of the Kinaaldá ceremony: Shirley M. Begay, *Kinaaldá: A Navajo Puberty Ceremony*; and Charlotte Frisbie, *Kinaaldá: A Study of the Navaho Girl's Puberty Ceremony*. My understanding of the ceremony and of Changing Woman has been further enhanced by my ongoing dialogue with Mark Bahti, an anthropologist and friend of the Navajo people, who lives in Tucson, Arizona.

30. *Exogamous* means outside the intimate family group.

31. Neumann, *Amor and Psyche*, a commentary on the tale by Apuleius. Amor is the Latin name for Eros.

32. The painting is titled *Amor and Psyche, or The Journey*. Its presence in my office is testimony to my long-standing friendship with the artist, Lynn Taber-Borcherdt. She also painted *The Altar*, which graces the cover of this book.

33. Neumann, *Amor and Psyche*, 6–8.

34. Kerenyi, *Eleusis*, 60–61.

35. *Shadow* is Jung's term for the undeveloped aspects of the ego, negative or positive. It appears in dreams and fantasies as a same-sex figure. See Jung, "The Shadow."

36. Wyman, *Blessingway*, 32.

37. Graves, *White Goddess*, 142.

38. Graves, *White Goddess*, 394–96.

39. Jung, "Transformation Symbolism in the Mass."

40. Jung, "Archetypes of the Collective Unconscious," 18, par. 37.

C H A P T E R   2
Adorning a Woman

1. Harding, *Woman's Mysteries*, 68.

2. Harding, *Woman's Mysteries*, 103.

3. Jung "Concept of the Collective Unconscious," 43–44, pars. 91–92.

4. Wyman, *Blessingway*, 46–47.

5. Wyman, *Blessingway*, 8.

6. Wyman, *Blessingway*, 50.

7. Begay, *Kinaaldá*, 15–21.

8. Frisbie, *Kinaaldá*, 12.

9. Lincoln, *Emerging from the Chrysalis*, 17.

10. Witherspoon, *Language and Art in the Navajo Universe*, 34.

11. Witherspoon, *Language and Art in the Navajo Universe*, 24.

12. Begay, *Kinaaldá*, 45.

13. Wyman, *Blessingway*, 14.

14. Frisbie, *Kinaaldá*, 183. Talking God Hogan Song No. 1, as related by Frank Mitchell. Blessing Way, 1957. I have taken excerpts from the individual songs of the Kinaaldá. The songs are recorded in their entirety in Frisbie's and Wyman's books.

15. Begay, *Kinaaldá*, 7, 9.

16. Lincoln, *Emerging from the Chrysalis*, 104.

17. Begay, *Kinaaldá*, 47–51.

18. Frisbie, *Kinaaldá*, 297. Combing Song No. 2, as related by Frank Mitchell. Marie Shirley's Kinaaldá 1963.

19. Reichard, *Navaho Religion*, 407–8.

20. Begay, *Kinaaldá*, 25.

21. Perera, "Ceremonies of the Emerging Ego," 69–73.

22. Reichard, *Navaho Religion*, 414.

23. Brown and Gilligan, *Meeting at the Crossroads*.

24. According to Mark Bahti, the Kinaaldá is still regularly performed for Navajo girls. There have been attempts to instill it with new life in recent years.

25. Neumann, *Great Mother*, 332.

C H A P T E R 3
Molding a Woman

1. Lincoln, *Emerging from the Chrysalis*, 20.

2. Frisbie, 350.

3. Begay *(Kinaaldá*, 55) says that the girl is massaged with a weaving tool, but neither Lincoln nor Frisbie mention a tool. And in the photograph "The Ideal Woman Molding/Massaging the Initiate" (figure 6), the Ideal Woman is using her hands.

4. Frisbie, *Kinaaldá*, 359.

5. Begay, *Kinaaldá*, 57.

6. Begay, *Kinaaldá*, 57.

7. Wyman, *Blessingway*, 515–16. Version 3, as related by River Junction Curly. I could find no recorded songs identified specifically by Frisbie as belonging to the molding ceremony. I chose this one from Wyman's compilation as being closest to the meaning of the enactment.

8. Reichard, *Navaho Religion*, 409.

9. Reichard, *Navaho Religion*, 407.

10. Begay, *Kinaaldá*, 59.

11. Begay, *Kinaaldá*, 63.

12. Lincoln, *Emerging from the Chrysalis*, 20; Frisbie, *Kinaaldá*, 361–62; Begay, *Kinaaldá*, 63.

13. Wyman, *Blessingway*, 47.

14. Link, *The Pollen Path*, 25–26.

15. Frisbie, *Kinaaldá*, 267. Racing Song No. 1, as related by Blue Mule. Solo Recording, 1963. The other two-thirds of the song consists of repetition and variation on the same theme.

16. Frisbie, *Kinaaldá*, 360–61.

17. In present-day Kinaaldá ceremonies, part of the corn is ground by hand as a symbolic gesture. The rest is machine ground for efficiency.

18. Begay, *Kinaaldá*, 67.

19. Lincoln, *Emerging from the Chrysalis*, 20–21.

20. Begay, *Kinaaldá*, 69.

21. Begay, *Kinaaldá*, 65, 83.

22. Begay, *Kinaaldá*, 99–100.

23. Begay, *Kinaaldá*, 107.

24. Begay, *Kinaaldá*, 111.

25. Begay, *Kinaaldá*, 115–17.

26. Begay, *Kinaaldá*, 121, 131.

27. Lincoln, *Emerging from the Chrysalis*, 22.

28. Begay, *Kinaaldá*, 125, 129, 139.

29. Begay, *Kinaaldá*, 139–43.

30. Begay, *Kinaaldá*, 147.

31. Begay, *Kinaaldá*, 149–51.

32. Lincoln, *Emerging from the Chrysalis*, 32.

33. Frisbie, *Kinaaldá*, 299. Combing Song No. 1 (Last Morning), as related by Blue Mule, Solo Recording, 1963.

34. Begay, *Kinaaldá*, 53.

35. Begay, *Kinaaldá*, 155.

36. Begay, *Kinaaldá*, 159.

37. Lincoln, *Emerging from the Chrysalis*, 32–33.

38. Wyman, *Blessingway*, 524, Version 3, as related by River Junction Curly.

39. Begay, *Kinaaldá*, 165–67.

40. Lincoln, *Emerging from the Chrysalis*, 96.

41. "The Navajo Puberty Ceremony," *The Indian Trader* 17, no. 10 (October 1986). P.O. Box 1421, Gallup, NM 87301.

42. Lincoln, *Emerging from the Chrysalis*, 65. The following description of the Festa das Moças Novas is paraphrased from chap. 5 of Professor Lincoln's book, 50–70.

43. Lincoln, *Emerging from the Chrysalis*, 55.

44. Lincoln, *Emerging from the Chrysalis*, 53.

45. Lincoln, *Emerging from the Chrysalis*, 52.

46. Lincoln, *Emerging from the Chrysalis*, 53.

47. Jung, Introduction to "Psychology of the Transference."

48. Reichard, *Navaho Religion,* 407.

49. Lincoln, *Emerging from the Chrysalis,* 55–59.

50. Lincoln, *Emerging from the Chrysalis,* 56–60.

51. Lincoln, *Emerging from the Chrysalis,* 60.

52. Lincoln, *Emerging from the Chrysalis,* 52.

53. Lincoln, *Emerging from the Chrysalis,* 61–63; fig. 22.

54. Lincoln, *Emerging from the Chrysalis,* 63.

55. Kerenyi, *Eleusis,* 136; Campbell, "The Ritual Love-Death," chap. 5.

56. Groesbeck, "Archetypal Image of the Wounded Healer."

57. Lincoln, *Emerging from the Chrysalis,* 64–65.

58. Lincoln, *Emerging from the Chrysalis,* chap. 4, "Tiv Scarification: The Pattern of Time," 34–49.

59. Lincoln, *Emerging from the Chrysalis,* 45.

60. Lincoln, *Emerging from the Chrysalis,* 47.

61. Lincoln, *Emerging from the Chrysalis,* 48–49.

62. Lincoln, *Emerging from the Chrysalis,* 65.

63. Lincoln, *Emerging from the Chrysalis,* 66–67.

64. Lincoln, *Emerging from the Chrysalis,* 67–68.

65. Lincoln, *Emerging from the Chrysalis,* 68–70. Lincoln also explains, 51, that agricultural people like the Navajo support fertility in all realms of nature whereas hunters and fishers like the Tukuna support a balance in nature without excessive growth. Therefore, for them, moderation in human fertility is the cultural expectation.

66. Neumann, *Amor and Psyche,* 77.

67. Moon, *A Magic Dwells,* 176.

68. Eisler, *Chalice and the Blade,* xvii.

69. Jean Baker Miller, "The Construction of Anger in Women and Men," in *Women's Growth in Connection,* 183.

C H A P T E R 4
Knowing the Power of the Womb

1. Craighead, *The Mother's Songs,* 6–7.

2. Cameron, *Symbols of Birth and of Death.*

3. Mellaart, *Çatal Hüyük.*

4. Cameron, *Symbols of Birth and of Death,* 1–3.

5. Gimbutas, *Civilization,* 9.

6. Cameron, *Symbols of Birth and of Death,* 21.

7. Mellaart, *Çatal Hüyük,* fig. 40.

8. Mellaart, *Çatal Hüyük*, figs. 26, 23.

9. Mellaart, *Çatal Hüyük*, plate 27.

10. Gimbutas, *Civilization*, 229.

11. Mellaart, *Çatal Hüyük*, plate 28.

12. Cameron, *Symbols of Birth and of Death*, 8.

13. See Fabricius, *Alchemy*.

14. Walker, *Woman's Dictionary*, 433–34.

15. Walker, *Woman's Dictionary*, 422.

16. "Litany of the Blessed Virgin Mary," *Emmanuel Prayer Book* (1946), 238–39.

17. Craighead, *Litany of the Great River*, 53, 54.

18. Cameron, *Symbols of Birth and of Death*, 10.

19. Cameron, *Symbols of Birth and of Death*, 12.

20. Porphyry (A.D. 233–c. 304) *De ant. nym.*, 18 and Antigonos of Karystos (c. 250 B.C.) *Hist. mir. 19*, quoted in Ransome, *The Sacred Bee*, 107, 114.

21. Brindel, *Ariadne*, 31, 49.

22. Cameron, *Symbols of Birth and of Death*, 22–25.

23. Gimbutas, *Civilization*, 236.

24. Mellaart, *Çatal Hüyük*, fig. 50, plates 78, 79.

25. Mellaart, *Çatal Hüyük*, fig. 52, plates 67, 68.

26. Gimbutas, *Goddesses and Gods*, figs. 200, 202.

C H A P T E R   5
Encountering the Goddess of Death

1. Cameron, *Symbols of Birth and of Death*, 30.

2. Cameron, *Symbols of Birth and of Death*, 28. Griffin vulture *(Gyps vulvus).*

3. Cameron, *Symbols of Birth and of Death*, 27–31.

4. Cameron, *Symbols of Birth and of Death*, 34–43.

5. The Chinese doctrine of *yin*, female, dark, and *yang*, male, light, are the two alternating primal states of being. They are described in *The I Ching, or Book of Changes*, translated by Richard Wilhelm and Cary F. Baynes, lvi.

6. I am grateful to Dr. Ruth Hill, who was responsible for my first viewing of a Jizo statue.

7. Yvonne Rand, personal communication. The ceremonies have gradually expanded to include women and/or men who have had a child die before reaching maturity or those who feel a need to come to terms with not having a child. For information, write Yvonne Rand, Goat-in-the-Road Dharma Center, Box 233, Star Route, Sausalito, CA 94965.

8. Lincoln, *Emerging from the Chrysalis*, 41–43. The entire description of the Tiv ceremony is paraphrased from chap. 4.

9. Lincoln, *Emerging from the Chrysalis*, 43–45.

10. Blofeld, *Bodhisattva of Compassion*, 20.

11. Wyman, *Blessingway*, 48.

12. *Synchronicity* is the experience of a meaningful coincidence between inner and/or outer events. See Jung, "Synchronicity: An Acausal Connecting Principle."

13. Stone, *Ancient Mirrors of Womanhood*, 29.

C H A P T E R 6
Divining the Dark

1. Harding, *Woman's Mysteries*, 113.

2. Harding, *Woman's Mysteries*, 114.

3. Boer, "Hymn to Demeter," 129–30.

4. Harding, *Woman's Mysteries*, 114.

5. Harding, *Woman's Mysteries*, 109.

6. Harding, *Woman's Mysteries*, 116.

7. Harding, *Woman's Mysteries*, 114.

8. Mellaart, *Çatal Hüyük*, fig. 83.

9. Baylor, *Moon Song*.

10. Harding, *Woman's Mysteries*, 114.

11. Neumann, *Great Mother*, plate 159B.

12. Kaplan, *Oneness and Separateness*, 61.

13. Hamilton, "The Quest of the Golden Fleece," chap. 3 in *Mythology*, 159–79.

14. Neumann, *Amor and Psyche*, 41–42.

C H A P T E R 7
Healing With Compassion

1. Neumann, *Amor and Psyche*, 112–14.

2. Blofeld, *Bodhisattva of Compassion*, 17. Kuan Shih Yin is the proper form of her name.

3. Stone, *Ancient Mirrors of Womanhood*, 28.

4. Hamilton, "Atalanta," in *Mythology*, part 3, chap. 4, 244–51; and *The Metamorphosis of Ovid*, trans. Innes, book 10, 261–66.

5. Jung, "Synchronicity," 437–38, 525–26, pars. 843, 982.

6. Mann, *The Black Swan*, 16, 18.

7. Monaghan, *Book of Goddesses and Heroines*, 170.

8. Neumann, *Amor and Psyche*, 112–14.

9. Graves, *White Goddess*, 45.

10. Blofeld, *Bodhisattva of Compassion*, 25, 102.

C H A P T E R   8
Celebrating the Mother-Daughter Mystery

1. Feyerabend, Karl, *Langenscheidt's Classical Greek-English Dictionary* (Berlin and Munich, 1991).

2. Kerenyi, *Eleusis*, 45–47.

3. Kerenyi, *Eleusis*, 46.

4. Burkert, *Ancient Mystery Cults*, 9.

5. Kerenyi, *Eleusis*, 45–47.

6. Boer, "Hymn to Demeter," 106–8.

7. Kerenyi, *Eleusis*, 38.

8. Kerenyi, *Eleusis*, 56, plate 12B, "The Purification of Herakles" on the Lovatelli Urn (Rome, Museo Nazionale Romano).

9. Kerenyi, *Eleusis*, figs. 23b (Priestess with the *cista mystica)* and 23c (Caryatid from the interior of the Lesser Propylaia) from the Eleusis Museum.

10. Kerenyi, *Eleusis*, 24–25.

11. Burkert, *Ancient Mystery Cults*, 10.

12. Burkert, *Ancient Mystery Cults*, 45.

13. Kerenyi, *Eleusis*, 13, 16.

14. Kerenyi, *Eleusis*, 7, 62.

15. Kerenyi, *Eleusis*, 52–59.

16. Kerenyi, *Eleusis*. Lovatelli Urn, 56–57, plates 12A–12D.

17. Kerenyi, *Eleusis*, 52–59.

18. Betty DeShong Meador, "The Thesmophoria: A Woman's Ritual," 92–103.

19. Harrison, *Prolegomena*, 546–47.

20. Harrison, *Prolegomena*, 305.

21. Henderson and Oakes, *Wisdom of the Serpent*, 40.

22. Meier, *Healing Dream and Ritual*, 108.

23. C. G. Jung, "The Symbolism of the Mandala," 145–46, par. 186.

24. Johnson, *Lady of the Beasts*, 132.

25. See Kerenyi, *Eleusis*, 61–66, for a description of the Mysteries from the beginning of the fast to the end of the ceremony.

26. The *cista mystica* and other objects were kept at Eleusis; they were brought to Athens before the ceremony.

27. Boer, "Hymn to Demeter," 108. Iambe is a less provocative form of Baubo.

28. Lincoln, *Emerging from the Chrysalis*, 80.

29. See discussion in Burkert, *Ancient Mystery Cults,* 108, on suggestions from scholars that the *kykeon* included a hallucinogenic drug. The possibilities have included ergot (a fungus that grows on grain), opium, or mushrooms. My belief is that walking fourteen miles after even a moderate fast of nine days would produce an altered state of consciousness. The *kykeon* was mildly alcoholic and would have enhanced the euphoric state. Also, it seems to me the mass participation in the Mysteries would have induced a communal trance state.

30. Kerenyi, *Eleusis.* The following description of the rest of the ceremony is selected and paraphrased from pp. 67–94.

31. Kerenyi, *Eleusis,* 141–42.

32. Jung, "The Dual Mother," 342–43, par. 530.

33. Shuttle and Redgrove, *The Wise Wound,* 140–41.

34. Gimbutas, *Civilization,* 236.

35. Graves, *White Goddess,* 161.

36. Boer, "Hymn to Demeter," 101–2.

CHAPTER 9
Emerging Through Ritual Separation

1. Jung, "Psychological Aspects of the Mother Archetype," 94–96, pars. 176–78.

2. Jung's concepts of *logos* and *eros* are not useful in describing outer gender differences that are vulnerable to patriarchal distortion.

3. Lincoln, *Emerging from the Chrysalis.* The description of this ritual is taken and paraphrased from chap. 2, "Talikettukalyanam: The Marriage of Opposites," 7–16. According to Professor Lincoln, 7, the rite was last performed in the 1930s.

4. See Harding, *Woman's Mysteries,* 144–45, for a discussion of sacred prostitution in ancient religions.

5. Lincoln, *Emerging from the Chrysalis.* The tree *(Ficus religiosa)* is sacred to both Hindus and Buddhists, 14.

6. Lincoln, *Emerging from the Chrysalis,* 16.

7. Wyman, *Blessingway,* 47.

8. Jung, "Components of the Coniunctio," 3–41.

9. Blofeld, *Bodhisattva of Compassion,* 150.

10. Bradley, *Mists of Avalon.*

11. Blofeld, *Bodhisattva of Compassion,* 152.

12. Gimbutas, *Goddesses,* fig. 165.

13. Reichard, *Navaho Religion,* 114–15.

Bibliography

Baylor, Byrd. *Moon Song.* New York: Charles Scribner's Sons, 1982.

Begay, Shirley M. *Kinaaldá: A Navajo Puberty Ceremony.* Rev. ed. Rough Rock, AZ: Navajo Curriculum Center, 1983.

Blofeld, John. *Bodhisattva of Compassion: The Mystical Tradition of Kuan Yin.* Boulder, CO: Shambhala, 1977.

Boer, Charles. *The Homeric Hymns.* Rev. 2nd ed. Dallas, TX: Spring Publications, 1980.

Bradley, Marion Zimmer. *The Mists of Avalon.* New York: Alfred A. Knopf, 1982.

Brindel, June Rachuy. *Ariadne: A Novel of Ancient Crete.* New York: St. Martin's Press, 1980.

Brown, Lyn Mikel, and Carol Gilligan. *Meeting at the Crossroads: Women's Psychology and Girls' Development.* Cambridge: Harvard Univ. Press, 1992.

Burkert, Walter. *Ancient Mystery Cults.* Cambridge: Harvard Univ. Press, 1987.

Cameron, D. O. *Symbols of Birth and of Death in the Neolithic Era.* London: Kenyon-Deane, 1981.

Campbell, Joseph. "The Ritual Love-Death." In *The Masks of God: Primitive Mythology.* New York: The Viking Press, 1959.

———. *Myths to Live By.* New York: The Viking Press, 1972.

Christ, Carol. *Diving Deep and Surfacing: Women Writers on Spiritual Quest.* Boston: Beacon Press, 1980.

Craighead, Meinrad. *The Mother's Songs: Images of God the Mother.* New York: Paulist Press, 1986.

———. *The Litany of the Great River.* New York: Paulist Press, 1991.

Eisler, Riane. *The Chalice and the Blade.* San Francisco: Harper & Row, 1987.

Fabricius, Johannes. Alchemy: *The Medieval Alchemists and Their Royal Art.* Copenhagen: Rosenkilde and Bagger, 1976.

Frisbie, Charlotte. *Kinaaldá: A Study of the Navaho Girl's Puberty Ceremony.* Middletown, CT: Wesleyan Univ. Press, 1967.

Gadon, Elinor W. *The Once and Future Goddess.* San Francisco: Harper & Row, 1989.

Gimbutas, Marija. *The Goddesses and Gods of Old Europe: Myth and Cult Images.* Berkeley: University of California Press, 1972.

———. *The Civilization of the Goddess.* San Francisco: Harper San Francisco, 1991.

Graves, Robert. *The White Goddess: A Historical Grammar of Poetic Myth.* New York: Farrar, Straus & Giroux, 1966.

Groesbeck, Jess. "The Archetypal Image of the Wounded Healer." *Journal of Analytical Psychology* 20, no. 2 (July 1975): 122–145.

Hamilton, Edith. *Mythology.* Boston: Little, Brown & Company, 1942.

Harding, M. Esther. *Woman's Mysteries, Ancient and Modern.* New York: G. P. Putnam's Sons for the C. G. Jung Foundation for Analytical Psychology, 1971.

Harrison, Jane Ellen. *Prolegomena to the Study of Greek Religion.* London: Merlin Press, 1962.

Henderson, Joseph L. *Thresholds of Initiation.* Middletown, CT: Wesleyan Univ. Press, 1967.

———. *Shadow and Self: Selected Papers in Analytical Psychology.* Wilmette, IL: Chiron Publications, 1990.

Henderson, Joseph L., and Maud Oakes. *The Wisdom of the Serpent: The Myths of Death, Rebirth and Resurrection.* New York: Collier Books, 1963.

I Ching, or Book of Changes. Translated by Richard Wilhelm and Cary Baynes. Bollingen Series 20. Princeton, NJ: Princeton Univ. Press, 1967.

Johnson, Buffie. *Lady of the Beasts: Ancient Images of the Goddess and Her Sacred Animals.* San Francisco: Harper & Row, 1988.

Jung, C. G. "The Dual Mother." In *Symbols of Transformation.* Vol. 5 of *Collected Works,* 306–393. Bollingen Series 20. Princeton, NJ: Princeton Univ. Press, 1956.

———. "The Self." In *Aion: Researches into the Phenomenology of the Self,* 23–35. Vol. 9, part 2 of *Collected Works.* Bollingen Series 20. Princeton, NJ: Princeton Univ. Press, 1959.

———. "The Shadow." In *Aion: Researches into the Phenomenology of the Self,* 8–10. Vol. 9, part 2 of *Collected Works.* Bollingen Series 20. Princeton, NJ: Princeton Univ. Press, 1959.

———. "Anima and Animus." In *Two Essays in Analytical Psychology,* 188–211. Vol. 7 of *Collected Works.* Bollingen Series 20. Princeton, NJ: Princeton Univ. Press, 1966.

———. "The Psychology of the Transference." In *The Practice of Psychotherapy,* 163–323. Vol. 16 of *Collected Works.* Bollingen Series 20. Princeton, NJ: Princeton Univ. Press, 1966.

———. *Alchemical Studies.* Vol. 13 of *Collected Works.* Bollingen Series 20. Princeton, NJ: Princeton Univ. Press, 1967.

———. *Psychology and Alchemy.* Vol. 12 of *Collected Works.* Bollingen Series 20. Princeton, NJ: Princeton Univ. Press, 1968.

———. "The Archetypes of the Collective Unconscious." In *The Archetypes and the Collective Unconscious,* 3–41. Vol. 9, part 1 of *Collected Works.* Bollingen Series 20. Princeton, NJ: Princeton Univ. Press, 1969.

———. "The Concept of the Collective Unconscious." In *The Archetypes and the Collective Unconscious,* 42–53. Vol. 9, part 1 of *Collected Works.* Bollingen Series 20. Princeton Univ. Press, 1969.

————. "The Psychological Aspects of the Kore." In *The Archetypes and the Collective Unconscious*, 182–203. Vol. 9, part 1 of *Collected Works*. Bollingen Series 20. Princeton, NJ: Princeton Univ. Press, 1969.

————. "Psychological Aspects of the Mother Archetype." In *The Archetypes and the Collective Unconscious*, 75–110. Vol. 9, part 1 of *Collected Works*. Bollingen Series 20. Princeton, NJ: Princeton Univ. Press, 1969.

————. "Psychotherapists or the Clergy." In *Psychology and Religion: West and East*, 327–347. Vol. 11 of *Collected Works*. Bollingen Series 20. Princeton, NJ: Princeton Univ. Press, 1969.

————. "Synchronicity: An Acausal Connecting Principle." In *The Structure and Dynamics of the Psyche*, 417–519. Vol. 8 of *Collected Works*. Bollingen Series 20. Princeton, NJ: Princeton Univ. Press, 1969.

————. "The Transformation Symbolism in the Mass." In *Psychology and Religion: West and East*, 201–296. Vol. 11 of *Collected Works*. Bollingen Series 20. Princeton, NJ: Princeton Univ. Press, 1969.

————. "The Components of the Coniunctio." In *Mysterium Coniunctionis*, 3–41. Vol. 14 of *Collected Works*. Bollingen Series 20. Princeton, NJ: Princeton Univ. Press, 1970.

————. "Woman in Europe." In *Civilization in Transition*, 113–133. Vol. 10 of *Collected Works*. Bollingen Series 20. Princeton, NJ: Princeton Univ. Press, 1970.

Kaplan, Louise. *Oneness and Separateness: From Infant to Individual.* New York: Simon & Schuster, 1978.

Kerenyi, Carl. *Eleusis: Archetypal Image of Mother and Daughter.* Princeton, NJ: Princeton Univ. Press, 1967.

Keuls, Eva C. *The Reign of the Phallus: Sexual Politics in Ancient Athens.* New York: Harper & Row, 1985.

Lincoln, Bruce. *Emerging from the Chrysalis: Studies in Women's Initiations.* Cambridge: Harvard Univ. Press, 1981.

Link, Margaret Schevill. *The Pollen Path.* Stanford, CA: Stanford Univ. Press, 1956.

Mann, Thomas. *The Black Swan.* Berkeley and Los Angeles: Univ. of California Press, 1990.

Matthews, Caitlin. *Sophia: Goddess of Wisdom.* London: Mandala, HarperCollins Publishers, 1991.

Matthews, Caitlin, and John Matthews. *Ladies of the Lake.* London: The Aquarian Press, Harper Collins Publishers, 1992.

Meador, Betty De Shong. "The Thesmophoria: A Woman's Ritual." In *Uncursing the Dark: Treasures from the Underworld.* Wilmette, IL: Chiron Publications, 1992.

Meier, C. A. *Healing Dream and Ritual: Ancient Incubation and Modern Psychotherapy.* Einsedeln, Switzerland: Daimon Verlag, 1989.

Mellaart, James. *Çatal Hüyük: A Neolithic Town in Anatolia.* New York: McGraw-Hill, 1967.

Miller, Jean Baker. *Toward a New Psychology of Women*. Boston: Beacon Press, 1986.

Monaghan, Patricia. *The Book of Goddesses and Heroines*. New York: E. P. Dutton, 1981.

Moon, Sheila. *A Magic Dwells: A Poetic and Psychological Study of the Navaho Emergence Myth*. San Francisco: Guild for Psychological Studies Publishing House, Wesleyan Press, 1970.

Moss, Leonard W., and Stephen C. Cappannari. "In Quest of the Black Virgin: She Is Black Because She Is Black." In *Mother Worship: Theme and Variations*, edited by James J. Preston, 54–74. Chapel Hill: Univ. of North Carolina Press, 1982.

Nathanson, Sue. *Soul Crisis: One Woman's Journey Through Abortion to Renewal*. New York: New American Library, 1989.

Neumann, Erich. *Amor and Psyche: The Psychic Development of the Feminine*. Bollingen Series 54. Princeton, NJ: Princeton Univ. Press, 1963.

———. *The Great Mother: An Analysis of the Archetype*. Bollingen Series 47. Princeton, NJ: Princeton Univ. Press, 1972.

Ovid. *The Metamorphoses of Ovid*. Translated by Mary M. Innes. Baltimore: Penguin Books, 1955.

Perera, Sylvia Brinton. *Descent to the Goddess: A Way of Initiation for Women*. Toronto: Inner City Books, 1981.

———. "Ceremonies of the Emerging Ego in Psychotherapy." In *The Body in Analysis*, edited by Nathan Schwartz Salant and Murray Stein, 59–85. Wilmette, IL: Chiron Publications, 1986.

Ransome, Hilda M. *The Sacred Bee in Ancient Times and Folklore*. London: George Allen & Unwin Ltd., 1937.

Reichard, Gladys A. *Navaho Religion: A Study of Symbolism*, Vol. 2. Bollingen Series 17. New York: Pantheon Books, 1950.

Rich, Adrienne. *Of Woman Born: Motherhood as Experience and Institution*. New York and London: W. W. Norton, 1986.

Sandner, Donald. *Navajo Symbols of Healing*. New York and London: Harcourt Brace Jovanovich, 1979.

Sappho. *Sappho*. Translated by Mary Barnard. Berkeley: Univ. of California Press, 1958.

Shakespeare, William. *King Lear*. Edited by T. J. B. Spencer and Stanley Wells. London: Penguin Books, 1972.

Shorter, Bani. *An Image Darkly Forming: Women and Initiation*. London and New York: Routledge & Kegan Paul, 1987.

Shuttle, Penelope, and Peter Redgrove. *The Wise Wound: Eve's Curse and Everywoman*. New York: Richard Marek Publishers, 1978.

Spretnak, Charlene. *Lost Goddesses of Early Greece: A Collection of Pre-Hellenic Mythology*. Berkeley, CA: Moon Books, 1978.

Stone, Merlin. *Ancient Mirrors of Womanhood.* Boston: Beacon Press, 1984.

Walker, Barbara G. *The Woman's Dictionary of Symbols and Sacred Objects.* San Francisco: Harper & Row, 1988.

Weigle, Marta. *Spiders and Spinsters.* Albuquerque: Univ. of New Mexico Press, 1982.

Witherspoon, Gary. *Language and Art in the Navajo Universe.* Ann Arbor: The Univ. of Michigan Press, 1977.

Women's Growth in Connection: Writings from the Stone Center. New York: The Guilford Press, 1991.

Wyman, Leland C. *Blessingway.* Recorded and translated by Father Berard Haile. Tucson: The Univ. of Arizona Press, 1970.